Richard L. Davis
and the Color Line
in Ohio Coal

CONTRIBUTIONS TO SOUTHERN APPALACHIAN STUDIES

1 *Memoirs of Grassy Creek: Growing Up in the Mountains on the Virginia–North Carolina Line.* Zetta Barker Hamby. 1998

2 *The Pond Mountain Chronicle: Self-Portrait of a Southern Appalachian Community.* Edited by Leland R. Cooper and Mary Lee Cooper. 1998

3 *Traditional Musicians of the Central Blue Ridge: Old Time, Early Country, Folk and Bluegrass Label Recording Artists, with Discographies.* Marty McGee. 2000

4 *W.R. Trivett, Appalachian Pictureman: Photographs of a Bygone Time.* Ralph E. Lentz II. 2001

5 *The People of the New River: Oral Histories from the Ashe, Alleghany and Watauga Counties of North Carolina.* Edited by Leland R. Cooper and Mary Lee Cooper. 2001

6 *John Fox, Jr., Appalachian Author.* Bill York. 2003

7 *The Thistle and the Brier: Historical Links and Cultural Parallels Between Scotland and Appalachia.* Richard Blaustein. 2003

8 *Tales from Sacred Wind: Coming of Age in Appalachia. The Cratis Williams Chronicles.* Cratis D. Williams. Edited by David Cratis Williams and Patricia D. Beaver. 2003

9 *Willard Gayheart, Appalachian Artist.* Willard Gayheart and Donia S. Eley. 2003

10 *The Forest City Lynching of 1900: Populism, Racism, and White Supremacy in Rutherford County, North Carolina.* J. Timothy Cole. 2003

11 *The Brevard Rosenwald School: Black Education and Community Building in a Southern Appalachian Town, 1920–1966.* Betty J. Reed. 2004

12 *The Bristol Sessions: Writings About the Big Bang of Country Music.* Edited by Charles K. Wolfe and Ted Olson. 2005

13 *Community and Change in the North Carolina Mountains: Oral Histories and Profiles of People from Western Watauga County.* Compiled by Nannie Greene and Catherine Stokes Sheppard. 2006

14 *Ashe County: A History; A New Edition.* Arthur Lloyd Fletcher. 2009 [2006]

15 *The New River Controversy; A New Edition.* Thomas J. Schoenbaum. Epilogue by R. Seth Woodard. 2007

16 *The Blue Ridge Parkway by Foot: A Park Ranger's Memoir.* Tim Pegram. 2007

17 *James Still: Critical Essays on the Dean of Appalachian Literature.* Edited by Ted Olson and Kathy H. Olson. 2008

18 *Owsley County, Kentucky, and the Perpetuation of Poverty.* John R. Burch, Jr. 2008

19 *Asheville: A History.* Nan K. Chase. 2007

20 *Southern Appalachian Poetry: An Anthology of Works by 37 Poets.* Edited by Marita Garin. 2008

21 *Ball, Bat and Bitumen: A History of Coalfield Baseball in the Appalachian South.* L.M. Sutter. 2009

22 *The Frontier Nursing Service: America's First Rural Nurse-Midwife Service and School.* Marie Bartlett. 2009

23 *James Still in Interviews, Oral Histories and Memoirs.* Edited by Ted Olson. 2009

24 *The Millstone Quarries of Powell County, Kentucky.* Charles D. Hockensmith. 2009

25 *The Bibliography of Appalachia: More Than 4,700 Books, Articles, Monographs and Dissertations, Topically Arranged and Indexed.* Compiled by John R. Burch, Jr. 2009

CONTRIBUTIONS TO SOUTHERN APPALACHIAN STUDIES

26 *Appalachian Children's Literature: An Annotated Bibliography.* Compiled by Roberta Teague Herrin and Sheila Quinn Oliver. 2010

27 *Southern Appalachian Storytellers: Interviews with Sixteen Keepers of the Oral Tradition.* Edited by Saundra Gerrell Kelley. 2010

28 *Southern West Virginia and the Struggle for Modernity.* Christopher Dorsey. 2011

29 *George Scarbrough, Appalachian Poet: A Biographical and Literary Study with Unpublished Writings.* Randy Mackin. 2011

30 *The Water-Powered Mills of Floyd County, Virginia: Illustrated Histories, 1770–2010.* Franklin F. Webb and Ricky L. Cox. 2012

31 *School Segregation in Western North Carolina: A History, 1860s–1970s.* Betty Jamerson Reed. 2011

32 *The Ravenscroft School in Asheville: A History of the Institution and Its People and Buildings.* Dale Wayne Slusser. 2014

33 *The Ore Knob Mine Murders: The Crimes, the Investigation and the Trials.* Rose M. Haynes. 2013

34 *New Art of Willard Gayheart.* Willard Gayheart and Donia S. Eley. 2014

35 *Public Health in Appalachia: Essays from the Clinic and the Field.* Edited by Wendy Welch. 2014

36 *The Rhetoric of Appalachian Identity.* Todd Snyder. 2014

37 *African American and Cherokee Nurses in Appalachia: A History, 1900–1965.* Phoebe Ann Pollitt. 2015

38 *A Hospital for Ashe County: Four Generations of Appalachian Community Health Care.* Janet C. Pittard. 2015

39 *Dwight Diller: West Virginia Mountain Musician.* Lewis M. Stern. 2016

40 *The Brown Mountain Lights: History, Science and Human Nature Explain an Appalachian Mystery.* Wade Edward Speer. 2016

41 *Richard L. Davis and the Color Line in Ohio Coal: A Hocking Valley Mine Labor Organizer, 1862–1900.* Frans H. Doppen. 2016

42 *The Silent Appalachian: Wordless Mountaineers in Fiction, Film and Television.* Vicki Collins. 2017

Richard L. Davis and the Color Line in Ohio Coal

A Hocking Valley Mine Labor Organizer, 1862–1900

FRANS H. DOPPEN

CONTRIBUTIONS TO SOUTHERN APPALACHIAN STUDIES, 41

McFarland & Company, Inc., Publishers
Jefferson, North Carolina

LIBRARY OF CONGRESS CATALOGUING-IN-PUBLICATION DATA

Names: Doppen, Frans H., 1957– author.
Title: Richard L. Davis and the color line in Ohio coal : a Hocking Valley Mine labor organizer, 1862–1900 / Frans H. Doppen.
Description: Jefferson, North Carolina : McFarland & Company, Inc., Publishers, 2016 | Series: Contributions to Southern Appalachian studies ; 41 | Includes bibliographical references and index.
Identifiers: LCCN 2016035363 | ISBN 9781476667393 (softcover : acid free paper) ∞
Subjects: LCSH: Davis, Richard L. (Richard Lorenzo), 1862–1900. | United Mine Workers of America—History. | African American labor leaders—Biography. | Coal miners—Labor unions—Organizing—Ohio—History.
Classification: LCC HD6509.D39 D67 2016 | DDC 331.88/122334092 [B] —dc23
LC record available at https://lccn.loc.gov/2016035363

BRITISH LIBRARY CATALOGUING DATA ARE AVAILABLE

ISBN (print) 978-1-4766-6739-3
ISBN (ebook) 978-1-4766-2667-3

© 2016 Frans H. Doppen. All rights reserved

No part of this book may be reproduced or transmitted in any form or by any means, electronic or mechanical, including photocopying or recording, or by any information storage and retrieval system, without permission in writing from the publisher.

Front cover: *top* pickaxes © 2016 iStock; *inset* Richard L. Davis, National Executive Board, United Mine Workers of America, 1897 (courtesy Ronald L. Lewis); *background* photograph of Mine #268 tipple in Rendville, Ohio (courtesy Little Cities of Black Diamonds Archives)

Printed in the United States of America

McFarland & Company, Inc., Publishers
 Box 611, Jefferson, North Carolina 28640
 www.mcfarlandpub.com

Table of Contents

Preface 1

Introduction 7

1—Richard L. Davis 15

2—Rendville 22

3—The Great Hocking Valley Strike 38

4—A Year to Remember 58

5—The Road to Prominence 70

6—A Year of Transition 104

7—National Recognition 115

8—A Private in the Ranks 131

9—A Life of Devotion 143

Chapter Notes 153

Bibliography 175

Index 181

Preface

This book is about the remarkable life of Richard L. Davis. Born in Virginia, he spent most of his adult life in Rendville, a community located on Sunday Creek in the Hocking Valley of southeast Ohio. Here, in a microregion known as the Little Cities of Black Diamonds, which encompasses Athens, Hocking, Perry and Morgan counties, Davis became an ardent mine labor organizer, most notably among his "colored brothers." Soon active in the nascent mine labor movement, he rose to prominence by being twice elected to serve on the National Executive Board of the United Mine Workers of America. During the last decade of the nineteenth century, his was a regular voice in letters to the editor. In this book I briefly review prior research that has been conducted on Richard L. Davis after which I proceed to chronicle his life as much as possible in his own voice and those of his contemporaries. There are many lessons to be learned from Davis' life that hold meaning for us today. I leave it up to you, the reader, until the final chapter to draw your own conclusions and analogies from his letters and experiences. It is my sincere hope his letters will inspire you as much as they have inspired me and those I have met along the way while conducting the research for and writing this book.

The following is the outcome of a serendipitous encounter I had when exploring southeast Ohio shortly after accepting a faculty position in what is now the Patton College of Education at Ohio University in Athens. During my 19 years as a middle and high school social studies teacher in north central Florida, I came to appreciate the importance of knowing the history of one's local school community. I organized field trips for my students to nearby small towns and engaged local historians to conduct walking tours to share their town's history. I quickly learned that my students loved the experience. Rather than learning history out of one of the many generic textbooks, they loved being able to make connections that had personal meaning to them. I took them to obscure and often largely forgotten cemeteries to visit not only, for example, the grave marker in Rochelle of Madison Starke Perry, Florida's fourth governor who led the state into the Confederacy, but also unknown markers of individuals who had lived in the area, including soldiers from various wars referenced in their history textbooks and early immigrants to northern Florida from the Carolinas. I'll never forget when one of my students discovered a stone marker overgrown with grass only to find out that a young woman had been buried there in the late eighteenth century. As a result, as a social studies teacher, I have made it my business to emphasize to student teachers the importance of getting to know the local school community in which their students live.

Upon my arrival in Athens, I therefore made it my personal mission to get to know the region so I might be able to make it part of my student teachers' experience. Having learned of a small local town that supposedly still had late nineteenth century store buildings standing with second story cantilevered balconies, I decided to take a drive out to Shawnee. It was late on a Sunday afternoon when my wife and partner Loraine and I got to town. Main Street appeared to be completely abandoned. Just as we got out of the car, a man came out of what appeared to be the only local community store asking us if we were from out to town and what the purpose of our visit was. After we admitted we were indeed from out of town, he pointed at our old Volvo station wagon, suggesting that "folks around here" don't drive such vehicles. Next he rushed back inside the store and emerged with a key in his hands. He motioned us to a building across the street and gave us a tour of the three floors of an amazing opera house built by the Fraternal Order of Red Men. This encounter was to be the beginning of a long relationship with John Winnenberg, a former hippie by his own admission turned community activist. It is in the context of this experience that I have found the inspiration to dig deeper and learn about Richard L. Davis.

In 1976, on a trip home from college, Winnenberg's friend Skip Rickets overheard a contractor at lunch in Shawnee discussing his plan to buy the deteriorating Fraternal Order of Red Men opera house, built in 1907, so he could salvage the steel I-beams supporting the building's roof. Concerned that this might mark the demise of yet another important historic building, Rickets borrowed $500 from his father to save the theater from demolition. Renamed the Tecumseh Theater, the building now serves as a venue for local events, including exhibits and concerts, as well as a classroom space where I have taught place-based courses for my college students.

Having decided to return to his hometown of Corning and abandoning a teaching career after one year, Winnenberg became director of the non-profit organization Residential Incorporated which focused on community release of institutionalized individuals with disabilities in Perry County. In Winnenberg's own words, "they were rejected by their families at a young age, no one knew their history, being subjects of the state they were moved around, were not treated as real people, and had deep wounds."

Along with co-worker Sandy Landis and colleague Jack Pealer, Winnenberg became known for his rather radical anti-medical establishment and anti-group home views on the normalization movement which at the time was an area of interest of the Highlander Research and Education Center in New Market, Tennessee. Founded in 1932 by Miles Horton as the Highlander Folk School, it has hosted social activists and civil rights leaders such as Septima Clark, Martin Luther King, Jr., Rosa Parks, John Lewis, Pete Seeger, and Ralph Abernathy. Having previously met Miles Horton, who over a glass of whiskey told him about spending a night in the local jail in nearby New Straitsville in Perry County during the 1927 coal miners' strike, Winnenberg was invited to attend a workshop at the center in 1981. While exploring the center's library, two large, black volumes in a section on coal mining history caught his attention. Taking the two volumes of the *History of the United Mine Workers of America from 1890 to 1900* of the shelf, he discovered that its author Chris Evans came from New Straitsville. He had never "heard of the guy," and this "stunning find" further motivated him to become involved in saving the local history of his native community and realizing that not only did he work professionally with wounded people but he also worked in wounded communities. Thus began his journey "to give voice to under-voiced people" in the boom-to-bust communities in the region, much like his and others' efforts to do so with formerly institutionalized people.

In 1970, when the New Straitsville community celebrated its centennial, based on word of mouth passed down from generation to generation, its residents sought to gain recognition of Robinson's Cave, located in the heart of their town, as the birthplace of the United Mine Workers of America. Not even in possession of a single copy of the Evans' volumes, the United Mine Workers of America unfortunately refused to recognize New Straitsville as its cradle, instead awarding that honor to Columbus where it was officially founded in 1890. In an effort to give their local community a voice after years of decline from the boom-to-bust cycle, Winnenberg then decided to start a local newspaper called *Community Live News* which later morphed into a community magazine called *Community Life Quarterly*. He and fellow community members began collecting oral histories and relying heavily on the dissertation research of Ivan Tribe, a professor of history at the University of Rio Grande. Through their efforts they came to realize that the Little Cities were home to three significant events: the rise of the mine labor movement in the Hocking Valley; multi-ethnic rural immigration, including the unique experience of the nearby integrated African American community of Rendville; and one of the nation's first ever government-sponsored environmental clean-ups. The clean-up began as a project for the Civilian Conversation Corps and Works Progress Administration during the Great Depression when the federal government bought up "the lands that nobody wanted" and put young men to work creating the Wayne National Forest through tree planting and erosion fighting efforts. This maturing forest now surrounds Rendville and makes "Little Cities of the Forest" a more accurate moniker for the former coal region. The effort continues as projects are underway to remove acid mine drainage from orange-colored streams in both the Sunday Creek and Monday Creek valleys.

Founded in 1990 by Winnenberg and Landis, Sunday Creek Associates took the view, reminiscent of George Santayana's admonition, that they had "lost their voice in history," and that in order "to heal [they had] to understand where [they had] been [as] it's hard to move forward if you don't know where you've been." After its first year in existence, Sunday Creek Associates obtained an Ohio Humanities Council grant which allowed them to bring in humanities scholars, including Ivan Tribe, Lorle Porter, a historian at Muskingum College, Ric Sheffield, an African American historian at Kenyon College, and Warren Van Tyne, a labor historian at The Ohio State University. The latter "got in hot water" when he informed the locals that the famous John L. Lewis, president of the United Mine Workers from 1920 to 1960, was "no friend of the Hocking Valley coal miners" even though he had been a hero whose picture was in many a miner's household, right beside that of John F. Kennedy. Lewis' success in 1924 in raising miners' wages under the Jacksonville Agreement led to the closing of most aging mines in the area as the operators were unable to pay their workers due to antiquated mining methods. The region has experienced economic and population decline ever since and now has about one-third of its original population.

Sunday Creek Associates also decided to feature a history tent at the New Straitsville Moonshine Festival which commemorates how the locals survived hard times by brewing whiskey in the abandoned mines during Prohibition. The exhibit was small and featured community elders sharing their memories, and other locals started bringing in items from their own collections to be put on display. Deciding to move forward, these folks started meeting monthly in a local antique shop which is now the home of the Monday Creek Restoration Project.

Recording oral histories resulted in two volumes of *Our Journey Con-*

tinues: *The History of New Straitsville, Ohio* as part of New Straitsville's quasquicentennial celebration in 1995–1996, to be followed by *Shawnee: Reflections Upon the First 125 Years*. Despite efforts to engage the neighboring communities of Corning and Rendville to publish a book on their shared history, due to a disconnect between the two towns, no Rendville residents participated. However, this initiative did lead to a series of seven of publications of the *Corning-Monroe Reader*, the last of which was published in 2003.

Through his involvement with the *Corning-Monroe Reader*, Winnenberg started attending social gatherings of current and former residents of Rendville to record their life histories as well as to collect the history of the town. Sunday Creek Associates adopted the name Little Cities of Black Diamonds in 1991, and three years later, in 1994, it was awarded a second grant from the Ohio Humanities Council to call attention to small town landmarks which enabled the non-profit to save six historic structures in Corning, Rendville, New Straitsville, Congo, Drakes and Shawnee. The project involved working with teachers and gifted students from Southern Local Schools, located in Hemlock, to produce drawings of the landmarks and in 1999 resulted in *The Story of Our Community: The Little Cities of Black Diamonds of Southern Perry County, Ohio*, a student-centered lesson unit plan developed in collaboration with the Millcreek Elementary School Local History Committee.

It was at a meeting in the Rendville town hall to present *Town Landmarks*, a publication on the buildings that had been saved and the cost of complete renovation, that Winnenberg met Cheryl Blosser, the mother of one of the gifted students from Southern Local Schools and history enthusiast who volunteered to conduct local historical research. Soon, large groups of other enthusiasts began attending monthly meetings sharing notes, drawing up budgets and making future plans. A grant from the Kellogg Foundation, designed to enhance technology access in rural areas, resulted in the creation of three teams in southern Perry County, each of which received a $15,000 grant which boosted the group's research initiative and in 2005 resulted in *Agents of Change: The Pioneering Role of the Miners of the Little Cities of Black Diamonds in the Nation's Labor Movement*, co-authored by Blosser and Winnenberg.

As I learned more and more about the history of the Little Cities of Black Diamonds, I began organizing field trips throughout the microregion for the teacher candidates in my social studies methods courses. This ultimately culminated in a series of week-long course offerings over several summers, co-taught by Blosser and Winnenberg, that took my students out of the Athens bubble. Their amazement at the rich history right outside of their college town continues to affirm to me why local history truly matters and place-based education is of paramount importance. It is against the background of this shared enthusiasm for local history that I became interested in the life of Richard L. Davis and his fascinating life. Much remains to be told about the history of Rendville and the Hocking Valley but it is my hope that this book will be part of a promising path on which we hope the next generation will continue.

This book would not have been possible without the incredible support of many individuals. Foremost, I want to thank John Winnenberg, Cheryl Blosser, Sandy Landis and Skip Rickets for their inspiring efforts to heal their communities. I am also thankful for the support for this project by Renee Middleton, dean of the Patton College of Education, and John Henning, chair of the Department of Teacher Education. The hard work by my graduate students Jing An, Matt Hollstein, and Jennifer Hinkle has not only been invaluable but also infectious as their enthusiasm and amazement about Richard L. Davis' extraordinary life was never-ending. Bill Kimok, archivist at the Mahn Center for Archives and Special Collections, deserves my gratitude for directing me to the United Mine Workers of America cash books for District 6. I also wish to thank Kristin Diki for her detailed attention to the chapter notes, and Ron Eller, renowned Appalachian Studies scholar who, along with Winnenberg, reviewed my manuscript and offered numerous suggestions for improvement. At the risk of forgetting anyone, for which I kindly ask forgiveness, I also thank Albert Siemer who drove me around to show me where some of the mines were once located, and Bryan Bailey, mayor of what is now Ohio's smallest incorporated town, Rendville, as well as the welcoming folks at Rendville Arts Works and the many student teachers who have completed numerous service learning projects in the Little Cities for the support they have provided me along the way. As we move forward with continuing to unearth Rendville's history, I also am grateful to Jerry and Anita Jackson, Denver Norman, Harry and Janis Ivory, Robin Muhammad and others for helping revive the annual Emancipation Day celebration in Rendville and founding the Rendville Historic Preservation Society. Finally, I must thank Loraine McCosker for being the one to have told me about Shawnee in the first place and for her ongoing support of my seemingly never-ending involvement in deepening and telling the history of the Little Cities of Black Diamonds.

Introduction

"I know that in former days you used to sing 'Give me Jesus, give me Jesus, you have all the world, just give me Jesus.' But the day has now come that we want a little money along with our Jesus, so we want to change that old song and ask for a little of the world as well. Don't you think so friends?"

These words are from a letter published in the *United Mine Workers' Journal* on April 21, 1892, in which "Brother Davis [offered some] Square and Manly Advice to [his] Colored Brothers."[1] At the time, Richard L. Davis, a young African American labor organizer and prolific letter writer to the *National Labor Tribune* and the *United Mine Workers Journal* from Rendville, had spent nearly a decade in Perry County, Ohio, the heart of the Little Cities of Black Diamonds.

In his annual report for 1892 to William McKinley, Jr., governor of Ohio, Robert M. Haseltine, chief inspector of mines, reported that coal production in Perry County exceeded two million tons, making it the top coal producing county in the state. There were 67 mines in the county, 56 of which employed more than ten men. Of these 67 mines, 49 were classified as drift, five as shaft, two as slope and 11 as small mines. The 2,994 men who were employed in these mines represented 14.2 percent of the total number of 21,002 miners in the entire state. The 25 mine accidents that occurred that same year ranked Perry County fifth in the state. With six fatalities, four of which were due to roof falls and two of which due to coal falls, it ranked highest in the state along with Jefferson County.[2]

Located in southeast Ohio's Hocking Valley, the village of Rendville, once a booming coal mining town, today lingers with a population of 36, which makes it the smallest incorporated community in Ohio.[3] Yet this easily bypassed community in the rural Little Cities of Black Diamonds microregion is a site of national historical significance. It is here that Richard L. Davis spent the last 18 years of his short life that ended in 1900 organizing a fledging labor movement and breaking the color line.

The Little Cities of Black Diamonds microregion includes sections of southern Perry, northern Athens, eastern Hocking, and western Morgan counties. The region is characterized by two major watersheds, Sunday Creek and Monday Creek, tributaries that flow southward into the Hocking River, which in turn flows east into the Ohio River. In 1774, Virginia's governor, Lord Dunmore, sought to secure the Ohio frontier after Chief Logan in retaliation conducted three murderous raids against white settlers who had killed eight Shawnee, including his brother and a sister-in-law. On October 11, one day after the Battle of Point Pleasant, in which Andrew Lewis defeated Chief Cornstalk, Dunmore departed from Fort Gower, today's Hockingport, with the intent to destroy Chillicothe, an important Shawnee village in the Scioto Valley. While traveling due west toward his target, Dunmore's party set up camp along the banks of the two creeks, first on a Sunday and next on a Monday. Lord Dunmore's War, however, came to an end on October 18 at Fort Charlotte, six miles east of Chillicothe, when he concluded a peace treaty with the Shawnee.[4]

The Little Cities of Black Diamonds derive their name from an article in the *Athens Messenger* which reported on the celebration in 1869 of the first trainload of coal that was shipped from Nelsonville, "the little city of Black Diamonds," to Columbus.[5] A century later, as the result of his dissertation research, Ivan Tribe's *Little Cities of Black Diamonds: Urban Development in the Hocking Coal Region, 1870–1900* led Sunday Creek Associates, a local community organization dedicated to promoting the historical, cultural, civic and environmental assets of the region, to adopt the name. Followed by *Sprinkled with Coal Dust: Life and Work in the Hocking Coal Region, 1870–1900*, Tribe's pioneering research on the numerous coal mining towns that once dotted the landscape in this part of the state provides an excellent starting point for an in-depth study of the life of Richard L. Davis.

According to Ronald L. Lewis, segregation by race was a common practice in American coal mines, and Rendville's blacks remained segregated in their own sections of town as well as in the workplace.[6] Whites often resented the presence of black miners, whom some believed had been brought into the valley "for the purpose of breaking down, driving out, or degrading the white workers in the mines."[7] After the Civil War thousands of former slaves found their way across the mountains of Virginia and West Virginia building railroads and opening coal mines in central Appalachia, and many found their way into the burgeoning coal fields of southeast Ohio. Black workers were sometimes recruited as strike breakers to replace white miners during labor disputes. In Rendville, Mine No. 3 was commonly known as the "Negro mine" since "blacks found themselves almost entirely excluded from work in other mines."[8] This racism was further fueled by local newspapers, such as the *New Lexington Tribune*, which referred to Rendville as a "pest place of industrial leprosy that has infested our valley" with a "horde of barbarian niggers" who "drove the white men out of their houses and compelled white women and children to settle in dugouts."[9]

Despite this segregation and racial hostility, however, Rendville proved to be a different kind of community. According to Charles Nelson, a great social experiment unfolded in Rendville as "its unique social and economic circumstances, allowed race relations to emerge without the usual obstructions and intimidation of Jim Crow institutions. Rendville had the advantage of being a partially isolated geographical entity."[10] Indeed, race relationships in Rendville appear to have been rather harmonious, as evidenced by the election and appointment of African Americans to public office. In neighboring communities racism often had a latent presence that would manifest itself, as it did, for example, in New Straitsville in 1894 when, after his sixteen-year-old sister, "a pretty little Miss scarcely out of short dresses," gave birth to "a negro child," Arch Lafferty then purchased a "Winchester repealing rifle" with which he laid Glenroy Payne, "a burly negro ... who has always born a bad reputation ... cold in death." Two weeks after Payne's hasty burial "in the colored graveyard without any ceremony," a grand jury in New Lexington failed to indict his murderer.[11] Being "a completely new community in the North," Rendville had no prior social structure.[12] As a "free space,"[13] the town gave its inhabitants the opportunity to engage in "a quest for identity, autonomy, and dignity" in "spontaneous face-to-face relations of family, ethnic community, church, fraternal and workers' organizations."[14]

In his 1963 reappraisal of the Gilded Age, Herbert Gutman argued that the relationship between employers and workers in small industrial communities was very complex and differed significantly from that in the large industrialized cities. In these small communities different social classes typically lived and worked side by side, yet every town was unique.[15] Later, in 1986, Gutman suggested that the "absence of detailed knowledge of the 'local world' inhabited by white and Negro workers ... leaves only an obscure and tangled reality—filled with scattered and contradictory but suggestive bits of information" and that "the world of men like Richard L. Davis awaits his historian."[16] While much information has been lost and hopefully remains to be discovered about Richard L. Davis, this book seeks to add to our understanding of his noteworthy life.[17]

The Gutman Debate Revisited

The philosopher George Herbert Meade suggested that history involves an ongoing reinterpretation of the past as each new generation seeks to reconstruct a communal past in order to better understand the present.[18] It is therefore useful to review the scholarly debate that erupted after Herbert Gutman first brought Davis back to the public's attention.

In 1922, more than two decades after the death of Richard L. Davis, the Industrial Workers of the World proclaimed, "The working class and the employing class have nothing in common and there can be found no peace so long as hunger and want are found among millions of working people and the few, who make up the employing class, have all the good things in life." These words could well have been spoken by Davis. Having been a dedicated early member of the inclusive Knights of Labor, he most likely would have agreed with the Wobblies' preamble's admonition "An injury to one is an injury to all," which was inspired by and adapted from the Knights' motto. He would have appreciated their assessment that "the sufferings of the coal-mine workers during the last hundred years are so appalling, that a study of the history of the industry is bound to make a flaming rebel of any fair-minded man or woman."[19] However, he likely would not have agreed with the Wobblies' radical stance that "it is the historic mission of the working class to do away with capitalism," and he would have been outraged by their lack of reference to black miners.

More than a decade earlier, William Scaife, then a retired editor of the *United Mine Workers Journal*, using the pseudonym Old Timer and who had first met Richard L. Davis at the founding convention of the United Mine Workers of America, described him as "a heroic fighter for the miners' organization in Ohio."[20] Although R.F. Warner of Ohio was the first African American to be elected to the National Executive Board of the United Mine Workers of America,[21] Old Timer wrote that while other colored men had "honors bestowed upon them ... none of them seemed to have the sticking qualities" of Dick Davis. Arguing that Davis, "by his devotion to the miner's union, deserved better treatment than that accorded to him in the last few years of his life," he strongly criticized "some of the mushroom growth of latter-day leaders" who were so "unmanly and unremindful of the past" as to designate Davis a "barnacle." He reminded them that "Dick was a union man since when the memory of man runneth not to the contrary" and, although "he was black, he had a heart as white as any man and a devotion to union principles that was second to no man in the movement." Reminding all miners to stand together against "incorporate greed ... no matter his color, creed, religious or political belief," Old Timer implored, "We need more colored men like Dick Davis, and we white men want to treat them right for the common good of us all."

In 1968, nearly a half century after *Old Timer* wrote his passionate letter in defense of Richard L. Davis' memory, Herbert G. Gutman reintroduced Davis to the world when he published *The Negro and the United Mine Workers of America: The Career and Letters of Richard L. Davis and Something of Their Meaning: 1890–1900*.[22] Based on his interpretation of several letters Davis wrote during the last decade of his life, Gutman depicted the United Mine Workers of America as a "secular church" to which Davis devoted himself as a "dedicated missionary ... influenced by a postmillennial evangelical protestantism."[23] He described Davis as an ardent defender of interracial trade unionism who found in the United Mine Workers[24] a labor organization in which he was able to overcome the "color line" between white and black miners.[25] Asserting that Davis was not a socialist, Gutman nonetheless found him to be "a radical by the standards of his time" because of his insistence on attacking the "race problem" and the issue of wage slavery.[26] Referencing two notably significant events in which the United Mine Workers' white leadership crossed the color line, Gutman argued that Davis found a home in the interracial organization. The first event occurred in West Virginia in June 1893, when its leadership compelled a white hotel owner to give Davis a room for the night. The second event happened in Ohio in August 1895, when the leadership walked out after the owner of the Mercer Hotel in Corning, Ohio, refused to serve Davis dinner.[27] According to Gutman, these events demonstrated that the early leaders of the United Mine Workers, "not without formidable difficulties, welcomed Negro members and drew them actively into the union," making it "a viable, integrated trade union and quite possibly ... the most thoroughly integrated voluntary association in the United States of 1900."[28]

In 1974, in *Organized Labor and the Black Worker, 1619–1981*, Philip Foner revisited Richard L. Davis in the broader context of the experience of black workers in the United States. According to the U.S. Census in 1860, on the eve of the Civil War, there were nearly half a million free blacks and nearly 4.5 million slaves among a population of 31.4 million. The prospect of free slaves competing with white laborers, particularly as strike breakers, increased significantly less than one month after the birth of R.L. Davis when, on January 1, 1863, Lincoln's Emancipation Proclamation went into effect. Although a labor congress met in Baltimore after the Civil War and resulted in the creation of a National Labor Union in August 1866, it did not call for the admission of blacks.[29] In 1868, one year after Karl Marx published his first volume of *Das Kapital*, William H. Sylvis, who by then had become an advocate of the First International and been elected president of the National Labor Union, at its third convention declared, "We are now one family of slaves together and the reform movement is a second emancipation proclamation.... The working people of our nation, white and black, male and female, are now sinking into a condition of serfdom oppressed by the center of slave power in Wall Street."[30] In January 1869, Sylvis and the Executive Committee of the National Labor Union decided to invite all persons in the labor movement, regardless of color or sex, to attend the next convention to be held in Philadelphia in August. Unfortunately, the National Labor Union convention that followed Sylvis' sudden death in July failed to honor the call for adopting a policy of integration but instead passed a resolution that encouraged the organization of separate unions for whites and blacks, which in December led to the creation of a Colored National Labor Union led by Isaac Myers, the first important black labor leader in America and who served as its president.[31]

That same year, nine garment cutters in Philadelphia, led by Uriah S. Stephens, created the Noble and Holy Order of the Knights of Labor, a secret society to represent all workers in a joint association that, except for bankers, lawyers, gamblers, speculators and liquor tradesmen, included men and women, regardless of color, with the motto "An injury to one, is a concern of all." From its beginning, the Knights upheld their commitment to racial solidarity. Uriah Stephens, who had been born into an abolitionist household, announced, "I can see ahead of me an organization that will include men and women of every craft, creed, and color." Because of its openness, by the early 1880s the Knights of Labor had a membership of diverse political persuasions that included amongst others Marxists, socialists, anarchists, reformers, temperance advocates, ministers, small employers, and trade unionists.[32]

Assuming that in the current state of relations between capital and labor it would not be a wise decision to reveal being a union member, the Knights adopted secret symbolic signs to greet one another and secret knocks to enter meetings that included an extensive array of rituals which can be found in a booklet known as the *Adelphon Kruptos* (*AK*), or Secret Brotherhood. The *AK* was not printed for internal use until sometime after 1872, and only a few copies circulated prior to 1879.[33] According to Weir, the meetings were permeated by strong Christian-based personal morality. It was not enough for a Knight to be a good comrade; he or she had also to be "sober, patriotic, law-abiding, trustworthy, and moral."[34]

By 1879, one year before Rendville was founded, and when Uriah Stephens resigned to run of Congress and Terence V. Powderly became the Knights'

Grant Master Workman, the order's membership had grown to nearly 52,000. Led by Powderly, on January 1, 1882, the Knights of Labor became a public organization, officially relegating its secret rituals to the dustbin of history. By 1886, some four years after Richard L. Davis had become a member, the Knights' membership reached its peak, estimated between 700,000 and one million members.[35] Having condoned the existence of segregated locals, in 1894, when the Knights' membership had plummeted to 20,000, James R. Sovereign, Powderly's successor, announced that the only solution to the "Negro problem" would be to deport them back to Africa.

When the United Mine Workers of America was founded in 1890, Richard L. Davis was one of about a thousand black Knights who came into the new union.[36] However, although Davis believed the United Mine Workers did more than any other organization to break the color line, he was nonetheless a severe critic who didn't "mince any words."[37] In 1980, historian Stephen Brier uncovered several previously unknown letters by Davis in the *National Labor Tribune*, which prior to the *United Mine Workers Journal* was the official organ of the Amalgamated Association of Miners of the United States and its successor, the National Federation of Miners and Mine Laborers. Brier suggested that these letters clearly demonstrated that while Davis was often critical of the United Mine Workers, he nonetheless "remained steadfast in his belief in the efficacy and importance of trade unionism as the mechanism through which black Americans would secure their final liberation as a people."[38]

In his dissertation, Michael McCormick in 1978 challenged Gutman's "mythical, almost utopian, setting" in which small town, non-industrial pre-capitalist "community consciousness transcends social class considerations and neighborliness social conflict."[39] In 1988, three years after Gutman's death, Herbert Hill similarly accused him of "myth making" and "romantic Marxism."[40] Led astray by the "wonderful, wonderful letters of this fellow, born a slave and victimized by racism on all sides,"[41] Hill argued that Gutman failed to recognize that letters published in the *United Mine Workers Journal* would have been subject to "a policy of containing controversy" and hence "susceptible to selective quotation."[42] Characterizing the Mercer Hotel incident as a trivial event that amounted to no more than an "isolated example of basic decency,"[43] Hill charged Gutman with ignoring "the role of racist ideology in working class history"[44] and asserted that Davis' two terms on the National Executive Board failed to have any lasting impact on any United Mine Workers policies or practices and that in fact, until forced to do so, its leaders simply ignored Davis' plight after he failed to gain re-election to the National Executive Board in 1898.[45] Furthermore, Hill added that while blacks made up over 20 percent of the United Mine Workers membership, Davis was one of a total of only six blacks, less than two percent, who held office at any district level during the 1890s.[46] In Hill's final analysis Davis was "significant less as a leader in the United Mine Workers ... than as the foremost representative of organized black miners,"[47] even more so because after Davis' last term on the National Executive Board, no African American would be elected to national office until 1973.[48]

As part of a series of responses to Hill's "ludicrous charges" that Gutman painted something that "amounts to an unqualified picture of harmonious race relationships," Brier and others came to Gutman's defense.[49] In his counter response, Hill derided Brier's suggestion that white workers began to shed racist attitudes and practices as "sheer nonsense" and unsubstantiated by history.[50] In a more balanced review of the Gutman debate in his study of union organizing among black miners in Alabama, Ronald Lewis has argued that these contending interpretations tend to "essentialize race and class into mutually exclusive categories" rather than acknowledge their inseparable interrelationship and that Richard L. Davis can only be truly understood in the local context of southeast Ohio.[51]

Suggesting that the debate is far from over, Brier, in a subsequent article reporting the discovery of a letter Richard L. Davis wrote to the *Cleveland Gazette* in 1886, reminded us that Hill's original article was "marred by professional and personal vitriol."[52] Suggesting that Hill utilized only 20-plus letters in the *National Labor Tribune* and 50-plus letters in the *United Mine Workers Journal*, Brier noted that the current narrative will instead be based on an additional hundred uncovered letters. In testament to Davis' prolificacy, this book's narrative will be based on 173 letters: 33 in the *National Labor Tribune*, 138 in the *United Mine Workers Journal*, and one each in the *Cleveland Gazette* and the *Labor Advocate*. While the Gutman debate centered on the issue of interracial solidarity in the United Mine Workers between 1890 and 1900, new knowledge gleaned about the life of Richard L. Davis from the additional letters I have discovered and other information will provide a fuller understanding of his local and national significance. While Davis' first known letter dates to 1886, the context of his life in early Rendville provides a foundation for better understanding his later writings and work.

Chapter 1

Richard L. Davis

Personal Background

Richard Lorenzo Davis[1] was most likely born on December 24, 1862.[2] According to the U.S. Census conducted on August 18, 1870, Davis was seven years old and living in Big Lick Township in the County of Roanoke, Virginia. His father, Lee Davis, was a 40-year-old black male who worked as a farm laborer, while his mother, Maria Davis, was a 33-year-old black female whose occupation was "keeping house." At the time Davis was the oldest of four children. Besides two brothers, five-year-old Lee and one-year-old Edmund, he had a three-year-old sister named Jane. When Davis was eight years old, he started to work in a local tobacco factory where he remained for nine years.[3] This suggests that he most likely started working in the factory in 1871 and left sometime in 1880.

The 1860 U.S. Census does not list Davis' parents as they most likely were slaves who then made up 90 percent of the 175,000 African Americans living in southern Appalachia. Although Virginia provided for registration of births as early as 1853, compliance during the Civil War and for African Americans was incomplete. Unfortunately, the Historical Society in Roanoke does not have any birth certificates.[4]

By the time of the 1880 U.S. Census, conducted on June 15, the Davis family consisted of the father and five children and was living in Gainsborough in the County of Roanoke. Davis' father Lee was 50 years old at the time; however, his mother is no longer listed and probably had died sometime during or after 1872. Richard, still 17 rather than 18 years old, as he was inaccurately listed, appears to also have lost his youngest brother Edmund. Yet the family had been enlarged with a younger sister, Lucy, who was now ten years old and a younger brother, William, now eight years old.

Founded in 1835 by Major Kemp Gaines, the Gainesborough settlement where the Davis family lived was located in what is today the city of Roanoke, Virginia, was referred to as Old Lick. In 1852 the settlement shifted slightly southwest after the arrival of the Virginia and Tennessee Railroad and the establishment of Big Lick Township, which was located on a large saltlick that attracted wildlife to a site near the Roanoke River. Developing into what was to become a predominantly African American community, Big Lick incorporated with Old Lick in 1882 as Roanoke. Today Gainesboro is located immediately north of downtown Roanoke.

Most likely sometime after the 1880 census was conducted, "disgusted with the very low wage rate and other unfavorable conditions of a Southern tobacco factory,"[5] Davis decided to leave for the Kanawha and New River region of West Virginia where coal mining, although first begun about 1817, was still a fledging operation and would remain so until the arrival of the Chesapeake & Ohio Railroad in 1870. Most African Americans in Kanawha County, including Booker T. Washington and his stepfather, still worked in the salt works near Malden, located about eight miles south of today's Charleston. Within a few years of his arrival in 1865, Booker T. Washington became a houseboy for General Lewis Ruffner and his wife Viola whose employ he periodically sought to escape to work in a local coal mine.[6]

After the Civil War coal from the Kanawha and New River region was shipped to the Great Lakes by river barge. By 1870 about a thousand of the state's 20,000 African Americans were living in the Kanawha Valley. Davis' decision to leave Roanoke made him one among the thousands of African American Virginians who after the Civil War migrated west to the Kanawha and New River region where in the early 1870s many found work in the construction of the Chesapeake and Ohio Railroad. Boosted by the initially slow opening of the coal mines, a result of the Depression of 1873, the C&O in combination with the coal mines contributed to a dramatic increase in the African American population in the region during the 1880s.[7]

Upon completion of the railroads many African American workers decided to remain in the Kanawha-New River coal field where they were hired by coal companies that sought to create a "judicious mixture" in order to counter union organizing by playing off whites, African Americans who were often perceived as opposed to labor agitation, and immigrants against one another.[8] Still, by 1880, despite a large influx of African American miners, nearly 95 percent of the miners in the Kanawha-New River region where either native born or had ventured from Pennsylvania and Ohio.[9]

Davis was likely first exposed to the world of labor organizing in the mines of West Virginia. Although they often worked alongside white miners when underground, African American miners typically were assigned poorer locations and jobs in the mine while facing discrimination above ground. First established in the Kanawha Valley in the mid–1870s, by 1882 when Davis left the region the inclusive Knights of Labor listed seven regular as well as four segregated assemblies. Several blacks served on integrated committees and helped persuade fellow black strikebreakers to leave. It is in this environment that Davis likely witnessed the first labor strike on the New River when the miners sought a ten cent increase per ton of mined coal.[10]

It wasn't until October 2, 1886, four years after his arrival in Rendville, that Davis' first letter was published in the *National Labor Tribune*. According to Gutman, although Davis attended the Roanoke schools during the winter months when there was no work in the tobacco factories, his letters are typical of those written by self-educated workers in the nineteenth century.[11] Davis' letters clearly suggest that he was a well-educated man who had mastered a commanding writing style. At various points it is evident that he had a broad general knowledge. For example, the valediction to his second letter to the *National Labor Tribune*, "I am yours for liberty, equality and fraternity," suggests a familiarity with the French Revolution.[12] Reminding readers of the *United Mine Workers Journal*'s motto "United we stand, divided we fall," words spoken by Patrick Henry in his last public speech, Davis later once more invoked the patriot's words, "Eternal vigilance is the price of liberty."[13] Raising "the question of education" in another letter, Davis wrote, "This is something we all need and should pay more attention to in the future." He argued strongly in favor of setting up reading rooms in "every little mining camp" so that the miners could get "as many good labor papers" as possible and "all the literature that we possibly can treating upon social and economic questions" because

R.L. Davis (*United Mine Workers Journal* 3, no. 7 [May 25, 1893]: 5).

reading and discussing such matters would have a "tendency to elevate us socially, politically and otherwise."[14]

The Hocking Valley

Davis was one of many African American miners from the Kanawha and New River region who were recruited by the Ohio Central Coal Company and Colonel William P. Rend to the Hocking Valley coalfields, today also referred as the Little Cities of Black Diamonds.[15] He most likely first arrived in Rendville by way of the Ohio Central and the Richmond and Allegheny's recently completed direct line from the lakes to the seaboard. At this time the Hocking Valley coal boom was in its fledging stages.[16] In 1830, James Knight, a merchant who had been born in England and settled in York Township in what is now Nelsonville, became the first local coal operator when he took two wagonloads of coal to Columbus.[17] Unfortunately, the Ohio Canal, which was completed in 1825 and connected Portsmouth on the Ohio River with Cleveland on Lake Erie, had bypassed the Hocking Valley. In response, local businessmen obtained a charter to build a canal to connect Lancaster with the Ohio Canal at Carroll, thus providing an outlet to the East Coast market.[18] To open up the Hocking Valley, soon the idea developed to extend the canal to Athens where north of Sunday Creek, according to Samuel Carpenter, an engineer commissioned by the Board of Canal Commissioners, there existed an extensive coal field.[19] Begun in 1837, the Hocking Canal reached Athens in September 1842. However, frequent winter and spring floods led to mounting costs and in 1861, as railroad companies began to construct their own network of transportation, the Ohio legislature decided to lease the Hocking Canal.[20] Languishing in private hands, the canal was finally abandoned for navigation in 1894, providing a route that could be easily used to construct a railroad.[21]

First discovered in the early 1830s, the Straitsville Great Vein, 10 to 14 feet in thickness, was opened at different places on Sunday Creek and Monday Creek as many landowners began to mine its coal for private use.[22] Still the demand for coal remained relatively limited in the Midwest until after the Civil War. However, after the war ended and as industrial development in cities such as Cleveland, Toledo, Columbus and Cincinnati began to take off, interest in the Hocking Valley Coal Field grew as railroad companies began to look for ways to build routes to more rapidly get the coal to market.

The first major railroad to arrive was the Columbus & Hocking Valley Railroad on which during the evening of Monday, August 16, 1869, the first coal was transported from Nelsonville, "the little city of Black Diamonds," to Columbus. The railroad was completed the following year, and regular service between Athens and Columbus began on July 25, 1870.[23] After the railroad opened, the production of coal increased more than nearly tenfold and in less than five years nearly 20 percent of Ohio's coal came from the Hocking Coal Field.[24]

After acquiring land about 12 miles northeast of Logan, John D. Martin, a Lancaster businessman, began organizing wagon excursions into the Monday Creek region to promote New Straitsville. Opened on January 7, 1871, the Straitsville Branch connected Martin's new town to the Columbus & Hocking Valley Railroad. A second railroad, further north and in the same region, the Sandusky, Newark, Somerset & Straitsville Railroad, was completed in 1872 with a terminal at Shawnee, which was to become the valley's second coal mining boom town.[25] Resolved that Toledo, Sandusky and Cleveland should also be connected by rail to the Kanawha Valley another group of business men conceived of a third railroad, this one, however, in the Sunday Creek region. Although construction was begun in 1870, it wasn't until 1879, after experiencing financial difficulties due to the economic depression that followed the Panic of 1873 and delays that resulted from the need to construct a 1,600-foot-long tunnel near Moxahala, that the Ohio Central Railroad reached Corning, another recently platted town.[26] That same year, William P. Rend, a Chicago businessman, founded his namesake town one mile north of Corning, where Richard L. Davis was to arrive some two years later.

Even though the coal boom in the Hocking Valley had taken off only one decade before Davis first arrived in Rendville, the region already had a rich history of labor conflict. The depression that followed the collapse of the banking house of Jay Cooke and Company in September 1873, led nationally to over 5,000 commercial failures by the end of the year and the collapse of nearly two-thirds of all national unions by 1877.[27] According to Andrew Roy, who in 1874, five years after the Avondale, Pennsylvania, catastrophe in which 109 miners died after a single shaft fire trapped them in the mine, became Ohio's first state inspector of mines, "the panic of 1873 fell upon the country like an avalanche." It "led to a series of strikes which crippled and finally destroyed" the American Miners Association, which had been founded by Daniel Weaver before the Civil War.[28]

Despite the depression, however, a new national organization, the Miners' National Association, was founded on October 13, 1873, in Youngstown, Ohio, and led by John Siney of St. Clair, Pennsylvania. Committed to "Arbitration, Conciliation and Co-operation," yet beset by Franklin B. Gowen in his pursuit of the Molly Maguires and union organizers, as well as by the ongoing economic depression and miners' opposition to Siney's stance against strikes as a means to settle disputes, in 1877 the Miners' National Association was forced to close its office in Cleveland as a result of an empty treasury.[29]

Soon after the depression hit the Hocking Valley a large percentage of its white miners went out on strike, which according to John James, secretary of the Miners' National Association, was one of the mining industry's most significant crises.[30] By 1873, when Nelsonville's population had doubled to 2,000 inhabitants, some 17 new coal companies had started up in addition to the 16 already existing ones, and nearly 2,000 men were working in the mines. By 1875 the Hocking Valley produced more than 20 percent of all coal that was mined in Ohio.[31]

Organized late in 1871, the Hocking Valley Miners' Union, which was a branch of the American Miners' Association negotiated a regional wage agreement. In response the operators organized the Hocking Valley Benevolent Association. Although it was open to miners, few joined. With an increasingly sizable regional labor force and competitive national market, in April 1873 the operators negotiated an annual contract that in fact lowered all miners' wages. By the time the depression started and the operators decided to cut production, the union had ceased to exist. Still, by December, miners in Nelsonville and New Straitsville once again organized locals belonging to the Miners' National Association. Soon after, the operators announced a new contract that would sharply cut wages and introduce screens, which meant the miners would no longer be paid for pea and nut coal.[32] On April 1, 1874, the day the new contract, which cut wages, introduced screens and proscribed the union, was to go into effect, the miners struck. After nearly two months, the operators still were unable to enforce the new contract. Although by mid–May, Miner T. Ames, a Chicago operator who owned part of the Lick Run Mine near Nelsonville, advised bringing in African American strike breakers, toward the end of the month, John D. Martin and the Shawnee operators decided to settle with the union. By early June, however, Ames had recruited between 400 and 500 African Americans, who knew nothing about the strike, to come to Columbus. On June 11, a special train with 11 railroad cars carrying the strikebreakers departed for the valley. Passing through Nelsonville the train stopped near Thaddeus Longstreth's mine, where they were issued muskets and provided extra protection by special policemen hired by the operators. The mine was turned into a military camp, and when the miners learned of the arrival of the strikebreakers, "anger swept the valley."[33] The next day between 600 and 800 miners, accompanied by their families and led by a brass band, headed for Longstreth's mine where they pled with the strikebreakers to leave. Although the miners and local citizens raised enough money to pay for 14 wagonloads of the strike breakers to leave, the majority did not. Rejecting compromise with the union, Longstreth employed 80 African Americans, protected by 45 white guards, at his mine. Similarly, W.F. McClung, at his mine in New Straitsville, employed 65 African Americans, protected likewise by 25 white guards. Expressing some of the latent racist resentment among the striking miners, the *Hocking Sentinel* wrote that "a gang of brutal Africans" had descended upon the valley whose "hills, vocal with independence and intelligence, were not formed to echo the crack of the negro driver's whip."[34]

Defeated by a "gang of Africans," according to the *Hocking Sentinel*, the Miners' National Association lost the strike as rehired workers left the union and went back to work at the lower wage.[35] The operators argued the miners should be happy with their new wages as mining coal required little skill. They boasted they had destroyed "the communistic principle that the miners have a proprietary interest in the mines" and broken the spirit of the French Commune.[36] Still, troubles and disputes continued, and by 1879, the Knights of Labor had become a nationally significant factor in the American labor movement.[37]

Unfortunately, little is known about what happened to the "gang of Africans" who first came to the Hocking Valley and, according to the *National Labor Tribune*, was "mostly composed of ignorant, dissolute villains" who threatened the livelihood of the "few hundred hardworking miners who have for years past been struggling to build themselves and their children little homes" in the "beautiful Hocking Valley."[38] According to "J.," a Nelsonville correspondent for the *Miners' National Record*, however, by July 1875,

> The negroes are getting quite scarce at the present. There seems to be a great demand for them elsewhere. It is their harvest time always when strikes are going on. A man was here from Brazil, Ind., and took some of them away with him to supplant the white labor now on strike there. A large number of them are professional "blacklegs," as well as being black. "We have," said they, "taken one valley, now go to take another." This was their farewell address, on entering the cars for other points.[39]

The voices of strikebreakers, unlike that of Richard L. Davis, are missing as they typically did not belong to organizations that would have left a written record.[40] Yet their recent arrival and history of labor conflict in the Hocking Valley helped create the world in which Davis arrived.

Chapter 2

Rendville

W.P. Rend

The life of Richard L. Davis was deeply intertwined with that of William Patrick Rend. When Rend passed away on November 30, 1915, 15 years after Davis' untimely death, his obituary which appeared in the *Chicago Tribune* the next day referred to him as a coal pioneer and the millionaire president of a consolidated coal company that included amongst others the Sunday Creek Coal Company and W. P. Rend & Company.[1] A prominent businessman and president of the Hibernian Banking Association in the city of Chicago, Colonel William P. Rend had played an important role in the drive of the "miracle city" to become the second largest manufacturing city in the country and the center of a steel industry powered by coal.[2] Rend had received his military title after the Civil War, while serving as a lieutenant-colonel in the Illinois National Guard, the Second Regiment of the Illinois State Militia.[3]

A controversial individual throughout his entire life, Rend was described in the *Biographical History of the American Irish in Chicago* in 1897 as one of the city's "most honored and eminent citizens," "cosmopolitan in character," and "better known [and] more highly respected" than any among those who could "lay claim to have been born in the Emerald Isle."[4]

Ever the businessman Colonel Rend reportedly told the Chicago Union League Club in January 1892 that they should welcome the smoke that clouded the Chicago skyline. "Smoke is the incense burning on the altars of industry," he said. "It is beautiful to me. It shows that men are changing the merely potential forces of nature into articles of comfort for humanity … smoke means manufactures and manufactures have built our city. You can't stop it." While he personally did not like choking on "this great mass of black smoke belching out of all our chimneys," Rend argued that smoke did not hurt people and might even promote good health and resistance to disease.[5]

Rend was born on February 10, 1840, in County Leitrim, Ireland, to Ambrose Rend, a farmer, and Elizabeth Cline, the daughter of a steward. He came to the United States in 1847 at the age of seven.[6] Settling in Lowell, Massachusetts, Rend graduated high school there at the age of seventeen. Unsuccessful in finding employment in New York City, he moved to New Jersey where he obtained a teaching position for one year in the city of New Brooklyn. Intending to visit an old friend in South Carolina, and on his way to Baltimore, he applied for another teaching position in West River, Maryland, where he ended up staying for three years during which he engaged himself in classic studies at St. John's College, located in what is now Annapolis.

However, when the Civil War broke out, Rend decided to give up his teaching position after receiving permission from the governor of Maryland to organize a company. Although he liked the South and counted several slaveholders among his friends, he had become convinced that slavery was "an evil of the greatest magnitude" and decided to oppose secession.[7] Unsuccessful in organizing the company, Rend decided to travel to Washington where he joined the Fourteenth New York Volunteers. He was engaged in several famous Army of the Potomac battles, including the battles of Antietam and Yorktown, and was honorably discharged in 1863. Shortly thereafter, during a visit with friends in Massachusetts, he met Elizabeth C. Barry, who like Rend was also of Irish descent but had been born in Nova Scotia. They married on December 27, 1864. Prior to his wedding, Rend traveled to Chicago where he secured employment in the surveyor's department of the Northwestern Railway Company. While working there as a freight clerk during the spring of 1864, Rend

William P. Rend, 1840–1915 (public domain).

decided to start a trucking business with his own line of teams. When his business prospered, he decided to enter the coal trade with Edwin Walker, a well-known corporate attorney, as his partner. Soon W.P. Rend & Co. became the largest merchant in eastern coal and the first coal operator responsible for transporting a train load of coal from the Hocking Valley to Lake Erie from where it was shipped to Chicago.[8] By 1894, after having entered the oil business as well, Rend owned 1,700 and 50 train freight cars and employed over 2,000 men in his mines in Pennsylvania and Ohio, the two largest coal producing states in the Midwest.[9]

As a businessman, Rend was a strong believer in arbitration and opposed to lockouts and strikes as he made clear in the role he played during the Hocking Valley Strike of 1884–1885 when a Christian Socialist publication referred to him as "a proprietor with a soul."[10] Five years earlier, Rend had stated that "capital represents the accumulation, or savings of past labor, while labor is the most sacred part of capital. Each has its respective duties and obligations toward the other.... Each is entitled to its equitable share, and there is no law, either human or divine, to justify the one impoverishing and crushing the other. God tells us, 'The laborer is worthy of his hire,' and threatens the vengeance of Heaven upon the oppressors of the poor."[11]

Remaining steadfast in his beliefs, in a speech at the Fourth Annual Joint Conference of Miners and Operators, held in Columbus, Ohio, on March 12, 1889, Rend said,

> We have got to employ one of two agencies: the agency of force or reason. Gentlemen, which shall we employ? Shall we resort to brutal strikes and lockouts again? Is that your wish? Is it the wish of any operator here to go back to the old system, to the old plan of fighting the miners, the plan that entails the loss of capital, the plan which brings ofttimes scenes of bloodshed and disorder to the State, and feelings of hostility, feelings of enmity between capital and labor? I do not believe that you want to go back to that old system. The other system is that of reason and intelligence, of using the highest power and the highest faculty that God Almighty has given us.[12]

Two years later, again putting his words into action, amidst such "poverty and distress ... that it became a question of whether the entire population would have to leave their homes," Rend "offered to give over the mine [in Rendville] to the miners for two months to work in for their own benefit as he claimed he could not work it without loss."[13]

Influenced by his Catholic faith, Rend was "a hater of bigotry ... and everything which tends to create animosity and ill-feeling between citizens and people of a common country." Yet he was also known for his "sanguine, lightly nervous temperament."[14] As reported in the *Hocking Sentinel* on September 2, 1897, Max Hayes, secretary of the Cleveland Central Labor Union, opined that Rend had "made it his business to besmirch every official who has ever been at the head of the miners' organization." Calling Michael Ratchford, then president of the United Mine Workers, an anarchist, Rend supposedly had stated that "he would like to be at the other end of the rope when Ratchford should be hauled over a tree or lamp post." In response Hayes suggested that he would like to be "one of a crowd who had hold of a rope to pull Rend up a lamp post."[15] Two weeks later, and reported in two newspapers, having been a witness to Rend discussing business with another mine operator in Pittsburgh, J.J. Steytler, manager of the Blythe Coal Company, gloated that it did him "good to see one millionaire snub another." After asking Steytler whether he had just been called a liar, Rend struck him, knocking Steytler down to the floor. As Steytler left the hotel stating he was going to get his gun, Rend went to get his. When Steylter returned an armed Rend asked him whether he was ready to fight, now or at any other time. When Steytler declined, the matter was dropped.[16] In 1901, on another occasion, while vacationing in Italy, Rend's daughter reported that after receiving a telegram from Chicago, he blew his temper so bad that she wondered which of "the two volcanoes put on a better show," Mt. Vesuvius or her father.[17]

In 1902, two years after Davis' death, Rend left Ohio when he sold all his mines in the Hocking Valley to the Continental Coal Company of Pittsburgh for $750,000 and turned his attention to Illinois where he opened two mines near Rend City in Franklin County.[18] There he and another operator apparently owned enough land in 1909 to sell 20,000 acres for $1.5 million to a representative of a group of New York investors.[19] Mirroring the story of Rendville, Ohio, Rend City, Illinois, quickly grew into a town of 1,500 inhabitants that faded rapidly after Rend sold his mine following a disastrous explosion that occurred in 1908. Rebuilt, but sold in 1920 and shut down in 1927, the mine and its town disappeared to the bottom of Rend Lake when it was constructed in 1972.[20] Adding to the reputation he had developed earlier in life, Rend was remembered by a Mrs. Agostine of Rend City as a "down-to earth" type of person who once asked her to hide a burlap sack with $36,000 on her horse-drawn cart from thieves so he could follow her in his buggy to personally deliver his miners' wages.[21] Indicative of his concern for the well-being of his miners, Rend gave the miners in Rend City the opportunity to paint their company-built houses "in different hues of orange, yellow and gray" as he had done in Rendville, Ohio, where houses "of different size, shape and color" gave the town "an agreeable and picturesque appearance."[22]

Although he was a frequent contributor to the press on political issues, throughout his life Rend generally did not actively involve himself in politics. After the Civil War, it was at the suggestion of Rend that Bishop Ireland of St. Paul sent Father Cotter, the future Bishop of Winona, on a temperance crusade across Ohio and Indiana in which 17,000 people took a pledge not to drink alcohol.[23] In 1880, Rend decided to no longer vote along with "the Irish people of this country and against the interests of a suffering and down-trodden race" for the Democratic ticket. Instead he decided to support James Garfield, declaring that he felt it his "duty to vote with the Republican Party," because "it has been the party of the freedom and progress, [has] entrenched a down-trodden people ... preserved the Union, and ... is the party of intelligence and enlightenment."[24] Later that same year, in a speech on the "Dangers of Free Trade to the Industrial Workers of the Country," Rend condemned the Democratic Party for opposing tariffs. Speaking at a time when the depression that followed the Panic of 1873 was coming to an end, Rend believed it had been the direct outcome of free trade that forced "one million men ... in enforced idleness," and reduced many of them "to a condition of beggary and want in a land of fertility and profuse abundance." Suggesting that the French Commune "has vanished into thin air and will never again show its head as long as our laboring men are employed and earning a decent living," Rend argued that as "never before in the entire history of the country has our currency been so good, or so plentiful, as at the present time; and our laboring, our business, and our commercial classes have never before enjoyed such general prosperity" turning "so-called communists [into] law abiding peaceable citizens."[25] Rend concluded, "Good wages gives our laborers a manhood independence, while starving wages, no matter what the form of government may be, means the abject slavery of the laborers."[26] In 1896, nearly two decades later, Rend served as marshal of Illinois Day, a parade held in Canton, Ohio, home of presidential candidate and tariff advocate William McKinley. During that same election year, he also helped organize a large parade for McKinley in Chicago.[27]

By the time of his death, Rend had fathered 11 children of whom five reached maturity, including three sons, Joseph P., James E., and Frank A.[28] In 1899, the year before Davis died, Joseph Paul, born on September 22, 1870, was serving as the president of six companies, including the W.P. Rend Co., which at the time was located in the McCormick Building on Michigan Avenue in Chicago.[29] That same year Joe managed three mines for his father in Athens County.[30]

Rendville

Rendville's history of African American miners and their families living side by side with its white inhabitants was so unusual in southeast Ohio that when published by the *New Lexington Herald* in 1909, *The Book of Perry County: An Historic, Industrial Portfolio* referred to the community as a "Dark-Town." Its author opined that "its people are thrifty, enterprising and have made good citizens" and that "while most of them work in the mines, many have become merchants, doctors and preachers, and are demonstrating in a quiet way what education and environment may do for the colored people."[31] According to John L. Jones, author of a fascinating family history written circa 1930, over time African Americans came to outnumber the white population and "instead of taking everything as they could have done they divided the offices with their white brothers and by so doing ... kept up a relationship akin to love."[32]

McCormick Building, W.P. Rend & Company, Chicago (Lake County [IL] Discovery Museum, Curt Teich Postcard Archives).

By the time of the 1900 U.S. Census, Rendville had grown from an all-white community of 349 inhabitants in 1880 to a racially mixed community in which approximately three-fifths of its 790 inhabitants were white and two-fifths African American. That same year Rendville's population was nearly evenly divided between males and females. While in 1880 males made up slightly more than two-thirds of Rendville's inhabitants, by 1900 the genders were nearly evenly divided, an indication that the town had become more stable and family-centered.[33] In 1879, when the economy had sufficiently recovered from the Depression of 1873, New York industrialist Erastus

Rendville, bird's-eye view, early 1900s (Little Cities of Black Diamonds).

Corning financed resuming construction of the Moxahala tunnel and the Ohio Central Railroad. Having supervised the final extension of the Toledo & Ohio Central Railroad, which connected Rendville with Moxahala and Corning and included finishing construction of the Moxahala tunnel and opening the Thomas and Lemert mine, Colonel Wilson C. Lemert was appointed superintendent of the Ohio Central Railroad Company and the Ohio Central Coal Company.[34] After consolidating with the Richmond and Alleghany and extending the Ohio Central Railroad with a distance of 150 miles from Corning to Williamson, West Virginia, a distance of 150 miles, in 1882 Lemert was appointed chief engineer on the staff of Governor Foster.[35]

In 1879, a syndicate of capitalists in the city purchased the Columbus and Sunday Creek Valley Railroad as well as the Central Ohio Railroad for $1 million to create the Ohio Central Railroad Company. The latter was capitalized at $4 million "to open up the coal trade of the Sunday Creek Valley." Among its directors was Governor-Elect Charles Foster of Ohio. In anticipation of finishing the railroad, which was expected to bring "an enormous business of carrying the Sunday Creek Valley coal into Columbus and Toledo," William P. Rend & Co. of Chicago leased land from the Ohio Central Railroad Company. By October of that same year, together with Captain Thomas J. Smith, a local investor, Rend had platted Rendville and personally overseen

the sinking three mine shafts in which he installed a large air compressor to run three Lechner cutting machines, known as "Iron Men," that were "kept at work both night and day."[36]

Throughout the first eight months of 1880 "U. No.," an unidentified local resident, regularly reported to the *New Lexington Tribune* on the progress that was being made in Rendville. By April, Captain Thomas J. Smith was planning to build a hotel with 16 rooms, while Frank Deaver, on whose farm Rendville had been platted, planned to erect a brick building with a hall for the Odd Fellows who organized their Sunday Creek Lodge No. 699 on January 19, 1881. Less than two months later, and in the typical tradition of the day,

Top: Rendville, Main Street with Scotch Hill, early 1900s (Little Cities of Black Diamonds). *Above:* Rendville, section of Main Street and Scotch Hill, today (photograph by the author).

the African Americans in Rendville organized their own separate Mineral Lodge No. 2220 on March 1.[37] In July, the Odd Fellows held a successful Independence Day picnic, Charles Mulharren lost his right hand after being hit by the train, five-year-old Ned Rodgers was fatally kicked by a horse, and

John Williston was fatally struck by a rebounding limb as he was cutting a tree. Succumbing to sun stroke, Rend's agent and operator, G.C. Weitzel, nearly lost "the opportunity to improve his French" speaking skills as he was wont to regularly communicate by telephone with the company's bookkeeper, Monsieur Frebault, in Corning.[38] In April, Rend's hiring practices led to early tensions when he brought about 35 Swedes from Chicago to Rendville which caused the "old hands" to worry they might be replaced as soon as the Swedes would become proficient at working in the mines.[39] Another three months later Rend brought in "a squad of fifty foreigners he had employed upon their landing in New York." According to the *New Lexington Tribune*, they were Irish, German and English. Very few of them had ever mined any coal, and they did not take very kindly to the work. Most of them departed in July and left Rend to pay their boarding bills. Since Rend had also paid their fares from New York to Rendville, that item could now also be charged "to the profit and loss account."[40] In mid-August, tensions re-emerged as Rend employed "some twenty colored men" to be paid "one half of the proceeds of all lump coal, nut coal and slack mined." According to U. No. the white miners who agreed to stay and mine at that rate "appear[ed] to be indifferent as to what the colored men [did]."[41] By early September, African American men and women in Rendville, most of who came from the New River region in West Virginia, numbered about 120. Although there had "been no actual collision between the white miners and colored men," the African American miners working at Mine No. 3 had to be guarded "both day and night" as, according to U. No., there had been "considerable threatening."[42]

By September 3, tensions escalated to such an extent that W.C. Lemert telegraphed Sheriff Henry Martin a request "to send troops at once." On Saturday, September 18, about 250 white miners marched downhill from nearby Millertown to Corning and demanded Lemert allow them to meet with the colored miners. After proclaiming that "it was not the colored race they were opposing" but rather their agreement to work on "the sliding scale," all but about a hundred white miners remained overnight in Rendville. The next morning, Sunday, September 19, Lemert once again called upon the sheriff, notifying him that "persons and property [were] in danger" as "about one thousand [men] from Nelsonville, Shawnee and elsewhere" had arrived at Rendville with two hay wagons that were falsely rumored to conceal rifles.[43] Lemert telegraphed the governor that he had to "detain by talk ... about two hundred men with arms ... they had stored in the mines at Rendville."[44] The would be "assailants finally scattered when Governor Foster called out the National Guard, complete with the newly developed Gatling Gun."[45] After they had gathered "about 30 shotguns and squirrel rifles," one of the miners, it is claimed, accidentally discharged his rifle which led to a "five minutes battle" that resulted in three or four wounded men. According to the *New Lexington Tribune*, "had it not been for that all disturber of the peace, 'King Alcohol,' there would have been no firing."[46]

The following Tuesday, as "all [was] quiet on Sunday Creek," at a Democratic rally in Corning, M.A. Foran, the first of two speakers, attempted to use the incident for political gain. "The negroes [are] the inferior race," he told the crowd, and he did "not wonder at the miners refusing to work with a race of people not their equals." Having claimed to have freed the negroes, he believed that, the Republican Party now had to take care of them and had done so by importing them into the Sunday Creek Valley and put them to work on the sliding scale.[47]

According to U.No., the trouble was over as long as the "soldier boys" with their Gatling guns which could "fire 300 shots per minute" stayed in town.[48] By early October the militia had departed and the Ohio Central Coal Company having done away with the sliding scale, Rend & Co. and the Sunday Coal Company each agreeing to pay 80 cents per ton, "all was peaceable once again."[49] Although rumors spread once again that the "negroes" intended "to come down and clean out the whites," and "the male portion of the place paraded the street all night, with their guns on their shoulder," all remained "peace and quiet" in "Ebony Hollow."[50] Thus the so-called "Corning War" had in effect come to an end. Rendville's African Americans were here to stay.

As the town continued to prosper, by November 1880, Rendville featured a grist mill, a meat market, several store rooms, boarding houses, a hotel, a drug store, a shoe shop and seven saloons. Still, life was not without its problems. In the midst of talk about incorporating Rendville and Corning in an attempt to control some of the rowdiness in both towns,[51] local resident Christopher Hock "was found hanging in an old slaughterhouse," the victim of a suspected murder after he had been seen "drinking quite heavily for some time."[52] In March of the following year, as "a young colored man" accidentally "shot himself through the head" and a drunken Pat Kelly fell to his death after he stumbled into a mine shaft, an effort was made to control the rowdiness in both towns and Rendville and Corning were incorporated as Corning.[53]

Rendville's incorporation with Corning, however, was short lived. As the 17 saloon keepers and several druggists in town failed to keep their agreement to close their businesses at 10 p.m. on week nights and be closed on Sundays, U.No. soon called for Rendville to incorporate as a separate town: "It would be a blessing to the peace loving citizens of this place if we were

Rendville, Baptist Church, early 1900s (Rendville Art Works).

incorporated. Then, perhaps, our saloon keepers could be made to respect law and decency enough to keep their saloons closed on Sundays. Yesterday they were in full blast, and were filled with loafers of our own and neighboring towns, as well as a number of excursionists who came on the train."[54] Less than one and a half years after it incorporated with Corning, on August 10, 1882, Rendville elected its first town officer, passed its first ordinances and made plans to build a town hall and jail.[55]

Although public drunkenness appears to have been a significant problem in the early days of Rendville, the Ohio Central Coal Company had a policy of donating "dollar of dollar for money collected," which enabled the town's African American population to construct two churches, one Baptist and one Methodist, before the end of 1881. One reason perhaps why they were so successful in building these houses of worship was that, as Colonel Wilson C. Lemert, superintendent of the Ohio Central Coal Company, claimed, the company paid "the colored and German miners" it had brought into the valley "exactly the same as the old miners" in all of its mines. In a report in the *New Lexington Tribune* in January 1882 on its 11 mines in the Sunday Creek Valley, Lemert asserted that the company had "no fight against organizations, color or creed" and that "any man who wants work, and is willing to work, is welcome to go into their mines and go to work any day. The company will do all

Rendville, Baptist Church, today (photograph by the author). It was relocated during the rerouting of State Route 13 during the 1960s. The church was moved to the short section of Main Street that still exists. Scotch Hill was part of Main Street but is now an unpaved hillside that leads up to the Rendville cemetery.

in their power to make them comfortable and happy."[56] An indication of the goodwill he had engendered, when Lemert "bid his goodbye" on April 1, 1882, the laborers of Mine No. 3 presented him with an inscribed "elegant gold watch, chain and charm." According to U.No., "Large crowds of the Coal Company employes [sic] assembled at the depots at Corning and Rendville, to bid the Colonel adieu when he started home on Saturday; his departure is universally regretted and the almost unanimous opinion of the people is that the coal company had made a mistake in the change of management."[57]

To distinguish between the locations of the mines, the Ohio Central Coal company assigned odd numbers to mines with shaft openings into big vein coal and even numbers to mines with drift openings into four- to six-feet coal veins.[58] One of eight shaft mines, operated by Rend, Mine No. 3 had a shaft 47 feet deep, a vein eight feet thick, and employed 140 men, all African-American. Rend also operated Mine No. 5 which had a shaft 45 feet deep, a vein eight feet thick, a double entry system and employed about 170 men of whom 75 were black.[59] In May 1882, as the coal business in the valley had "about come to a standstill," Rend sent 40 black miners to work in his mine at Midway, Pennsylvania. With a hundred more expected to follow soon, by the end of the month several had already come back to move their families.[60] Still, Rendville's black mining families organized their own Thanksgiving celebrations that year, to be followed by their first annual Emancipation Day, which they celebrated on September 22, 1883, with an "old fashioned southern barbeque."[61] On Thursday, August 3, 1882, the narrow valley where Rendville was located was struck "by the most destructive floods that ever occurred on Sunday Creek. In about half an hour's time the water had risen thirteen feet, and was destroying everything in its course," including Clifford's saloon, and flooding several mines.[62] Amidst efforts to rebuild the town and reopen the mines resident Owen Murray opened his door on Friday, August 18, "surprised to find a basket on his doorstep in which was found a pretty infant about four months old with a note telling her age (and that her) name was Mary, and promising half the mother's earnings for the care of the child. Nothing is known about who the mother is or why she left the child. Mr. Murray will adopt the child."[63]

Violence continued to be a problem during Rendville's early years. On February 3, 1884, for example, Peter Clifford, a white resident, became a victim of crime when Richard Hickey, "the dissolute keeper of a saloon and bawdy house" and member of "a notorious and worthless" white family committed "one of the most cold blooded murders that has ever been known in the history of the Sunday Creek valley." After Peter's brother James Clifford had "scandalized his family and friends by marrying Mary Ann Hickey," Peter Clifford had "taken no pain to conceal his opinion of his new sister-in-law." After Peter's wife had been insulted by Mrs. Hickey in downtown Rendville, he went over to Hickey's place "to settle the affair." In the fight that broke out, "Hickey got the worst of it." That night, at 12 o'clock, when Peter Clifford answered a knock at his door, "a revolver flashed before him and a ball passed entirely through his body from side to side." His dying words, "Molly, Hickey

Rendville, Emancipation Day (Little Cities of Black Diamonds).

has shot me," led to the arrest of three suspects. Soon "upwards of one thousand people gathered at the house in which the prisoners were confined and surrounded it all day." Although "a guard of fifteen colored men [had] been placed over them for protection," that evening at 8 o'clock, "Richard Hickey was taken out of the custody of the officers by twelve masked men and hanged to a sycamore tree," which still stands today next to the city hall. The remaining two prisoners were ordered out of town.[64]

Two months after her husband's lynching, Mrs. Hickey "paid the tax and again opened the saloon at the old stand."[65] Perhaps not surprisingly, she once again made the front page when on Sunday, December 23, 1888, when Mrs. Whitfield, "better known to the public as Mrs. Hickey," got into a fight with her new husband and after running downstairs to get a revolver went back upstairs and fired two fatal shots. The *New Lexington Tribune* noted that her house was well known "as the resort of all masses of evil disposed persons and a stench in the nostrils of the good citizens of Rendville for many years. Negros and whites—the offscourings of the valley made her doggery a place for all kinds of debauchery." The paper wished "that Justice, with an iron hand,

Rendville, Town Hall (Little Cities of Black Diamonds).

be meted out to her," and Mrs. Whitfield was convicted of second degree murder.[66] Five years later, Peter Clifford's drunken and axe-wielding brother Billy, "a notorious character" and "for many years a Corning desperado," met a violent death at the hands of Dick Craney in a saloon dispute after which many citizens silently rejoiced "that the life of such a desperate character is ended."[67]

Despite such rowdiness, construction of a new school house at Rendville progressed, and on Monday, October 2, 1882, the Rendville Academy opened with three teachers, including Sadie D. Broadis, who according to her future husband John L. Jones "beat [him in] getting to the school" to become "the first colored person to teach school in Perry County and the first of any race to teach in Rendville, Ohio."[68] The Ohio school act of 1848 had established that African American children could attend the regular schools in districts where there were less than 20 colored children. In districts where there were more than 20 colored children the African American population was allowed to form its own self-supported school district. Beginning in 1849, however, colored school districts also began receiving state funds and four years later colored schools were placed under the same administration as the white schools.[69] In 1878, a new state school law dropped the requirement of a separate district when there were more than 20 colored children. While school boards were allowed to continue the practice of two districts, the law required they offer a free education to all children in the state.[70]

At the opening of the second school year, U.No. reported that principal J.E. Kintz of Somerset was assisted by Sadie Broadis, Ella Addison and Alice Wigten.[71] As families with children continued to move to Rendville, on May 15, 1884, the *New Lexington Tribune* reported that the town's school building was no longer big enough to accommodate the children of school age and that a room outside the school had to be rented. On February 16, 1887, one month after Richard L. Davis had married Mary Bailey, the Ohio legislature repealed the last of Ohio's "Black Laws," thus officially ending "separate schools for white and colored children."[72] Named the Arnett bill, the 1887 law was introduced by Benjamin W. Arnett, a bishop in the African Methodist Episcopal Church and Republican representative from Wilberforce in Greene County.

That same year, the school board in Rendville was composed of "two colored directors and one white," and thus controlled by African Americans. Therefore passage of the Arnett Law was not an issue in Rendville, unlike in some other southern Ohio communities, such as Xenia and Gallipolis, which continued to defy desegregation well into the twentieth century.[73] Interestingly however, according to John L. Jones, a member of Rendville's prominent Jones family, his brother J. McHenry, integrated Ohio's Pomeroy High School nearly ten years prior to the Arnett bill and in 1882 graduated as its valedictorian.[74]

In September 1887, the *New Lexington Tribune* reminded its readers that "the distinctively colored schools have been abolished and pupils, white and colored, are all to be graded and classified in accordance with what they know."[75] In a special report from Rendville the *Ohio State Journal* reported,

> Our schools will be mixed according to law. Our principal will be white. Our board appointed three white teachers and two colored to represent the ratio in population. Everybody seems to take the situation kindly save a few who will ere long learn that a man is but a man. This will be the first year of our grade schools; also a High school will be established. We are compelled to give undying praise to the Ohio Legislature and our present directors for a perfect school system at last in Rendville, the first town to elect a colored man, Dr. I.S. Tuppins, as mayor.[76]

This was the dynamic, changing community of early Rendville where Richard L. Davis would be joined by other prominent African Americans, including Isaiah Tuppins, Rend's company doctor, and Adam Clayton Powell, Sr., miner and future founder of Abyssinian Baptist Church in Harlem, New York. In June 1884, as the Great Hocking Valley Strike was about to break out, "Nuptisp" reported in the *Cleveland Gazette* that 250 to 300 African American families were living in the valley. In urging his black neighbors to subscribe to the *Gazette*, Nuptisp offered a telling description of Rendville's racially mixed population: "Our city officers largely are colored, our grocery keeper is colored, our doctor [I.S. Tuppins] is colored, also our hotel keeper is a colored man."[77]

Chapter 3

The Great Hocking Valley Strike

Two years after Richard L. Davis arrived in Rendville, major upheaval struck the Hocking Valley. Although no letters have been uncovered he might have written during this major strike that drew national attention, it doubtlessly must had a deep impact on his personal life as well as his thoughts about the labor movement. Among all letters he wrote, his only reference to the Great Hocking Valley Strike was published in the *National Labor Tribune* on April 20, 1891, in which he reminded the Hocking Valley miners that they only had to "look back at the great strike of '84' and '85' to remember to 'take heed' and stand together in a national movement."[1]

Chris Evans

Although we don't know for certain whether Richard L. Davis and Chris Evans ever met in person, Davis must have been well aware of Evans' status as a giant in the labor movement, especially because of his leadership role during the Great Hocking Valley strike. It is likely, however, that their paths crossed in 1897 while organizing labor in West Virginia. In a letter, Frank J. Weber, a labor organizer for the American Federation of Labor, informed Evans that "Richard L. Davis is here," and that he "had him speak to the colored men."[2]

Chris Evans was born on March 8, 1841, in Upper Gornal, South Staffordshire, England, to parents of Welsh descent. By the age of ten he was already working as a miner's son. By 1861 his father had died and Evans still lived with his widowed mother and younger siblings and worked as a miner. Eight years later, in 1869, the year the Knights of Labor were first organized and construction began on the Columbus & Hocking Valley Railroad, Evans immigrated to America with his wife Caroline and their young daughter

Rachel. That same year, the nation's first effort at a national miners association, the American Miners Association, had failed after an eight year effort, to be superseded by the Miners' Benevolent Association, first organized in the anthracite coal fields of eastern Pennsylvania.

Evans soon accepted a job as a miner in the Shenango Valley coal fields of western Pennsylvania, just across the border from the Mahoning Valley Coal Fields near Youngstown, Ohio. Changing its name to the Miners and Laborers' Benevolent Association, by 1872 the nation's second miners' organization had established branches in the bituminous coal fields of western Pennsylvania and eastern Ohio. Although the cause of labor was spreading, the Knights of Labor and the Miners and Laborers Benevolent Association, feared being seen as a militant labor unions. Organized in December 1873, a local lodge of the Miners' and Laborers' Benevolent Association was organized in Mercer County with Chris Evans as its president. The following year the lodge joined the Miners' National Association, formed two month prior in Youngstown, Ohio.

Chris Evans, 1854–1924 (Evans, *History of the United Mine Workers of America, 1914–18,* 1920).

In 1875, a few months after he joined the Knights of Labor and a year after a bitter strike in the Hocking Valley Coal Fields, a then 34-year-old Chris Evans first entered the history of the Hocking Valley as he traveled to collect money for his fellow striking miners back in Mercer County. His love for the cause of labor, however, in the years to come would be shaped by the ongoing ideological struggle between the inclusive Knights of Labor and the exclusive trade unions which were organized on the basis of trade-specific skills and typically were more militant in their use of strikes and confrontation.³

While traveling the Hocking Valley, rather than speaking of the Miners' National Association, Evans spoke to the miners of the secret Knights of Labor movement. Telegraphing organizers back in Pennsylvania to suggest the Knights of Labor should send an organizer into the Hocking Valley, local Master Workman John M. Davis instructed Evans to undertake that very role. As a result before returning to Pennsylvania, Evans organized Local Assembly No. 120 in New Straitsville, Ohio's second assembly of the Knights of Labor and its first in the coal fields.

Disappointed to find out upon his return that the strike in Mercer County had failed, Evans did receive the good news that on February 6, 1876, Thomas Lawson had successfully organized Local Assembly 169 in Shawnee, Ohio's fourth assembly of the Knights of Labor and its second in the coal fields. Encouraged by the pro-union sentiments he had encountered in the Hocking Valley, in the spring of 1876, Evans, along with his wife Caroline and three children moved to New Straitsville where the family would add four more.

On July 14, 1877, a seemingly small strike in Martinsburg, West Virginia, culminated in the Great Railroad Strike. Spreading into Hocking Valley, the local miners began to make their own demands. Describing the situation, Evans wrote, "The Hocking Valley became very uproarious, and the strike feeling intensely increased as the days passed by."⁴ During the strike the miners held secret meetings at Robison's Cave, an overhanging sandstone rock shelter, in downtown New Straitsville which is now considered the cradle of the United Mine Workers of America. Fortunately, according to Evans, the local coal operator and founder of New Straitsville, John D. Martin of Lancaster, "a fluent talker, mild in his expressions," who had "a persuasive power of eloquence such as a few men possess," helped end the strike by agreeing to a raise of ten cents per ton, after which the miners decided to return to work.⁵

By the early 1880's after the Knights of Labor had come out of secrecy, its membership in the Hocking Valley was widespread. However, Evans started showing signs of doubting the effectiveness of this organization for the miners' cause. Although he remained a member of Local Assembly 1560 in Carbon Hill until April 1887, when its charter was abruptly revoked by the national Knights of Labor office due to "insubordination," he began to increasingly emerge as a leader of the trade union movement for miners.⁶

In 1882, the year Richard L. Davis arrived in Rendville, the call for a state convention in the *National Labor Tribune* led to the creation of the Ohio

Miners' Amalgamated Association and the election of John McBride of Massillon as state president and Evans as president of District No. 1, Hocking Valley. When on June 27, the following year, the Hocking Valley miners decided to go out on a strike, Evans was appointed to a committee of three "to prepare an address to the miners of Ohio, setting forth the situation and necessity of their aid and support" and elected president of the Straitsville district relief committee.[7] Illustrative of his leadership skills during the strike, the relief committee secured donations from cities all around Ohio.

On February 27, 1885, a conciliatory Evans testified before the legislature's Investigative Committee, on behalf of the miners as President of District No. 1, of the Ohio Miners' Amalgamated Association. After the strike came to an end a few weeks later on March 18, elected executive secretary of the newly founded National Federation of Miners and Mine Laborers, Evans began to work closely with William P. Rend on plans for a joint conference between the operators and miners that on February 24, 1886, resulted in the nation's first ever jointly negotiated interstate labor contract.[8]

According to Evans, the Knights of Labor's decision on May 20, 1886, to organize National Trades Assembly No. 135 on behalf of the nation's coal miners started "a rivalry ... for supremacy [that] covers pages of history that for pure, unadulterated, caustic, pungent and satirical sarcasm could hardly be substituted on lines of the severest criticism."[9] During the next four years Evans played a key leadership role as a mediator in the struggle to unite the two distrustful rivals. On December 10–14, 1889, however, just one month before the scheduled convention for the purpose of combining the Knights of Labor and the National Progressive Union, which had succeeded the Federation in December 1888, the American Federation of Labor held its annual convention in Boston, Massachusetts. It was at this convention that Evans, representing District No. 10 of the National Progressive Union, was elected secretary, a position he would hold for the next five years while serving under founding president Samuel Gompers until John McBride's election in December 1894 as the president led him to the decision to step aside, arguing that it was wrong for two miners to serve as both president and secretary.[10]

Saying his goodbyes to the Ohio miners of District No. 10 on January 20, 1890, Evans stated,

> I have nothing but words of praise and commendation for the kind assistance given in the performance of my official duties. Our relations with each other have been of the kindest nature, at all times, and while the duties I have been called upon to perform by our co-workers in the trades union movement in America, will, for a time, cause our personal visits to be less frequent, you can rest assured that my voice and pen will be always with you, no matter where I am, or what duties I may be called upon to perform.[11]

After his resignation, Evans returned to the United Mine Workers as a statistician and organizer, and visiting, among others, convict mines. Already in his sixties, in 1905, Evans was attacked and beaten unconscious by three armed and masked men on a train near Trinidad, Colorado, where he was working as an organizer. After recovering from this traumatic experience, he wrote two volumes entitled *History of the United Mine Workers of America* from the year 1860 to 1890 (Volume 1) and from the year 1890 to 1900 (Volume 2) that were published sometime between 1914 and 1920 and dedicated to the "officers and members of the National Executive Boards" as well as the union's "rank and file." Having retired to Nelsonville, Evans lived with his never married daughter Elsie until he died in 1924, the same year Powderly and Gompers passed away.

Although the United Mine Workers desired to erect an elaborate marker on his grave, Evans' family felt that their humble father, who never sought fame, would not have approved. He is buried under a simple style marker in the New Straitsville cemetery, next to his wife Caroline and daughter Clara.

Prelude

It is in the person of Chris Evans that organized labor first entered the Hocking Valley in 1875. According to Fink, the Gilded Age "turned the plowshares of a consensual past into a sword of class conflict,"[12] as the Knights of Labor in its Declaration of Principles sought "by peaceful processes [to] evolve the working classes out of their present condition in the wage system into a co-operative system." Although it "did not propose to organize a political party," labor conflict led many Knights to seek political office.[13]

In 1880, a year after the Knights of Labor went public after a decade of secrecy, the miners in Rendville organized Local Assembly #1602. According to John L. Jones, two years later when Davis arrived in town, Rendville's African American miners organized their own Local Assembly # 1935. By June 1883, according to "Henry," "the colored assembly (1935) at Rendville [was] doing first class" and its members were "taking advantage of the free reading rooms recently established."[14] The following year Local Assembly 1935 counted 41 members, while by 1885 this number has increased to 83.[15]

In the early part of 1882, five years after the demise of John Siney's short-lived Miners' National Association, and as the economy continued to recover, the *National Labor Tribune* issued a call to the mine workers of Ohio for a convention to be held in Columbus for the purpose of organizing a state union. A joint conference in Pittsburgh on May 15, 1883, of the Ohio Miners'

Amalgamated Association and delegates from Pennsylvania, Illinois, and Maryland led to the creation of the Amalgamated Association of Miners of the United States. John McBride of Massillon was elected president, while Chris Evans was elected president of District 1 to represent the Hocking Valley.[16] In addition, the conference adopted the *National Labor Tribune* as its official organ.[17]

Representative of the growing consolidation of the coal industry and the disappearance of old economic patriarchal relationships, the coal operators in the Hocking Valley grew increasingly nervous about the labor movement and decided to organize as well.[18] In March, 1883, 17 mining companies in the Hocking Valley consolidated as the Columbus and Hocking Coal and Iron Company, better known as The Syndicate, with an appraised value of nearly $4.5 million. Samuel Thomas served as its president while John R. Buchtel, Walter Crafts, and Thaddeus Longstreth served as vice-presidents.[19] That same spring 12 other operators formed the Ohio Coal Exchange, which marketed coal on behalf of several firms.[20]

Although in 1878, to prevent strikes, the miners and operators in the Hocking Valley had come to an agreement to set the rate for mined coal at 70 cents in the summer (May 1–September 1) and 80 cents in the winter (September 1–May 1), unfortunately, in January 1883, the region was once again struck by an economic depression. Seeking an opportunity to improve their market position and perhaps force a strike to break the miners' union, the coal operators met in Shawnee in January, 1884.[21] They decided to ask the miners to accept a wage reduction from 80 to 60 cents per ton on March 1, arguing that they faced stiff competition from other coal fields, especially those in the Pittsburgh area. Rend, however, believed that a reduced rate in the Hocking Valley would be followed by other coal fields across Ohio, as well as in neighboring states, which would leave the Ohio operators in relatively the same position toward each other on the competitive market.[22] Advised by McBride and Evans that a wage reduction in the Hocking Valley would lead to similar wage reductions in coal fields across Ohio, the miners decided not to accept the wage cut. Concluding an agreement could not be reached, on Friday evening, June 20, the Syndicate posted notices that effective Monday, June 23, the rate of mining would be reduced to 60 cents per ton. At a district convention held in New Straitsville on June 27, the miners rejected the operators' reduction and walked out on strike.[23]

Rend claimed that before the depression his mines made a profit equal to 30 percent of his investment, and 20 percent during the depression year 1884, in part because he had the advantage of the Ohio Central Railroad's low freight rates for three of his four Hocking district mines.[24] However, most of the Hocking mines served by the Columbus, Hocking Valley & Toledo Railroad earned little or nothing in 1883 and 1884. In 1883, the Syndicate only earned a token profit. The Syndicate's iron business never earned a profit, and after February, 1884, the coal business of the Syndicate also ceased to be profitable.[25]

At a meeting on June 30, the Syndicate decided to end the 60 cents offer and instead bring in strikebreakers and mining machines. Next, on July 11, it discharged 1,800 miners ordering them to collect their back pay and remove their tools from the mines. The operators further decided on an additional wage cut to 50 cents per ton and stipulated the miners had to agree to "ironclad contracts" which required them to agree to work at a fixed rate for one year and not to join in any strike or belong to any union under penalty of immediate discharge and forfeiture of all pay. According to Andrew Roy, Ohio's first state inspector of mines, as many as 46 mines were shut down and more than 3,000 miners went out on strike.

> The anger of the strikers knew no bounds on reading these contracts and rules. The leaders at once prepared for a desperate and enduring struggle.... The great majority of the strikers, owing to the dull work of the preceding year, possessed neither money nor credit to carry themselves and families through any prolonged suspension. These needy families must be supported if the strike was to continue. The leaders at once organized committees of appeal, who were sent out among the surrounding farmers and to distant mining districts, to solicit aid. Money and provisions came pouring in from every quarter; many operators in other fields contributing liberally, feeling that the action of the syndicate in making such a sweeping cut in wages, and following it up with so hard and exacting a contract, was outraging the American spirit of fair play."[26]

Estimating that 4,000 to 5,000 miners participated in the strike, J.P. Burton, a coal operator from Massillon, guessed that immediately preceding the strike about 6,000 to 7,000 miners were employed in the Hocking District.[27] During the early 1880s, it was general knowledge that there were too many miners in the Hocking Valley for the amount of work that was available. By the spring of 1884, most major mines offered their men only three days of work per week. Reasons for the labor surplus included that the thick Straitsville Vein attracted a lot of miners because it was easier to mine the coal and therefore earn higher wages, that the operators deliberately employed too many miners and only paid them a month or sometimes even six weeks later after they had performed their services so they would end up spending their entire wages on credit at the company store, that expenses for mining tools exceeded earnings, and that the miners encouraged others to come to the Hocking Field and rather share the work than have some of their fellow miners leave.[28]

By the end of the year there were about 1,500 strikebreakers as well as slightly over a hundred Pinkerton guards in the valley. About a quarter of the strikebreakers were African American miners who came from Pennsylvania and Virginia. Germans, Poles, Italians, Hungarians and Swedes made up most of the others. According to Andrew Roy,

> The Pinkertons accompanied the needy adventurers, who were quartered in barracks improvised for the purpose—port holes being left in the barracks for the Pinkies to shoot through. Dead lines were established beyond which no striker was permitted to pass, and orders given to shoot every man, who on being halted, refused to turn back. In addition, a company of militia was sent to the Valley by the governor of the State on the requisition of the sheriff of Perry county.[29]

Ultimately it was their presence that allowed the operators to successfully break the strike.[30]

Andrew Roy, Ohio Inspector of Mines, 1874–1878 (Roy, *History of the Coal Miners*, 1906).

On June 27, the relief committee which was organized with Chris Evans as chairman, even though he was member of the Knights of Labor, an organization officially opposed to striking as a means to settle disputes. On the eastern side of the Hocking District, Rend, who had decided to remain an independent coal operator rather than join either the Syndicate or the Ohio Coal Exchange, continued to operate his mines at 70 cents per ton. Representing "a vanishing breed," Rend successfully sued the Columbus and Hocking Valley Railroad when it refused to supply him with railroad cars.[31] At one of his mines where he had employed 250 men on day shifts, he now employed over a thousand men in three shifts.[32] At the start of the strike his miners even voted to have one dollar per week checked off from their pay to help striking miners, a deduction which they later raised with another 50 cents. As donations came in from other coal fields in Ohio and across West Virginia and Pennsylvania, Rend also made a personal donation of $100 to the miners' cause. By the end of the strike the relief committee had received $26,740.37 in food and clothing and $70,333.48 in money, making a total of $97,074.15 to support of the strike, "all of which was distributed among the poor and needy of the strikers."[33] Although impressive, this amount was "only half" compared to donations collected for a smaller strike by Cincinnati cigar makers, which in the eyes of the miners affirmed the need for strong national union.[34]

According to historian George Cotkin, the miners "vented their anger in an essentially pre-industrial mode" by imposing "clear limitations upon the forms of violence they employed and the objects towards which their violence was directed."[35] During the early stages of the strike, local miners viewed the strikebreakers as misguided and uninformed. Despite the increasing tensions and misery, the strike witnessed relatively little violence. The reception of the strikebreakers was so mild that on July 26 the operators decided to send away the Pinkerton guards.[36] However, toward the end of the month news spread quickly that the operators would soon begin to evict strikers.[37] Despite warnings of violence, on July 31, the Syndicate began to evict some miners' families and simultaneously filed suit in court to remove all strikers from company-owned housing. As McBride implored the strikers not to resort to violence, most miners simply ignored their eviction notices. Fearing increased violence the operators failed to act upon most of their eviction notices. On August 2, James Hippel, a mine boss, was assaulted in Nelsonville and a train was fired at in Carbon Hill.[38]

On August 25, a court ruling allowing the operators to evict striking miners, however, led to riots in Buchtel involving nearly 400 miners. As bitterness over the evictions and restlessness continued to increase, during the weekend of August 30–31, the hopper at a New Straitsville mine was set on fire. With more than a thousand strikebreakers in the valley, masked miners fired shots at several mines, including at the Longstreth mine in Nelsonville, where despite his plea for mercy, William Hare, a mine guard, was shot and killed. As a result of this outburst of violence the miners lost much of their public support.[39]

On September 1, after the price of coal had dropped nationally to below what he was paying his miners, Rend felt forced to announce that he could not go back up to 80 cents. When his miners decided to go out on strike, Rend and Evans, who replaced an ill McBride, were able to persuade them to accept a wage cut and go back to work.[40] The day before, on August 31, when after "a night in riot and murder" and the hoppers at mine No. 7 in New Straitsville had been set on fire, Hocking County sheriff J.J. McCarthy called upon Governor George Hoadly, a Democrat, to send the militia. In response, Hoadly decided to not only send in the National Guard but to also make a personal visit. When asked during the visit what was to become of the evicted families, Hoadly replied, "I will send them tents." With the arrival of the militia, violence abated as miners' families continued to take in the evicted families. As a result, by mid–September Hoadly decided to withdraw the bulk of the militia.[41] In frustration over Hoadly's apparent unwillingness to use the militia to more severely suppress the strikers, many operators decided to shut down all operations in hopes of starving out the union miners. Later that year Hoadly would be soundly defeated in his attempt to gain another term as governor and would be replaced by Joseph B. Foraker, a Republican more sympathetic to the owners.[42]

By late summer the strike had gained national attention in New York's *Harper's Weekly Illustrated Magazine* and in newspapers around the country. On October 25, 1884, Frank Leslie's *Illustrated Newspaper*, also published in New York, featured a wood engraved image that depicted four officers leading a Hocking Valley miner through a large crowd of women in Buchtel. In the picture, sketched by artist Joseph Becker, some women held clubs that were raised in threatening positions and spoons to beat on pie pans, while the rest had faces that were contorted with rage. This image of the women of the Hocking Valley became a familiar one and drew national attention to the miners' plight. With the approach of fall and winter additional news accounts and images were published, including those of starving children huddled in cold tents in the arms of their despondent mothers.[43] On October 2, the *Athens Messenger* reported that while Rend's mine was the only one still operating, striking miners in Shawnee in search of food had raided the stock of farmers and that "scarcely a night passes but that cattle are butchered in the field and carcasses carried away."[44]

The strike also drew the attention of the International Working People's Association in Chicago. Decrying that every newspaper in the city was published by "capitalists in interest of profit-mongering, labor-robbing, slave driving schemes," and vowing to bring about "the abolition of economic slavery, and the complete emancipation of the working class from the tyranny of capital," its first issue of the *Alarm*, published in Chicago on October 4, 1884, under the heading "Modern Slavery" featured an article on "our starving friends in the Hocking Valley" where "10,000 men, women and children have been condemned to choose between unconditional submission to their masters and a slow starvation process, or resistance and a rapid process of starvation." Ironically, the only substantive population of African Americans in the valley was still at work and not among the starving. An army of "Pinkerton loafers, armed with Remington rifles," had arrived and declared martial law, and "the strikers were treated as criminals and every available political 'vag' or loafer in general was sworn in as a special policeman to guard the mines and other property of the syndicate against the strikers. This banditti of what is called 'law and order' live in grand style and were on an everlasting spree. Beer, whiskey and cigars were furnished gratuitously to them by the syndicate."

On October 18, the *Alarm* reported that on the previous Sunday, the mines in the Hocking Valley "were set on fire by parties unknown," and that evicted "families have been camping in the woods on the hillsides without shelter, and only such food as their sympathizing fellow-laborers have sent them from abroad."[45]

On the night of October 12, 1884, two weeks after the last national guardsmen went home, new trouble flared as unknown persons set fire to the Upson Mine near Shawnee. Three days later, on October 15, five mines of the Syndicate in the New Straitsville area, another mine at Sand Run, and W.A. Schoemaker's mine hopper at Nelsonville were set on fire as well.[46] In response, John Brashears, member of the Executive Board of the Ohio Coal Exchange, declared, "Mr. John McBride, I am sure, would be well satisfied and would like to see those men punished who did that deviltry, and I want to say that I know who the men are, and that they will get their deserts at the hands of the courts. It is not policy for us to say right now who these men are, but they will be brought to justice, you can rest assured of that."[47] However, no one was ever arrested or convicted for starting the "Devil's Oven," the underground fire that today, more than a century later, continues to burn.[48]

Although during the last few months of the strike there were no more mob actions, between November 1884 and March 1885 there was a constant succession of burnings of company houses, mine buildings, railway cars of coal, and even mines. On November 5, about 300 men attacked and fired on a house in Murray City where strikebreakers were lodging but they were driven off by Pinkerton Guards.[49] On December 4, the *Athens Messenger* reported that the hopper at an abandoned mine in New Straitsville had burned but that nonetheless "the backbone of the strike may be regarded as virtually broken."[50] Four days later, the *New York Times* quoted Judge Stevenson Burke, vice-president of the Columbus, Hocking Valley and Toledo Railroad Company, that the "backbone of the strike [had been] broken." The *Times* also reported on rumors of "gross mismanagement or fraud being practiced by those in charge of the distribution of money and supplies contributed for the relief of the distressed miners" and that two men from Nelsonville visiting Springfield, having "been very successful in collecting funds for the destitute miners," "at once proceeded to 'paint the town red' and were several days doing the town's saloons and places of low resort."[51] At the end of the month strikers set the Bristol tunnel on the Shawnee branch of the Baltimore and Ohio on fire, and in January, 85 more mines were set on fire.[52] In early December, the *Alarm* reported that the strike seemed to be nearing its end, "the outcome of coercion, of bayonets, of force." And by the end of the month, the "capitalistic cannibals" in the "Valley of Death," with "the aid of the State of Ohio, the detectives, the negro rabble of West Virginia, the refuse of Castle Garden, and the profound sympathy of the great guilds of monopoly, rapacity, and squeezing all over the land," were "devouring their propertyless victims."[53] According to Andrew Roy,

> The summer passed away into fall; the fall into winter; the winter into spring, and still there was no sign of yielding on the part of the determined strikers. Although liberal contributions in the shape of provisions, clothing and money came pouring in week after week, and month after month, there was much want and suffering in the Valley during the later months of the strike. Men without shoes waded through the frost and snow to the commissary; children subsisted on apples for days at a time; corn was grated on empty fruit cans and baked into bread, and still the strikers had their colors nailed to the mast.[54]

By February 1885, however, the *New York Times*, reported that the "very cold weather" precipitated that "the great Hocking Valley strike is at an end" and that due to "the reduction in the price of mining" in other states, "the commissary stores have been closed because of the lack of supplies" while "2,000 new men are at work" and "the efforts to prolong the misery of this strike come from individuals who do not want to work."[55]

Meanwhile, however, the strike received much interest in the Ohio legislature where Rep. Jones introduced a bill against the payment of wages in scrip that passed.[56] At a state convention, with State President John McBride in attendance and held in Columbus in early January 1885, the delegates asked the legislature to investigate the causes that led to the strike.[57] At a session of the General Assembly, at the instigation of John McBride, since his election in 1884 now also a Representative in the Ohio Assembly, a joint resolution passed to appoint what came to be called the Hocking Valley Investigation Committee.[58]

Hocking Valley Investigation Committee

The Hocking Valley Investigation Committee was appointed under House Joint Resolution No. 73 and consisted of senators John V. Lewis, Simon P. Wolcott and George F. Elliott and representatives G.H. Bargar, Jacob A.

Kohler and D.J. Stalter. Between February 25 and March 19, 1885, the day after the strike officially ended, the committee took the testimony of 13 witnesses on behalf of the miners. Next, between March 19 and March 25, the committee took the testimony of 16 witnesses on behalf of the operators. Its official report, *Proceedings of the Hocking Valley Investigation Committee*, was published after the committee adjourned on April 9. In its report the committee explained, "The first and primary object was to see what legislation is required to prevent, if possible, a recurrence of like troubles and to discuss a means for the adjustment of the same when so inaugurated; and secondly, to lay before the public the grounds of complaint as understood by both sides."[59] Because one of the committee's first actions was to elect a stenographer to record the testimonies, the report includes the unique original voices of each witness.

The witnesses for the miners included three coal operators, J.P. Rend and two operators from Massillon. Chris Evans and John McBride represented the Ohio Miners' Amalgamated Association. The remaining six miners and two checkweighmen all resided in the Hocking Valley and ventured from New Straitsville, Shawnee, Carbon Hill, Nelsonville, Orbiston, and Happy Hollow.

The first witness to appear before the committee was W.P. Rend, age 45 years and residing in Chicago. Rend blamed the strike on "human greed and avarice" among the operators as well as "the general depression." Referring to an "intense feeling of hostility" among the miners in response to the operators' demand for iron-clad contracts, Rend stated, "These men, from what I have learned, felt that this demand was insulting to their manhood; that it was degrading, and that it was an outrage in this free country to prevent men from meeting in defense of their common interest to discuss their labor rights." He thought that "it would be advisable for parties having mine stores to give up that branch as it is a constant cause of discontent and outcry on the part of the miners," and that it would be a great improvement "to pay the miners every two weeks, so as to give them an opportunity of buying for cash what they now have to buy on credit." "In treating with men," Rend argued, "I find that the proper way is to treat them with justice, to meet them as men, and to treat them as men; not to treat them as animals, not to treat them as slaves."

> A great many men who are now employing labor, are men who have never done any work; they don't understand the privations, trials and sufferings of the men, and often do not care anything for them.... If they were to mingle more among their men; if in our industry they were to go into their mines and converse with their men, and ascertain fully the difficulties they have to contend with, if they were to try to settle in a friendly manner the questions which come up from time to time, if they were to under-

stand the difficulties their men have in supporting their families on their paltry earnings, with their wives clad oftentimes in rags, and their children suffering for the necessaries of life; in other words, if they were to go among their men and view the picture as it really exists, and open up their hearts towards these men, and treat them as fellow-beings, and act towards them in a spirit of humanity, the relations between capital and labor would be very different from what they are at present.

He concluded his testimony by stating, "What I think ought to be done is this: let arbitration be authorized by the Legislature as much as possible, and establish, if you can, a friendly relationship between the two great interests."[60]

Chris Evans, age 44 years, and residing at New Straitsville, was the second witness to appear. Referring to the iron-clad contract, Evans called it "one of the most infamous designs upon freedom that was ever presented to an American citizen." He further testified,

> I believe that the present system which is inaugurated in the Hocking Valley, known as the "truck system," has, to a great extent, been very injurious, and in all probability has given about as much trouble in connection with the opposition that has been made to the proposed reductions as anything else that I know of.... There is a great difference between some of the working places in the coal mines, and in my experience has been such that the miner who deals most at the company's store, as a rule, receives best working places in the mines, and in a great many instances, while they will not discharge a miner direct, yet they will place him in some of these working places where he will be compelled to discharge himself.

Interestingly, Evans also called attention to a December 23, 1883, report by a legislatively appointed commissioner who wrote that "one signal merit" of the mine store is that "they sell no intoxicating liquors, and thus they save large bodies of miners from the temptation to waste their earnings in the worst possible way, viz.: in indulging in strong drink." However, although "the mine owner can often furnish to the miner better goods and more favorable rates than he would otherwise secure … it is obvious that the system opens the way to grave abuse." Striking a conciliatory tone, Evans also stated to the Investigation Committee,

> I would say, that I, for one, am not desirous of giving any encouragement to such troubles as we have had in the past and are at present having there. I believe that some steps should be taken in order to create a better feeling between the employer and the miner, and I know no other methods, as far as legislation is concerned, than voluntary arbitration.... I would suggest that some efforts be made to bring about an understanding between the two parties; and further, I believe that both parties could be greatly relieved by the abolition of the "truck" system that we have been referring to. I think there would not be so much trouble in regard to prices as there has been in the past, if that system was abolished.

Finally, deploring the use of scrip, Evans remarked that personally,

> hav[ing] always received cash when I have not received anything from the stores … my experience, however, is that with regard to the reason why the companies have such

stores at all mines in the Hocking Valley, or nearly so, is because there are generally employed more than is required, and as a rule all the money that can be earned by the miner is taken out at the store, from the fact that he has not got sufficient to provide for his family without doing so.[61]

According to John McBride, age 30, residing at Massillon, and the last witness for the miners to appear before the committee, "The principal cause of the strike was a reduction in the price of mining" and that "[t]he excessive freights charges of the Hocking Valley Railroad were one of the principal causes which led to the strike ... and that the coal operators have been compelled to pay such rates as the railroad company made them, or close their mines." The officers of the Hocking Valley Railroad, he alleged, "could not understand, or would not, that a change of price in the Hocking Valley would necessitate a change in all other districts." Defending the Ohio Miners' Amalgamated Association's position that the strike had been forced on the miners, McBride asked, "how can our Union be justly charged with having acted arbitrarily, when the miners plainly showed that they desired to amicably adjust the differences, and were willing to have this matter settled honestly, fairly and amicably?" Similar to Rend and Evans, McBride concluded his testimony by suggesting, "Arbitration would be a means to adjust differences between employes [sic] and employers, provided, we would secure by legislation a system of arbitration that would in some manner compel employees and employers to arbitrate by the awards."[62]

The witnesses for the operators included two company officials of the Columbus, Hocking Valley and Toledo Railroad, respectively from Cleveland and Columbus, three company officials from the Ohio Coal Exchange, including Vice-President W.B. Brooks, four representatives of the Syndicate, including Vice-President John R. Buchtel, and five miners from Columbus, New Straitsville, Corning and Sand Run as well as the superintendent of a foundry and machine works in Columbus.

The operators' first witness, Stevenson Burke, age 50 and upward, residing in Cleveland, attorney-at-law, vice-president of the Columbus, Hocking Valley & Toledo, and "a very large stockholder," did "not know any other reason" for the cause than that the union "ordered the miners down in the Hocking Valley to strike."[63] John R. Buchtel, now from Akron, and age 64, agreed that the miners had as much a right to organize as the operators, and stated that he "let them have a piece of ground to erect a hall for the meetings of their Union and ... did everything [he] could to be in harmony with them." He admitted that the operators had more miners than were needed, that "we did not need to have so many men around the mines, but they were there and we could not get rid of them" and that "there was not a word of truth in it; nothing at all" that this was a deliberate attempt by the operators to force the miners to buy their "necessaries" at the company store. Insisting that he had always enjoined upon the superintendent at his store "not to ask for any more than a reasonable profit on the goods and not to sell goods any higher than the same goods could be bought for in any other markets, Buchtel presented a detailed list of the amount of "liquor consumed in Buchtel," which he believed had "as much to do with [the strike] as any other reason.... I think that it has had more than anything else to do with poverty in the h— this extensive use of beer and whisky."[64]

According to Walter Crafts, age 46, residing in Columbus and vice-president of the Ohio and Hocking Coal and Iron Company, "The Pittsburgh district was a sharp competitor for the lake trade," which led to "the necessity on the part of the coal operators to have a lower price for coal mining." When asked whether the Syndicate had been able to pay any dividends in 1883 and 1884, he answered, "We have never been able to pay any." Stating that he could not exactly remember whether the Syndicate had six or seven company stores in the valley, he argued that the miners were "perfectly free to deal wherever they choose" and that "we think our stores are as much a convenience to the miners as they are an advantage to us." Indicating that since the start of the strike now about "one quarter of our present force is colored," Crafts stated, "We have no objection to laboring men organizing for the protection of their own interests in any legitimate way. We simply ask that in the management of our property we shall be free to manage as we please, and that men who are willing to work for us at our price shall not, in any way, be disturbed by the men who are not willing to work for such wages."[65]

W.B. Brooks, age 65, residing at Nelsonville and vice-president of the Ohio Coal Exchange, also argued that Pennsylvania "took the lake trade from us entirely" and that prices at the company stores were "as cheap as they are in the city of Columbus." He suggested that when the operators posted the notices that led to the strike the miners did not understand it was a demand instead of a request: "They think you are in fun.... They sat around on the street corners like turtles on a log, and didn't say anything, and would not work." His objection to miners organizing was that "when they associate and get together, they undertake to do business as they please, and not as we want them to do it."[66]

Serving as secretary of the Ohio Coal Exchange, Brooks' son Frank, age 37, also testified, adding, "Our miners are paid in cash, and they are not compelled to trade with us, under any circumstances; but it frequently occurs that a man starts in working for us, and before pay-day he wants something in groceries, etc., for his family. There are probably 15 to 20 stores in Nelsonville;

he can go to them and get credit, or he can come to us and get it." On the issue of the miners' union, he stated, "Wherever we have been able to get at our employees directly, and talk to them, there has always been room for argument on both sides. We could consider their grievances and get at them and rectify them, but wherever we have had a Union to deal with, or to deal with a committee, it has been our invariable experience that we have accomplished nothing."[67]

End of the Strike

By January 1, 1885, as all Syndicate mines were open except in New Straitsville, rumors abounded that the union was ready to call off the strike.[68] With the investigation about to get under way, on February 2, 1885, the State Executive Board of the Ohio Miners' Amalgamated Association met in Columbus. In order to be able to compete with the 50 cents wage rate in the Hocking Field, the Board voted that the wage rate in all fields in the state should be 60 cents per ton and only if the operators would not enforce an iron-clad contract.[69] Two weeks later at a meeting the miners in New Straitsville agreed they would return to work at 40 cents per ton.[70] On February 18, a "still very sick" McBride wrote Evans that "affairs have reached the point in your valley when it is policy for you to settle on any terms except to sign the contract. I am very sorry I cannot be with you in your darkest hour. I trust for the best, however." Throughout the month, Evans reported, "the working force continued to increase until the entire district, outside of Shawnee and Straitsville was filled with imports, and while the character of the men, so far as mining coal was concerned was not as good as the old miners, the fact remained that those working were producing all the coal needed to supply the trade without any coming from either Shawnee or the New Straitsville division." It became apparent to Evans that "it was of little use to continue to fight any longer" and "although the great conflict is ended, much suffering still exists, owing to the fact that many of our miners are unable to obtain employment, by reason of the foreign labor together with miners from other States, that have flooded into our district with the continuance of our trouble."[71]

With the economy still in decline, the price of coal in other coal fields dropping below that in the Hocking Valley, and "the operators getting as much coal as they had trade for," the official end of the strike came on March 18, 1885, when after a long plea from Evans to the miners to admit they had been defeated, they agreed to return to work at 50 cents per ton.[72] However, the miners in New Straitsville held out for another two months before they too ended their strike and, although having won the right to have checkweighmen and miners' grievance committees, they went back to work at the rate of 40 cents per ton.[73]

In a circular to the public, Evans, Alexander Johnson and Thomas Lawson wrote,

> Fellow citizens—for the last nine months a relentless war has been waged on the miners of the Hocking Valley by their employers ... assisted by the Columbus daily press.... These monster monopolies that are daily growing to such immense proportions and which in the near future will pauperize every industrious workman in our land, demand the closet attention of the toiling masses. Millions of dollars from the scanty earnings of the industrious classes have been squandered by them in order to pauperize their employees. Hundreds of the most degraded specimens of humanity, selected from the filthiest haunts of almost every city, have been hired to intimidate and demoralize the miners of the Hocking Valley. The pauper Labor of every land has been strewn in our midst by the thousands.... To organized labor, the public press and the generous and sympathetic public that has so nobly responded to our appeals during this bitter conflict, we return our sincere thanks.[74]

Although he remained employed in Rend's mine during strike, Davis must nonetheless have realized that both sides in the conflict suffered. In fact, both the operators and miners lost so much in the strike that in the future they were willing to resort to arbitration to settle their differences. The miners realized they needed a strong national organization while the operators came to the realization they would have to treat the miners on an equal basis.[75] In a conciliatory gesture, on April 7, 1885, Walter Crafts announced that the Syndicate would abandon the truck system and pay all future wages in cash.[76]

In the summer of 1885 the question of organizing a miners' national union was discussed both in the *National Labor Tribune* and at conventions. Daniel McLaughlin, who was the miners' state president of Illinois and a contributor of articles published in the *Tribune*, together with John McBride of Ohio issued a call for a national convention to be held in Indianapolis, Indiana, on September 9, 1885, which was attended by 35 delegates from seven states. It led to the formation of the National Federation of Miners and Mine Laborers, which became commonly known as the Federation. The same convention passed a resolution to adopt the *National Labor Tribune* as its official organ and established New Straitsville, located approximately ten miles west of Rendville, and the residence of Executive Treasurer Chris Evans, as its headquarters.[77]

Although some have argued that little came of the investigation except that the miners and operators were able to air their grievances with one another before the state legislature,[78] they gained three notable victories. In its final report to the legislature, the Investigation Committee noted, "It is contended that a law providing for arbitration of disputes between employer and employee would create a healthy public sentiment and promote the settlement of such controversies in the future. To this it may be proper to answer that a law intended to meet this demand has already been passed by this General Assembly, and is now in force." It further noted, "Again it is contended by many miners that the abolition of the truck system—the business of establishing company stores and paying the miners for their services from these stores by issuing checks and orders for goods, instead of payment for cash—would promote the interest of the miners, remove a fruitful source of complaint, and largely prevent future strikes, and since this investigation began it has become law."[79] Furthermore after two failed joint meetings between miners and operators, initiated by the National Federation of Miners and Mine Laborers, and with the crucial leadership of Chris Evans and W.P. Rend on October 15 in Chicago and on December 15 in Pittsburgh, a third meeting, held on February 23–24, 1886, in Columbus, led to what has come to be called the First Joint Conference of Operators and Miners. It established the "Pittsburgh scale," an agreement to take effect on May 1, 1886, that set differential wage rates for ten of the 14 mining districts across Pennsylvania, Ohio, West Virginia, Illinois, Indiana, and Iowa.[80] This historic agreement marks the first ever jointly negotiated interstate labor contract in the history of the United States, hailed by Chris Evans as a striking example of the change of feeling that had taken place:

> It was like a feast of enjoyment over a renovated treatment for the ills of life the coal operators and miners are heir to and the methods required to further the best interests of both. The reasoning powers of men engaged in one of the leading hives of industry had awakened to a sense of duty that said to the world, "Our joint interests are a common heritage, and we will build a structure worthy of the calling we follow," and the citizenship voice of the nation acquiesced.[81]

Negotiated annually, the Interstate Joint Agreement system broke down in 1889 and was not re-established until 1898 following the first successful strike organized by the United Mine Workers of America.[82] Thus the year 1886 marked a triumphant year for the labor movement across the country, and it was the year Richard L. Davis wrote his first letter to the *National Labor Tribune*.

In a paper he presented at the Second Annual Meeting of the American Economic Association, held in Boston on May 23, 1887, Edward W. Bemis reported that during a visit to the Hocking Valley he was struck by

> the remarkable harmony and good feeling now prevailing between operators and miners. For a year and a half this sentiment has been growing until now both parties appear fully convinced that all differences can and will be settled by peaceful arbitration between strong organizations of laborers and employers.... On all sides was nothing

heard but praise of the working of this system of arbitration and conciliation.... Operators who fought the miners most bitterly in 1884 and 1885, now acknowledge their mistake, and admit that inestimable benefits of the present system of arbitration in Ohio were only made possible by the organization of the laborers.[83]

A less optimistic Andrew Roy wrote, that despite the creation of a state board of arbitration, "as long as the present industrial system endures, there will be conflict between employer and employe [sic]. Political economist may tell us that the interests of labor and capital are identical' but that is only a half truth; if it were wholly true, strikes would never be resorted to by labor, nor lockouts by capital, to enforce demands."[84] Yet in seeming agreement with Bemis, he argued that, although "both sides came out of the conflict covered with wounds, the lesson taught was worth the sacrifice to the miners and operators alike, not only in the Hocking Valley of Ohio, but in every coal filed in the United States. It taught the miners the necessity of a national organization, and made the operators ready and willing to treat with their employes [sic] on equal terms."[85]

Chapter 4

A Year to Remember

The First Letter

When Richard L. Davis arrived in Rendville he found employment in Mine No. 3. Operated by Rend, the mine's eight-foot vein of coal was reached by a shaft 47 feet deep and provided jobs to 140 men, all African Americans, except Thomas Andrew, the mine superintendent. In addition, Rend owned and operated Mine No. 5 at Rendville whose eight-foot vein was reached by a shaft 45 feet deep and gave work to 175 men, 75 of whom were African American. Another mine, a mile and a half north of Rendville, No. 2 also employed 40 African American miners.[1] Reflecting shifting ownership, Mine No. 3 in Rendville, where Richard L. Davis was employed, was owned by the Ohio Central Coal Company and operated by Corcoran & Wilson. In 1889 it was listed as "owned and operated by W.P. Rend & Co." That same year Rend also owned and operated Mine No. 4 in Jacksonville in Athens County. In addition, he owned and operated Mine No. 5 and No. 9 on the Ohio Central Railroad as well as the Chicago and Shawnee mine on the Straitsville Division of the Baltimore and Ohio Railroad.[2]

In September 1886, 18 months after the Great Hocking Valley Strike had come to an end, a 23-year-old Richard L. Davis sent his first letter to the *National Labor Tribune* in which it was published on October 2. A second letter appeared on October 30 in the same newspaper, which the previous year had been voted the official organ of the National Federation of Miners and Mine Laborers. It was followed by an identical letter in the *Cleveland Gazette* on November 13.[3] These three letters were followed by a period of four years, which lasted until December 1890, during which Davis did not write any letters.[4]

In his first letter Davis criticized the Rev. T.H. Williams, a Baptist minister, for advising the members of his congregation not to participate in a picnic organized by the Knights of Labor and Odd Fellows since it was "not a suitable place for Christians." Foreshadowing his strongly opinionated letters to come in future years, Davis wrote that he would have liked to say a lot more about "the *reverend* gentleman" who appeared to have been insulted by not having been "selected as a speaker on this occasion, so that he could pocket ten or fifteen dollars."

Davis' second letter, however, more clearly marks his future as an organizer in the labor movement. In his role as R.S. (recording secretary) of L.A. (local assembly) 1935 of the Knights of Labor, he addressed the following letter to the editors of the *National Labor Tribune*:

> Work is fair in this district. The miners are poorly organized, but I think the time not very far distant when the workingmen of this country will see the necessity of organization, when we can receive a just and fair renumeration for our labor. May God speed that day. I will also send you for publication a copy of the preamble and resolution offered by brother J.L. Jones, and adopted by our assembly, 1935, K. of L. [Knights of Labor], viz.
>
> WHEREAS, Seeing the position taken by our G.M.W. [Grand Master Workman] T.V. Powderly and D.A. [District Assembly] 49 of New York, and the whole of the G.A. [General Assembly], assembled at Richmond, Va., in the heart of the Southern Confederacy, with reference to our race, and seeing the disposition manifested by our white brethren to elevate us, and especially our down-trodden brethren in the south, therefore it be
>
> *Resolved*, That we as members of L.A. [Local Assembly] 1935, K. of L. [Knights of Labor], renew our obligations to the order, and pledge ourselves to do all in our power to swell the number in our ranks, and declare that we will never relinquish our work until the bulk of our brethren in city, town, county, and state are brought within the fold of our noble order.
>
> Wishing your paper a grand success, I am yours in liberty, equality and fraternity.[5]

Although no evidence survives that L.A. 8223 ever sent any membership dues to the United Workers of America, in 1886 L.A. 1935, presumably merged into L.A. 8223, an interracial local.[6] Instead, the Cash Book of District 6 (Ohio) of the United Mine Workers of America shows that between 1892 and 1896, L.A. 1935 regularly sent in its membership dues.[7]

A Turning Point

In his annual report to Governor Hoadly, Thomas B. Brancroft, Ohio's chief inspector of mines in 1886, reported that "labor troubles have been frequent, and while no great strike, such as that in the Hocking Valley last year, has characterized the year, yet local strikes and lockouts have been frequent and widely distributed." While Muskingum County had the largest number of mines, Perry County's 51 mines employed the largest number of miners in the state. The 2,228 miners in the county worked an average of 30 weeks and mined 1,259,592 tons of coal, furnishing about 16 percent of the coal mined in the state, the highest in Ohio. It mined more than 400,000 tons compared to Athens County, the second highest producer, and together Athens, Hocking and Perry counties were responsible for 35 percent of the total coal output in the state. Although the state's total annual production of 7,816,179 tons still fell short of its all-time 1882 high of 9,450,000 tons, it marked a mild recovery since the Hocking Valley strike. There were 32 fatalities in the state, six in Athens, two in Hocking and one in Perry County, resulting in "one death ... to each of 616 men employed."[8]

A list of the mere number of fatalities was a recurring item in the Chief Inspector of Mines annual reports. However, a coroner's transcript such as that of the death of Reese Jones on May 23, 1888, in Shawnee, Perry County, adds a human face to this reality that affected many a miners' family life. Standing five feet and nine inches tall at 20 years of age, according to Dr. O'Farrell, Reese Jones died about ten minutes after he was "crushed under a large chunk of coal." The testimony of Reese's brother, one of four witnesses who also signed the report, illustrates the grief a mine accident would bring to a family:

> My name is John Jones. My age is fourteen. I live in Shawnee with my parents. I work at the XX mine [Mine No. 20]. I was present when Reese Jones was killed. He is my brother. He was leaning in on his knees when it fell. It was top coal come in on him. He did not speak or make any noise when it fell. There was about a ton fell. Only one chunk fell on him. It was about five hundred. It struck him on the head first. He fell back and the chunk was lying on his breast. I called for some men to come and help get if off. John Kistler and his buddy came. He was under it about five minutes. He was not dead. I do not know how long he lived. I came home and he was dead when he was brought home.[9]

On February 23–24, 1886, after two failed joint meetings between miners and operators, a third meeting, in Columbus, the First Joint Conference of Operators and Miners established the "Pittsburgh scale."[10] In response to the formation on September 6, 1885, of the National Federation of Miners and Mine Laborers, which was led by John McBride as president and Chris Evans as secretary-treasurer, the Knights of Labor, not having participated in the Hocking Valley strike, on May 20, 1886, decided to organize its own National Trades Assembly 135 led by William H. Bailey as Master Workman and Lewis James as secretary-treasurer. Since the secretary-treasurer of both organizations lived in New Straitsville this meant the national offices of the two mine workers organizations were both located in the same town.[11]

On September 5, 1879, when Terence V. Powderly became its grand master workman and a decade after having been founded as a secret organization,

4. A Year to Remember

Terrence V. Powderly, 1849–1924, Knights of Labor, Grand Master Workman, 1879–1893 (Library of Congress, LC-H261-5410 [P&P]).

the "Noble and Holy Order of the Knights of Labor" had reached a membership of somewhere between 9,000 and 20,000. On January 1, 1882, the year Davis arrived in Rendville, the Knights of Labor abandoned its secret rituals, encrypted in the *Adelphon Kruptos*, and went public, partially in response to opposition from the Vatican to its seemingly religious nature. Committed to its motto, borrowed from Solon, the ancient Greek lawmaker, and proposed by Powderly, "That is the most perfect government in which an injury to one is the concern of all," the Knights were open to any worker, including after 1878 to African Americans and women, except to those in professions associated with idleness, corruption or parasitism, such as bankers, lawyers, liquor dealers, and gamblers."[12]

A devout Catholic, Powderly believed that "the great power that came to Christianity through the teaching of Jesus Christ has been largely frittered away through the practice of Christianity." He found little evidence or no evidence to prove that the ordained teacher and preacher of Christianity has attempted to walk directly in the footsteps of the crucified one in driving the waterer of stocks, the gambler in life's necessities, the despoiler of children, the exploiter of labor, or the grabber of profits from the temple wherein the products of industry are exchanged.[13] To make a point Powderly once invited Father Thomas Ducey, who he had met on the ferry from Jersey City to New York, to come spend a few days in Scranton, Pennsylvania, so he could take him "through hell." After running from a blast, breathing in foul air, being exposed to flickering lights and constantly dripping water, listening to the heehaw of mules in the distance, feeling "the rushing of a rat across [their] feet now and then and occasionally the sight of several pairs of eyes that shone like diamonds through the gloom, [as well as] treading the yellow ooze and slime that lay ahead of every step," Father Ducey could not wait to see daylight again, while admitting, "That is hell, sure enough," and that he would "never complain of the price [he paid] for coal again."[14] In many ways remarkably reminiscent of the life of Richard L. Davis, in his autobiography Powderly wrote that during all the years, from 1879 until 1893, when he was General Master Workman of the Knights of Labor,

> I had a picture above my desk representing the world's greatest, most sublime agitator. He whose heart, moved to indignation and pity, condemned the wrongs inflicted on the toiling poor by the rich and powerful. Did they not call Him an agitator when they said: "He stirreth up the people?" Did He not pay the penalty for being an agitator when they pressed the thorns into His flesh, and nailed his hands and feet to the cross? Had Christ sanctioned or condoned the practices of the rich and great do you suppose He would have been crucified? Had He looked on in silence and uttered no protest against wrong do you believe He would have ascended the cross as He did? Christ, if I read Him alright, did not die for the unjust rich man any more than He did for the lazy, poor man? He lived and worked for the industrious poor, for them He agitated, for them He died. He could have lived and been honored by the rich of that day. He elected to die rather than pay such a price of life.[15]

Philosophically opposed to strikes, except as a last resort,[16] by the early 1880s the Knights had become an organization with members of a wide variety of sociopolitical persuasions that often unwillingly found itself at the center of such conflicts.[17] Due to its success in 1885 in the Wabash railroad strike against Jay Gould, and despite its failure to prevail in the Hocking Valley strike, the Knights began a meteoric rise in its membership. And, although its membership in the Hocking Valley was on the decline due to the Hocking Valley strike and Evans' leadership, by 1886 the organization reached a peak membership of 700,000 to one million members, including 60,000 African Americans and 50,000 women.[18]

Foreshadowing Richard L. Davis' Mercer Hotel incident in 1895, when the General Assembly of the Knights of Labor met in Richmond, Virginia, in 1886 Colonel Murphy refused to accommodate Frank J. Ferrell, an African American member of District Assembly 49 of New York City, at his hotel.[19]

Although he believed that "the color line cannot be rubbed out, nor prejudice against the colored man be overcome in a day,"[20] an outraged Powderly allowed Ferrell to introduce an embarrassed Governor Fitzhugh Lee.[21] In the largest black-white affair in the history of Richmond, nearly half of the 3,000 participants in the parade and picnic that followed the conclusion of the convention were African American.[22] Despite the fact that the *Cleveland Gazette* condoned the existence of segregated assemblies in the Knights of Labor, because it believed organizing with other workers would secure African Americans an ally, many black spokesmen were not happy with their existence.[23] Although it "did not propose to organize a political party," labor conflict led many Knights to seek political office. In November 1886 the Knights of Labor claimed to have elected a dozen members to the U.S. Congress and reported electoral victories in 59 municipal elections, including the election of Isaiah S. Tuppins in Rendville.[24]

Early in the year, May 4 also witnessed the Haymarket Square riots in Chicago, which marked the launch of a determined attack against organized labor and its efforts to seek political power. Having counted many Knights among the demonstrators, including four men who were eventually hanged, and now associated with anarchism and terrorism, members began to leave the Knights of Labor in large numbers.[25] By November 30, 1893, when Powderly was deposed and replaced by James R. Sovereign, its membership had dropped to less than 75,000. In 1894 after it announced that the only way to solve the "Negro problem" in the United States was to deport blacks to the Congo Basin, the Knights' Executive Board instructed Sovereign to raise funds for that very purpose.[26] That year membership fell to below 20,000 and by 1900, the year Davis died, the Knights had become a mere shadow of its former self. Finally, in October 1949, the organization officially ceased to exist when Local Assembly 3030 in Boston decided to merge with the American Federation of Labor.[27]

Isaiah S. Tuppins

In 1884, two years after Richard L. Davis arrived in Rendville, its "free space"[28] welcomed yet another African American who was soon to rise to local prominence as W.P. Rend's company doctor and the town's mayor. Dr. Isaiah S. Tuppins was born in Nashville, Tennessee, on April 19, 1854. His family moved to Xenia, Ohio, in 1858 where although he received a common education at a segregated school he was denied a high school education due to the color of his skin. In 1868, at the age of fourteen, he returned to Franklin,

Tennessee, where he held a teaching position until he decided to go north again in 1871. By 1877 he was working as a barber in the Civil Rights Barber Shop in Columbus, which he purchased soon thereafter along with other property in order to "do something and be something." A sign posted over the door of his barbershop referred to Tuppins as the "Judge," apparently reflecting his interest in and opinion on matters of the day. This same year he also married Ella Guy. Although her untimely death in 1886 left him with two children, less than one year later he remarried a Miss Simpson from Zanesville.

In 1881, at the age of 27, Tuppins entered the Columbus Medical College which at the time had "a national reputation because of the connection with it of Dr. J.W. Hamilton, one of the greatest surgical physicians in the country." When Tuppins received his M.D. degree in March 1884, he became the "first colored graduate from a medical college in Ohio." The *Cleveland Gazette* proudly reported, "The throng that attended the commencement at Comstock's Opera House, Friday evening, March _, and witnessed the giving of a diploma to I.S. Tuppins must have been impressed with the fact that our race are advancing and are knocking at the door of all professions and asking admission." The paper went on to say that Tuppins "borned in obscurity, nursed in the lap of poverty, mid adversities, he was not without an ambition that lured him on. He was determined to be something and at last he finds himself an honor to his family, to himself and to his race."[29]

After opening an unsuccessful medical office in Columbus, Tuppins decided to leave for Rendville where William P. Rend hired him as the company doctor. He regularly reported to the *Cleveland Gazette* on events in Rendville, praising the town for its accomplishments, yet also pointing out its weaknesses when it came to the plight of African Americans. As early as 1884, Tuppins began writing letters to the editor protesting, among others, Philadelphia's Jefferson Medical College's refusal to admit Villroy Simpson, Postmaster of Rendville, on account that "Negro students because of their presence would give rise to tumult and would thus be offensive to all parties," making a case for equality and "stickiness ... to the principles of the Republican Party," calling for the abolition of the sundown laws and endorsing various African-American political candidates.[30]

Urged by Quincey to "stand united ... in the exercise of our prerogatives of citizenship" and while whites still constituted a majority of the voters, Tuppins was elected mayor of Rendville in 1886 while serving on the school board and having opened a drug store,[31] As a result, he became "the first colored man to attain that distinction in the Central and Eastern United States" and north of the Mason-Dixon line.[32] A loyal member of Lincoln's Republican

Party, Tuppins was also the first African American ever to represent Perry County at the Republican State Convention held in Springfield in 1886. In addition, that same year he served as chairman of the Perry County Republican Convention. Tuppins also rose to leadership in the Order of Odd Fellows fraternal organization in Rendville, being elected three times as Grand Master of the Ohio District. Furthermore, he was elected Perry County Coroner in 1888, holding two public offices at the same time.³³ In a letter on March 24, 1888, and the same again two weeks later, to the *Cleveland Gazette* and signed off with "Yours for the race and G.O.P.," as "Ohio's only colored mayor," with further support from John L. Jones, Tuppins recommended that Harry C, Smith, publisher of the *Cleveland Gazette*, an "organ devoted to our race," should be elected to "represent Ohio's thirty-thousand colored voters on the State Ticket and in the National Republican Convention."³⁴

Isaiah Tuppins, 1854–1889 (*Cleveland Gazette* 5, no. 9 [October 15, 1885]: 1).

Unfortunately, Tuppins' rise came to an abrupt end during his second term as mayor when he became ill and died.³⁵ In its January 19 issue, the *Cleveland Gazette* mourned Tuppins' death on January 10, 1889, from "a serious illness" as follows:

> The death of Dr. I. S. Tuppins of Rendville, O, is indeed a loss to the colored people of this state. An enthusiastic, progressive, scholarly and useful member of the race is gone, and the progressive young colored men of Ohio, with whom he associated, will miss him most. Mayor Tuppins was wholly a self-made man. He had succeeded well in life by hard work and his success should serve as a beacon light to the hundreds of our youth now toiling to make their mark. No more staunch friend or zealous worker in the interest of The Gazette dwells in the Buckeye State than was our friend Tuppins and none of the obituary notices or portraits of him, given by numerous publications can do him justice.³⁶

Eulogized, among others, by John L. Jones, Tuppins' funeral at the African

Methodist Episcopal Church and burial in the Cherry Grove cemetery in Xenia on January 13

> was probably the largest funeral ever held in this city, the crowd filling the audience room of the church, the vestibule, and for half a square on both sides of the church the streets were crowded with people. The services were conducted by Rev. T.H. Jackson, of Wilberforce University, and were very impressive. The crowd from out of town was a big one, prominent colored people from all over the state being present. The procession was the largest that ever followed a colored person to the grave in this city. It was headed by the (Colored) Allen College Coronet Band, and then came lodges of Odd Fellows from Columbus, Springfield, Dayton, Jamestown, Yellow Springs and this city. They were followed by the Knight Templars in full uniform. Then came prominent Knights in carriages, followed by the hearse and a line of carriages many squares long.... One thing noticeable at the funeral was the presence of a large number of white people. Dr. Tuppins was well-liked in his home and birth place and every citizen was proud of his achievement, and it was with a feeling of universal sorrow that his death was heard in this city.[37]

Adam Clayton Powell, Sr.

Another African American who also arrived in Rendville the same year as Richard L. Davis, and who went on to rise to national prominence after he left, was Adam Clayton Powell, Sr. One of 15 children,[38] Powell was born to slaves on May 5, 1865, in Franklin County, Virginia, where his family lived in dire poverty as share croppers in a remote rural area. This was 15 miles distant from the Big Lick market in Roanoke where, according to the 1870 U.S. Census, seven-year-old Richard L. Davis was living with his family. Upon enrolling in school on October 1, 1871, Powell learned the 26 letters of the alphabet in one day and was able to say them backwards the next. Challenged by his stepfather to read aloud the Gospel According to St. John before the end of school, "on the last Sunday in March, 1872," Powell "sat down under a walnut tree in front of our cabin and read the entire Gospel to my stepfather and the astonished men and women he had invited." As a reward, on his seventh birthday, his stepfather gave him a subscription to a weekly newspaper. Powell recalled, "Then I became a world citizen and contracted a disease called *wanderlust*. Through this weekly paper we learned that men could earn a dollar a day, and women 12 dollars a month in West Virginia." Thus his family decided to sell all its livestock and moved to a farmstead on the Kanawha River across from Colesburg, West Virginia, where it was his job to take care of the cows. Two years later the family moved to Paint Creek, on the other side of the Kanawha River where he enrolled in school. Describing his eight years in West Virginia as a "mental and moral disaster," Powell wrote that "the chief aim of the average man was to possess a pistol, a pair of brass knuckles, and a jug of hard liquor. Fights were numerous and life was cheap. I soon became a part of all I met." Having learned everything his teacher knew in less than two years, Powell decided to quit school.[39]

Two years younger than Davis, portraying himself as "a cheap edition of a desperado" and "to keep from being lynched or murdered," he moved to Rendville in August 1884, at age 18. "This was the most lawless and ungodly place I have ever seen," he wrote. "Every house on Main Street, except the mayor's office and post office, was used as a gambling place. To the vices brought from West Virginia, I added gambling, the most vice-like of all the vices." Although he secured a job in Rend's mines and made $80 to

Adam Clayton Powell, Sr., 1865–1953 (public domain).

$100 a month, "every dollar of this and all I borrowed was sacrificed to the demon of gambling which possessed me, soul and body."[40]

But his life of vice met its match in Rendville. On March 1, 1885, having lost all his wages and $40 of borrowed money, something "stranger than any piece of fiction that [Powell] had ever read" happened. A powerful religious revival in the Methodist and Baptist churches drew in so many that "the saloons and gambling dens deserted." More than 50 persons in the Baptist church, including Powell himself, "joyfully accepted Christ." Then, as he stood outside, as far as he could see

> in every direction, people were seeking and finding the Lord. I had often heard ex-slaves pray that the day would come when the hillsides would be covered with mourners and the church doors would be crowded with young converts. Here at Rendville on that Sunday and the remainder of the week I saw a literal answer to that prayer. The

churches were kept open night and day until the following Saturday. The coal mines shut down for a week, businesses of all kinds were suspended and the whole town ... was converted to Christianity. That week I saw saloon keepers roll their liquor barrels in to Main Street and empty them. I saw gamblers gather their gambling apparatus and make a bonfire on the same street. In one week every saloon and gambling house disappeared.[41]

Having paid off his gambling debts by his twentieth birthday, that winter Powell enrolled at the Rendville Academy where he worked as a janitor in exchange for tuition. As he continued to repair his "sin-broken vessel" he received strong support from John L. Jones as well as later from mayor Tuppins, who appointed him deputy town marshal.[42]

Powell's stay in Rendville came to an end in 1888 when he decided to enroll at Virginia Union University in Richmond where he studied theology. After graduating in 1892, he served as pastor at several Baptist churches in St. Paul, Philadelphia and New Haven, Connecticut.

While in Connecticut, Powell decided to enroll in the Yale Divinity School where after delivering an unsuccessful sermon he considered going to law school instead and entering politics to get elected to the U.S. Congress, an idea that had first come to him in Rendville.[43] Deciding, however, to stay in divinity school, during a return trip from preaching in St. Paul, Minnesota, on July 3, 1892, Powell visited Rendville where he delivered three Sunday sermons. While in Rendville, having been too poor to visit his mother during the past four years during divinity school, he received a telegram she had died and would be buried that same day. Unable to return to West Virginia in time, "she was buried without [his] seeing her face."[44]

In December 1908, however, Powell Sr. was called to Harlem, New York City, to pastor at the Abyssinian Baptist Church which two decades later boasted 14,000 members. His son Adam, born that same year, often spent his summers with relatives in Rendville where he was watched over by a young Sophia Mitchell, who in 1969 became Ohio's first woman African American mayor, serving until 1978.[45] As is Richard L. Davis, she was buried in the Rendville Cemetery.

In deference to his love for catching large fish and the swift eight-feet-high inlet tide of Lake Worth, Florida, that he was required to pass before reaching the waters of the Atlantic Ocean, Powell Sr. interpreted his years in Rendville as his most prominent battle: working to overcome prejudice against African Americans—a never ending tide he faced throughout his life. When Powell died in 1953, he passed his leadership role in Harlem on to his son Adam Clayton Powell, Jr., who was to gain notoriety as a controversial Congressman, representing Harlem between 1945 and 1971.

Unfortunately there is no documented record of any personal relationship between Davis and either Isaiah S. Tuppins or Adam Clayton Powell, Sr. However, it is evident that during the first decade of its existence Rendville constituted a unique "small town" community whose social, economic and political opportunities and freedoms cradled several major African American leaders.

Chapter 5

The Road to Prominence

Not until four years after his first letters appeared in the *National Labor Tribune* and the *Cleveland Gazette* did Davis write any letters to the editor. However, between December 1890 and April 1896, when he was first elected to the National Executive Board of the United Mine Workers of America, he wrote a total 130 letters: two letters in December 1890, 41 letters in 1891, 31 in 1892, 23 in 1893, 13 in 1894, 22 in 1895, and three more before his election in 1896. Although he wrote another 35 letters after his election, the number of letters he wrote became less and less from year to year, from 15 in 1896, to 12 in 1897, to ten in 1898 and one final letter in 1899. Through these letters, in his own eloquent voice, for nearly an entire decade Davis tells us the story of his life.

Few details about Davis' personal life during the four years between 1886 and 1890 are known. It is likely, however, that personal affairs dominated his life during these years. On January 10, 1887, Perry County probate judge Frank A. Kelley issued a marriage license to a 25 years old Davis and Mary Bailey, both affirming that they were "not nearer kin than second cousins" and there were "no legal impediments" to the marriage[1] Most likely a 23-year-old at the time of her marriage to Davis, according to the 1870 U.S. Census Mary Bailey was five years old and living with her parents Joseph Bailey and Nelley [sic] Bailey of Cheshire in Gallia County, Ohio, along with three brothers and one sister: John, Samuel, Lucy and Isaac. Davis' marriage with Mary resulted in the birth of two daughters. On September 7, 1891 "Mary Baily [sic], a white female, wife of R.L. Davis," gave birth to a daughter, named Edith, in Pleasant Township, Perry County. Less than two years later, on March 3, 1893, "Mary Bailey, a colored female, wife of Richard L.," gave birth to a second daughter, named Beatrice Blanche, in Rendville.[2]

National Executive Board, United Mine Workers of America, 1897. Standing: Fred Dilcher; W.C. Pearce, Secretary-Treasurer; Richard L. Davis. Sitting: Patrick Dolan; John Kane, Vice-President; M.D. Ratchford, President; J.H. Kennedy. Two members, Henry Stephenson and J.M. Carson, failed to attend this group exposure (courtesy Ronald L. Lewis).

United Mine Workers of America

The founding convention of the United Mine Workers of America was the outcome of the divisive struggle led by John McBride and Chris Evans of the National Federation of Miners and Mine Laborers, then commonly referred as the Federation, and Shawnee resident Master Workman William T. Lewis of District Assembly 135 to unite all miners in one union. After a series of secret meetings, the struggle led to the dissolution of the Federation and, on December 7, 1888, the creation of the National Progressive Union. Accused by Terence Powderly of treason and deceit, Lewis was replaced by John B. Rae of Illinois. While the two competing unions were unable to settle on terms to unite, the coal operators were able to play each side off against the other. Despite efforts by W.P. Rend, the failure to reach a joint agreement at the Fourth Annual Joint Conference, held in Indianapolis on February 5–

5. The Road to Prominence

7 and in Columbus on March 12–14, 1889, further emphasized the miners' need to unite.[3]

On December 10–14, 1889, the American Federation of Labor, which had been founded in 1886 in Columbus, Ohio, held its annual convention in Boston, Massachusetts. It was at this convention that Chris Evans, representing District No. 10 of the National Progressive Union, was elected secretary, a position he would hold for the next five years serving under founding president Samuel Gompers until John McBride's election as president led him to step aside, arguing that it was improper for two miners to serve as both president and secretary. A few days after, on December 19, John McBride and John Rae appeared together at the convention of the National Progressive Union and called for a national convention of miners to be held in Columbus, Ohio, on January 24, 1890.

The founding of the United Mine Workers of America must have marked an exciting event for Richard L. Davis as he was among the delegates who cast a vote at the joint national convention of the National Progressive Union and District Assembly 135 of the Knights of Labor, held at City Hall in Columbus, Ohio, on January 22, 1890, that led to its creation.[4] Although some reports indicate there may have been five African Americans at the founding convention of the United Mine Workers of America,[5] a photograph taken that day on the steps of the Ohio Statehouse includes two such identifiable delegates: R.F. Warren, a delegate of the National Progressive Union,[6] and Richard L. Davis, both from Ohio.[7] Although R.F. Warren was elected as a member of the first National Executive Board and among the delegates who addressed the Fourth National Annual Convention in 1893, nothing further is known about him.[8]

On January 21, 1890, the executive board of the National Progressive Union met at the Farmer's Hotel while the executive board of National District Assembly 135 met the next morning in City Hall to draft resolutions in favor of amalgamation. In his farewell address, delivered the previous day to representatives of the National Progressive Union, Chris Evans called for removing the obstacles that stood in the way of progress: "The overproduction of organizations," he argued, "that has played such a disgusting part in reducing the powers of practical organized efforts in the past few years, should find no resting place among the miners in the future. Every miner should go hand in hand with his fellow-worker and take away the

Opposite: First National Convention of the United Mine Workers of America, January, 22, 1890, Columbus, Ohio. Davis is standing in the second row behind the fifth person from the left in the front row (District 6 Collection, MSS71, Mahn Center for Archives and Special Collections, Ohio University Libraries).

substance that gives life to the full destroyer of your future happiness and comfort."[9]

On Thursday morning January 23, the two unions met in joint convention. Although the previous year had witnessed "much strife" between the two organizations for "supremacy" and that "much hard feeling" had been engendered, according to the *Columbus Dispatch* they were believed to be "in favor of one organization."[10] Introduced by President John McBride, N.R. Hysell, Speaker of the Ohio House of Representatives and a miner from Corning, addressed the National Progressive Union convention arguing that "[t]here can be no two organizations in line and have harmony. You must agree to sink all things and come to an organization." Samuel Gompers of the American Federation sent a telegram urging consolidation.[11] President John Rae of National District Assembly 135 received a letter from Grand Master Powderly in which he wrote: "I see by the papers and am reliably informed by your officers that something grand is promised for the 23rd; and by the way, as that happens to be on my birthday, I hope it will be celebrated by something being done for the permanent good of the miners of America."[12]

John B. Rae, first president, United Mine Workers of America, 1890–1891 (Roy, *History of the Coal Miners*, 1906).

In the late afternoon of that Thursday, which indeed marked Powderly's birthday, following the advice of Secretary Watchorn of National District Assembly 135 that "we can weld the two together," the joint convention adopted the proposition to "unite under one head and not give up the essential features of either organization." While 103 of the 109 delegates of National District Assembly 135 voted in favor, 81 of the 91 National Progressive Union delegates did the same. With seven additional "aye" votes by unorganized miners, the total vote was 191 in favor with 16 against. The *Colum-*

5. The Road to Prominence

bus Dispatch reported that "[t]here was enthusiastic cheering over the result" while Andrew Roy, who also was present and had addressed the convention about the department of mining engineering at Ohio State University, reported that "the officers of the rival organizations [had] sat on the platform ... listening with breathless interest to the speeches of the delegates, and dreading lest some rash orator would excite the two factions, while discussing the question of consolidation" which required a three-fourths vote. However, once it had passed, "the scene that followed beggars description. Delegates shouted themselves hoarse; threw their hats aloft; and tears coursed down the cheeks of gray-haired men."[13]

After passing a resolution

John McBride, second president, United Mine Workers of America, 1892–1894 (Evans, *History of the United Mine Workers of America, 1914–18*, 1920).

on Friday that included "declaring [that] no local union or assembly [would be] justified in discriminating against any person securing or retaining work because of African descent" and completing adopting the constitution the following morning, the delegates in accordance with Article II, Section 1, elected Master Workman John Rae as president or Master Workman, W.H. Turner of the National Progressive Union as vice-president or Worthy Foreman, and Robert Watchorn as secretary-treasurer. Representing the miners' interests in the different middle–American coal fields, others who were elected to the executive board included "Patrick McBryde, Pennsylvania; William Scaife, Illinois; R.F. Warren (colored), Ohio, John Kane, Indiana; W.C. Webb, Kentucky."[14]

In the closing session, which took place on January 27, the new labor union voted to create a defense fund into which each member would pay 25 cents per month until May 1 and 15 cents per month thereafter. These funds

National Executive Board, United Mine Workers of America, 1890. Top Row, left to right: R.F. Warren, John Kane, Wm. Scaife, W.C. Webb. Bottom Row, left to right: Robert Watchorn, Secretary; John B. Rae, President, Patrick McBryde (*Evans, History of the United Mine Workers of America, 1914-18*, 1920).

were to be used only for supporting locked out or striking miners at weekly rate of $3.50. Finally, after having decided to meet again in Columbus on the second Tuesday in February 1891 and just before the convention adjourned, "an affective scene" took place when "John Nugent and Alexander Johnson who led the rival organizations in the Hocking Valley, shook hands and swore allegiance to the miners' union, and to show his sincerity, Mr. Johnson kissed Mr. Nugent in the mouth."[15]

The Constitution

A member of Local Assembly 1935, Davis must have been pleased with the constitution the United Mine Workers of America adopted as it included many of the organizational ideas espoused by the Knights of Labor.[16] According to the opening sentences of the Preamble:

> There is no fact more generally known, nor more widely believed than that without coal there would not have been any such grand achievements, privileges and blessings as those which characterize the nineteenth century civilization, and believing, as we do, that those whose lot it is to daily toil in the recesses of the earth, mining, and putting out this coal which makes these blessings possible, are entitled to a fair and equitable share of the same. Therefore, we have formed 'The United Mine Workers of America' for the purpose of the more readily securing the objects sought, by educating all mine workers in America to realize the necessity of unity of action and purpose in demanding and securing, by lawful means, the just fruits of our toil.

To accomplish these objects, the Preamble declared the United Mine Workers would seek to secure wages that would be compatible with the dangers of mine work and receive weekly payments in lawful money rather than scrip. It also called for safety legislation to protect the lives of miners and to reduce the number of "awful catastrophes which have been sweeping our fellow craftsmen to untimely graves by the thousands." Due to "the very nature of our employment, shut out from the sunlight and pure air, working by the aid of artificial light," the union "uncompromisingly" demanded legislation to establish the eight-hour workday and to forbid child mine labor until the age of 14 in order to "provide for the education of our children."

Finally, the union would seek to abrogate all laws that enabled coal operators to cheat the miners from having their mined coal properly weighed or measured and prevent them from employing Pinkerton detectives or guards. Most notably, the union pledged "to use all honorable means to maintain peace between ourselves and employers; adjusting all differences, as far as possible, by arbitration and conciliation, that strikes may become unnecessary."

The Preamble was followed by five articles. Article I declared the union's name and stated that its purpose was "to unite mine employes [sic] and ameliorate their condition of conciliation, arbitration, or strikes." Article II listed the officers' duties, including that the Executive Board would act as an arbitrator, execute the orders of the national convention, and have the authority to direct the union between conventions. It could be convened by the president or the secretary-treasurer or at the request of three board members. Article III stipulated that representatives of each local assembly or local union at the annual national convention, to be held on the second Tuesday in April, would have one vote for every first hundred or fewer members and one additional vote for each hundred more or a fraction thereof. Declaring the union's intent to seek "amicable adjustment" of local trouble, Article IV required that all local strikes be first approved by the district which then had to seek approval from the national office. In case the district refused approving a strike, the local had the right of appeal to the national office. Article V defined the qualifications of the officers and set their salaries. While it set the annual salary for the President at $1,500 and for the vice-president and secretary-treasurer at $1,000, it set the salary for the board members at "$3 per day and expenses" when performing duties for the union. Finally, Article VI outlined the nomination process for national officers and, notably important for Richard L. Davis and other black miners, that "no person a member of the organization, who holds a financial or clearance card, showing him to be a financial member (and in good standing), shall be debarred or hindered from obtaining employment on account of race, creed or nationality."

According to Secretary-Treasurer Robert Watchorn's Report at the Annual National Convention on February 10, 1891, at the time of consolidation the union had "not quite 17,000 members in both unions, sixty percent of said membership being with N.T.A. 135," amongst whom were about a thousand blacks,[17] "and forty percent with the Progressive Union. We now have a total membership of over 70,000 members, with less than twenty members of a difference in net membership in the two branches."[18]

District 6

Following the national convention, on April 14, 1890, a five-day-long joint meeting was held in Columbus between miners belonging to the National Trades Assembly 135 and the National Progressive Union. This convention resulted in organizing District 6 of the United Mine Workers. Similar to the national union, it declared as its purpose "to unite the mine employes [sic] of Ohio and ameliorate their condition by methods of conciliation, arbitration or strikes." On the fourth day of the convention, Davis was elected to serve as a member of its Executive Board, a position to which he would be re-elected each year until 1895.[19] Reflecting a more militant approach in case an operator decided to close down a mine, the convention resolved that "if causes are unjustifiable, that the board call a suspension of the mines located by such operators in this competitive field, until the miners that are already closed be started up." On the final day of the convention, after passing a long resolution to address numerous grievances, Davis was among the four board members who gave a final speech. Subsequently, during future annual state conventions Davis regularly served on committees that dealt with matters of grievances, moved resolutions, or audited the treasury books. During each of these five years he also represented Ohio at the national convention held in Columbus.[20]

Unfortunately the Cash Books of District 6 of the United Mine Workers only offer an incomplete insight into the work in which Davis was engaged between 1890 and 1894.[21] Typical entries include reimbursement for travel to board meetings, attending conventions, expenses for hotel and dinner, as well as payment for "work" which involved travel throughout the region and state to organize miners.

In May 1890 Davis was reimbursed for expenses to attend a four-day District 6 board meeting in Columbus. However, it was not until four years after he wrote his three initial letters in 1886 that Davis wrote the first of his 170 letters to come until his death in 1900. In rather typical fashion of the many letters he would write in the following years, his first letter, written on December 7, 1890, started off reporting, "Work around the mine here is somewhat dull owing to the scarcity of cars. Just how long this may last I am unable to say. Our miners here, although they call themselves organized, are certainly in a deep slumber, comparatively speaking." He also reported that at all the mines, with the exception of Mine No. 3, which was operated by Rend, the miners were not paid anything for breakthroughs which typically was considered "dead work." Despite the existence of a scale of wages for breakthroughs in Hocking, Perry, and Athens counties, to which Rend had agreed, he nonetheless had not paid for a single break through having claimed the previous year's summer that it was impossible for him to do so due to the expense of having to repair the pipes in Mine No. 3 that were corroded due to the presence of sulphur in the water. In another letter the following week Davis reported that "the mines in this part of the valley are working slow as yet, owing to the scarcity of [railroad] cars" and that the Sunday Creek Coal Company wanted to return to "the old thieving system" of docking the miners at Mine No. 8, "the dirtiest seam in this section of the valley," 500 to 1,000 pounds for the least bit of dirt it could find in a car.[22]

Wage Slavery

Resuming his letters to the editor of the *National Labor Tribune* in late January 1891, Davis typically wrote on a Sunday so his letters would be published the following Saturday. At the national convention of the United Mine Workers, held in Columbus, Ohio, February 10–17, John B. Rae, "of a religious turn of mind" and "by nature a cautious man [who] carried the precepts and example of the man of Galilee into his official duties, striving to heal up the wounds which have been inflicted during the internecine war," proposed establishing an official journal whose first issue was published on April 16, as the *United Mine Workers Journal*.[23] According to its editor John Kane, the journal was "established by the miners and for the miners, not by the white miners nor for the white miners, no more than by the colored nor for the colored miners."²⁴ Eight weeks after its first publication, on June 4, the journal featured the first of Davis' many letters, which he typically wrote on a Monday so they would appear in its weekly Thursday issue. Although Davis continued to send letters to the *National Labor Tribune*, on five occasions he also sent a second letter to the *United Mine Workers Journal* on the same day. However, after November 14, with one exception in 1897, he only sent his letters to the editors of the *United Mine Workers Journal*.

In a letter he wrote on January 25, having been re-elected to the executive board of District 6 at its six-day convention in Columbus, Davis expressed a "sincere thanks for the honor" conferred upon him. "Being a colored man," he wrote, "I feel proud of the recognition received from the miners of Ohio."²⁵ The last week of January Mine No. 3 worked only half a day while Mine No. 8 was idle. When Mine No. 8 was shut down the miners were told they could work at Mines No. 10 and No. 19. Rumor spread, however, that the miners at Mine No.19, located at nearby Buckingham, had passed a resolution to not allow any colored men in their mine. Described by the editor as "a tempest in a teapot," after a visit, unauthorized by President Jones of District 6, Davis found the rumor to have been false and expressed relief the colored men had decided to stick to the United Mine Workers.²⁶ The next week he wrote, "If there is a mine in the state or the United States that has a rule to not allow colored men to work in them, for God's sake at once remove that barrier, for the sooner it is removed the better it will be for all concerned" and "if the mines were thrown open to all miners irrespective of color it will do away with the fear that is entertained by the white miners that the negro will take their places in times of trouble."²⁷ Retelling the story a year later, Davis was happy the visit succeeded in saving "some three hundred colored men from withdrawing from the organization."²⁸

In February, after attending the second annual national convention, also held in Columbus, Davis was delighted "the baby is having a wonderful growth," and believed the United Mine Workers "will be one of the grandest and most gigantic organizations that ever existed." He was excited that the union was committed to bringing about the eight-hour day and expressed his support for the organization's efforts as it would allow the miners to spend more time with their families as well as give them more time for reading and developing their "physical and moral conditions."²⁹

Ever the maverick, W.P. Rend, in addressing the convention said, "I believe the time is coming when eight hours will prevail all over the globe. Postpone the decision as you may, I believe it will be adopted in time in all mechanical trades. I stand here before you favoring eight hours. All my colleagues are against me, and but for my efforts would have refused to discuss the matter." He then proposed adopting a nine-hour day for the first year and then if it worked satisfactorily to move to the eight-hour day.[30]

By March 1, Davis reported there was a virtual lockout as there was "no work and plenty of men" and called for an investigation arguing that the men would not be satisfied until President Rae paid them a personal visit to explain matters. Expecting the men to have some strong language for Rae, Davis wrote he could not do so himself as "it is not found in the Bible." By mid-March he reported that "hundreds of men" were "walking around," and that many had left for Pennsylvania and other coal fields look-

John Kane, editor, *United Mine Workers Journal*, 1891–96 (Evans, *History of the United Mine Workers of America, 1914–18*, 1920).

ing for work. Davis argued the lack of work constituted "a complete case of lockout" and called on President Rae and the national officers to support the miners of Rendville rather than spend all their efforts, time and money in Pennsylvania. While "Brother" Nugent, who at the time served as District 6 vice-president but in 1907 switched sides and went to work for the mine operators, paid a visit to express his support,[31] the $100 sent by the national officers for the relief of the miners "did not go very far." To make matters worse, the *Cincinnati Enquirer* falsely reported that "fifty of our miners broke into the company store here and took thirty barrels of flour and several hundred pounds of meat, saying that they had either to steal or starve, and I don't wish the public to believe that we have become outlaws yet. Yet I don't think a man would be justified in starving while there is plenty around him."

Still, an optimistic Davis was happy to learn President Moran's success in District 17, West Virginia, was having with the assistance of "Bro. John L. Edmonds [sic] ... in getting the miners of New River into the organization," showing that "the prejudice that once existed in West Virginia is dying out."[32] After being blacklisted in April 1892 Edmunds was succeeded by J.J. Wren who became the first full time African American organizer in West Virginia. When President Moran died in 1893 Wren finished out his term.[33]

On March 16, national president Rae and District 6 president J.P. Jones and vice-president Nugent paid a visit during which they convincingly rejected the miners' argument of a lockout. During a meeting that same afternoon at the opera house in Corning, W.P. Rend, being the only operator present, agreed to reopen Mine No. 3 "as soon as necessary repairs could be made." Rumor, however, had it that Davis would not be allowed to work in the mine, as in the meeting Rend had "classed [him] among those generally termed agitators ... who keep up trouble around the mines." However, Davis was most surprised "by the fact that of all those who have anything to say against me are of my own race (colored men), and why I can not tell unless it is ignorance. While Mine No. 8 remained idle, Rend blaming delays on water in the mine did not reopen Mine No. 3 until March 25, employing 72 men compared to the about 240 men in the past.[34] Simultaneously, a new controversy emerged at the mine on account of the blacksmith." After being "asked to do more than his share of work," by serving as carpenter and stable boss as well, the blacksmith decided to quit while the company continued to charge the miners for his services.

By mid–April, as work in the valley had improved somewhat, new trouble emerged as some men refused to pay their union dues. Arguing for a closed shop, Davis wrote:

> Let me say that experience has taught me that where there is one man who refuses to pay his dues, no matter if every other man in the pit is paying, just as soon as you allow one to go free, others will follow and say such and such a fellow won't pay and I won't pay either. This I have seen tried, and although it was only in the beginning, in a month or so half of them were not paying. Nip such a procedure in the bud and make them pay or get out. These human parasites, for such I think is their proper title, keep up more disturbance around the mines than the organized men do; they are satisfied with nothing; nothing is done right. They say the committee has not done this or that, when they themselves are the cause of certain reforms not being accomplished. Don't let these scalawags enjoy any of the reforms that we may get through our organized efforts, for such men are traitors to their country, enemies to their God and a curse to humanity. Boys, let us get rid to them.[35]

As Mine No. 3 production increased to employ about 130 mean, the Sunday Creek Coal Company reopened Mine No. 8 on April 17. Three months prior, in January, Mine No. 8 experienced a similar blacksmith experience as when Mine No. 3 reopened. Having to sometimes wait for several hours or even days as the blacksmith had to do the company's work first, the men at Mine No. 8 had decided to open their own shop and employ their own blacksmith. As a result, the company shut down the mine supposedly for repairs.

Even though it had made no repairs, the company hoped to build up its supply of coal before mining rates would increase on May 1. When Davis learned that the men in the Hocking Valley were not in favor of striking and anticipated they would be paid whatever they asked for, he reminded them to "only look back at the great strike of '84 and '85, of the danger of not standing together."[36]

On May 10, after having attended a state convention of nearly a hundred Ohio miners, held at Druids Hall in Columbus to discuss a new scale, Davis reported that while Mine No. 3 was idle, the Sunday Creek Coal Company had restarted Mine No. 8 where the men had hired their own smith. While things appeared to be going smoothly, on pay day the miners were surprised to find out that they were still being charged "one cent on the dollar for smithing."[37]

Arguing for the need to have "more colored organizers in the field," yet ever advocating for the men to stick together, Davis also criticized the colored "kickers" in the UMWA who threatened to leave the organization for not having any "colored salaried officers" and merely paying "money to build up the white man" while never reaping any benefit.[38] As work remained dull and mines No. 3 and 8 idle and men were leaving for other coal fields, National vice-president Phil Penna paid his first visit "to these parts"

Phil H. Penna, third president, United Mine Workers of America, 1895–1896 (Evans, *History of the United Mine Workers of America, 1914–18*, 1920).

and succeeded in "finishing off on the kickers," as he "did give it to them" so well that "some of them could not stand it and had to leave."[39] Simply put, Davis wrote, "I am one of those who believe that every man or woman who earns their bread by the sweat of the brow should and ought to belong to a labor organization."[40]

On April 30 Davis attended an Ohio Miners' Special Convention that, "to end the trouble at the mines in Rendville," led to a wage scale agreement between the district and W.P. Rend in the Hocking Valley to mine coal at 70 cents per ton until May 1, 1892.[41] In May, having attended another state convention in Columbus, Davis received his first packet of the *United Mine Workers Journal*. After distributing copies among the miners to recruit subscribers, he wrote his first letter to the journal, published on June 4.

In early July Vice President Nugent, against the wishes of President Rae, successfully persuaded the miners in nearby Jacksonville and Glouster "to lay down their tools" until the miners in Rendville received their fair share of work. "A more jolly or happier set of men could not be found" than the men in Rendville, who were only too happy as Nugent's "mistake" led to an agreement. By the middle of the month Mine No. 8 was working full while Mine No. 3 was promised the same by the end of the month.[42]

Later that month, addressing the "labor question" in response to a letter in the *United Mine Workers Journal*, Davis condemned "blacklegging." Believing "that the negro should be allowed to work anywhere that he please so long as he proves himself to be a man" and that blacklegs "should not be allowed to live among decent people," Davis wondered what the colored letter writer to whom he responded would do if the company brought in white strikebreakers. Rejecting as "utterly false" that former slaves, as the letter writer argued, were now free American citizens, Davis argued:

> Today we are, one and all, white and black wage slaves.... I think the time has come that the negro should know better than to run from place to place to break down wages, etc. He can plainly see that the money kings of this country are only using him to fill their own coffers with gold. Does any negro think that an operator thinks any more of him than he does of a white man? If you do, you are sadly mistaken, for I remember several instances in this valley: whenever the colored man asked for that which was something like right and just, the answer was, whenever you colored men want the same as the white do then we have no further need for you. This was the answer. Now then I would say to the negro, of which race I am proud to be connected, let us be men; let us demand as much for our labor as any other nationality; let us not suffer ourselves to be trampled upon any more than any other people. We are a people; we are men; we constitute one-sixth of this great country so far as numbers are concerned, consequently it is not a white man's country; it is partly ours as well, so let us prove ourselves men and the equal of any others. We can do it.[43]

Echoing his conviction that "we are all slaves, white and black alike" and that the color line must be broken now,[44] more than a year later Davis once again wrote, "We must assert our manhood and no longer allow ourselves to be the slaves, and should now with one mighty effort burst asunder the chains of wage slavery that now bind us."[45]

In August, a scarcity of railroad cars caused Mine No. 3 to still not work full. With the men of Mine No. 3 having practically been out of work since early December, the promise of enough railroad cars to work the mine full, turned out to have been false.[46] Davis attended a one-day District 6 executive board meeting.[47] He reported that Rend had agreed to a Hocking scale for Jacksonville, Glouster and Rendville.[48] Also, a recruiter came to Rendville to look "as is the usual custom" for "colored men" to go to Raymond City, West Virginia, where white miners were on strike. In response, invoking his Knights of Labor past, Davis wrote:

> Well, Mr. Stuart, we don't think you will get any from this place. True, our men are hard up, but they will suffer a little longer before they will go to Raymond to blackleg the honest miners who have been so long struggling for their rights. No, no! we have learned better than that now, so you may go a town further for your scabs, for we have quit breeding them. We are beginning to learn that an injury to one is the concern of all, and we cannot better our conditions running from place to place, taking the places of our fellow men. It has long been an understood fact that the miners of Raymond would not let a negro with them. We wish to show them that we are human beings, and want the same wages for our labor as they do, and we earnestly hope that they will remove the barrier that stands between them and the negro, and let us work along peaceably and brotherly alongside each other.[49]

On September 7, the day his daughter Edith was born, Davis wrote another long letter. With work being "somewhat better," he worried about the coming winter "with its chilling blasts of wind, ice and snow" and that "the children will need heavier clothes, shoes, &c., and these things cannot be gotten without the money." The docking issue once again re-emerged. Although W.P. Rend had agreed to accept the prevailing docking scale, Davis did not think this was fair as the mines in the valley had from three to three and a half feet of dirt whereas those "just over the hills have only from six to eight inches to throw away."[50] Fortunately by the end of the month, Davis was able to write that "work is very good at present," and referring to the Raymond strike reminded the "boys" to "mix up in our mines and work together as men for it is well known but that the negro is in this country and here to stay."[51] After the miners in Raymond City rejected the mine superintendent's offer they could come back to work at the old prices provided he'd be allowed "to fill the mine with one-half colored men," and went back on strike, Davis thought they would no longer be bothered.[52]

On September 22, Rendville also celebrated the Emancipation Proclamation, a tradition recently revived by the Rendville Historical Preservation Society. Davis wrote:

> There was no work at either of our mines and a nice day we had, everything passed off smoothly. It seemed that all were interested, both white and colored. After all our sports and speeches I wonder sometimes if we ever think of the system of slavery that we are now living under, viz: wage slavery. Under this system we are all slaves, black and white alike, and I do think it is about time we were getting together as unit and trying to work out our emancipation in this line.[53]

This same month Davis also traveled five days of across the state to organize miners in Dillonvale, Zanesville, Bellaire, Portland, Long Run, and Bowerston.[54] Taking note of not only "the encroachment of capital" but also the "Huns and Polanders to contend with," he hoped that the miners at Long Run and Dillonvale would "see the necessity of sustaining the organization and check weighman" and "stick together."[55] Worried also that lethargy among his fellow workingmen was so low that attendance at the L.U. (Local Union) 398 meetings had become alarming, Davis cautioned against indolence.[56] Admitting that he had "certain ideas" of his own on the "labor question,"[57] Davis encouraged the men to attend union meetings and asked, "Boys, how long will you continue in this go-as-you-please way?"[58] Urging them to openly voice their opinions," Davis wrote:

> As a rule when a man advocates what he thinks to be right, he is termed an agitator. It has been said that if you put a colored man on a horse he will ride it to h-l. Now as to the truthfulness of that statement, I don't think it's true. I am one of that particular race, yet I don't think I would take such a risky ride. I have certain ideas of my own on the labor question, as I feel as though I should be free to express an opinion should I deem it necessary. But I don't like to give gent to the feelings of everyone else while the go along are contented with nothing to say whatever.[59]

Finally, in October Davis also received a last payment for "1 day work."[60] By November 2, as attendance at union meetings was improving, work in the Sunday Valley" was "very good." This was likely due to "the Pittsburg strike." When "a gentleman" came to the valley to solicit aid for the striking men, the Sunday Creek Valley miners "contribut[ed] very liberally."[61] A week later, in his last letter to the *National Labor Tribune*, Davis reported that the Pittsburg strike was over hoping it had taught the men the importance of being united.[62]

While the strike in Raymond City continued and the railroad cars were filled and almost as rapidly disappeared as they arrived, Davis was sent to organize the miners at Finleyville and Snowden, where he found that a hundred colored men had been lured there during the Pittsburg strike with promises of employment as hotel waiters and carriage drivers only to find themselves forced to work in the mines and be treated like slaves working and sleeping in the same clothes in and out of the mine. Confronted by "cutthroats" and failing to organize the miners, after three to four days Davis returned unsuccessfully to Rendville.[63]

Urging his fellow black miners to not give in to blind allegiance to Lincoln's Republican Party simply because it had granted them their freedom, Davis now also turned his attention to politics arguing "that we must learn to vote. This old system of voting that we have been carrying on for so many years, voting a certain ticket because our fathers vote it, must be stopped if we would wish a better condition of things."[64] By coincidence perhaps, in December Davis learned that his name "had been sent in to be placed on the list of nominees of District 6 for vice president." Wanting "to have a little something to say in the matter" and suggesting that in the face of "no taxation without representation," it was "high time to give the poor negro a chance," Davis nonetheless wrote that he was "not an aspirant for the office for I do not think that it would be possible for prejudice to step aside long enough for me to be elected and I am one of those fellows who don't want to run for office for the sake of running." However, foreshadowing future aspirations, he added, "No, no, if I run for anything I want to be elected."[65] Then, in the new year, echoing some of today's political discourse, Davis added:

> I was not a politician nor am I likely to become one because of the fact that in former days politics was a matter of principle, but today it has become a science and it takes a very sleek scoundrel to understand it. I think it is about time for us—the working people—to make a change and stop supporting the two old political frauds. As a negro I am tired of being pointed at as a Republican simply on account of my color.... I believe the day is not very far distant when we will awaken to the full sense of our duty and put a stop to the nefarious work of the political tricksters. What say you fellow working men? Will you join in and by your united efforts make this country what it should be? I think you will, and God knows that it is about time that something was being done in the matter and I don't believe that any of the reforms need can be gotten at the hand of either of the two old political parties for they are owned solely by wealthy corporations, the monopolists and money kings and it would be follow to expect anything from them.[66]

Although still listed in the *United Mine Workers Journal* on January 14, 1892, as a candidate for Vice President, on December 27, Davis, expressing his "heartfelt thanks for their kind appreciation," declined the nomination as in his "weak judgment ... it would prove detrimental to myself, if to no one else, were I to run for the office as I don't like to get left."[67]

The Color Line

Having apologized the week before Christmas to his readers that they must be getting tired of his dull letters he nonetheless kept writing them in the new year because doing so would keep him "out of other mischief" and help him "to develop the intellectual faculties."[68]

On January 19–22, 1892, Davis once again attended the Ohio Miners' Convention, the "largest state convention of miners ever held," which passed a resolution, supported by Davis, to endorse "the speedy passage of a law to prohibit Chinese immigration."[69] In his notes on the convention, "J.K." wrote about Richard L. Davis, "Although his skin is black, I will vouch for his heart is as white as the average Caucasian's, and a good deal purer than a very large portion of them. He is characterized by a persistent, continuous, unflagging zeal in the cause upon which he has set his mind, and the tenaciousness with which friend Davis sticks to his guns is really refreshing to the true friends of unionism."[70] Others, such as Wm. Carmack of Tennessee, expressed similar sentiments, stating that "some of the smartest men we have in this country are men whose skins are black."[71]

Thanking the miners of Ohio for "the handsome vote" he received for his election to the Executive Board, Davis thought it demonstrated that "race prejudice will soon be a thing of the past if other states do as the grand old state of Ohio." Pledging that he would always be "the lad" to speak his mind on anything that he thought unjust, he praised the United Mine Workers for doing more than any other organization, "the church not excepted," by "placing all men on an equal standing without regard to race, creed, color or sex." Not quite ready yet, "all I ask," Davis wrote, "give me a chance to develop myself to the callings of my craft."[72]

The Cash Book records of District 6, show that between January 1892 and February 1896 L.U. 398 and L.A. 1935 K. of L. (Knights of Labor) of Rendville regularly made separate membership contributions, consistently on the same date. While the contributions of L.U. 398, of which Davis must have been a member, typically ranged between $6 and $9, with occasionally a significantly larger contribution, L.A. 1935, typically contributed approximately one dollar, suggesting it had a significantly smaller membership. Although, according to Brier, in 1886 black and white miners formed L.A. 8223 I have not been able to locate any records to validate its existence.[73] However, the cash books do include two one-time, one dollar contributions by L.A. 2488 K. of L. and L.A. 2611 K. of L., and one one-time $13.10 contribution by No.3, presumably Rend's mine, all made in 1892.[74]

While work in the Sunday Creek Valley remained dull, Davis wondered about a supposedly new union, "The Little Nickel Plated Knights," in Indiana:

> Is it a reference to the Knight of Labor? If so I think the brother is treading on dangerous ground inasmuch as the Knights of Labor and the National Progressive Union

joined hand and buried past differences, it would be well for us as individuals to do likewise, for I tell you that when a fellow casts any insinuations at the Knights of Labor then he rumples my feathers and I feel like saying some things not found in the Bible, nor are they taught in our everyday schools, and there are others just like myself. I am a United Mine Worker, but I am Knight of Labor just the same and would not like for anyone to trifle with my feelings on that score.[75]

Having returned from the Annual National Convention, in February President Nugent once again sent Davis and Vice President Cameron Miller on a successful six-day trip, made possible by the kindness of the local mine superintendent in helping them set up meetings, they organized the more than a thousand Ohio miners in Bowerston, Jewitt, Long Run, Dillon, and Laurelton, two-thirds of whom included a "foreign speaking element, consisting of Hungarians, Polanders, Slavs, Bohemians and Belgians."[76]

In March an optimistic Davis found "a good deal of Buckeye blood" in the Pittsburgh district at the Laurel Hill mine in Reissing. However, after successfully organizing "an assembly of colored men" in Finleyville, he failed to do so in McDonald, "hell's half acre," where there were "entirely too many men" as the companies were "bringing in new men from North Carolina and other places" so they could grind the miners "further into the dust." After attending service at the First Baptist Church in McDonald and reflecting upon the sermon, Davis wondered while God had sent his son to save the world, who he would send "to save this place."[77] Despite posting notices all over town, and some even written out "in the Belgian language," not more than 40 out of the 800 to 900 men who worked in the mines here attended the meeting. On a more positive now, however, Davis learned that the local superintendent in Canonsburg, Mr. Hitchman, had started to hire union men, supposedly as he had come to the conclusion that he had no other option. In April, reporting two fatalities at Congo and Mine No. 19 at Buckingham, he traveled to Coshocton with "Brother J.P. Jones," where "the boys" were "beginning to see the injury done to themselves and their fellow-craftsmen by remaining on the outside."[78]

In a remarkable letter, worthy of extensive quotation and written on April 18, in which, according to the editor, Davis offered "some square and manly advice to Colored brothers," Davis wrote:

> Why is it that the colored people are so hard to conceive the proper idea of organization? Now, while I speak thus, I am aware of the fact that some of them are connected with our organization and are good, loyal members too; but, it is the great number on the outside that I now want to talk about. I have noticed in my travels that they always make the plea that the organization will not do them any good, that it is a white man's organization, that the only cause for asking them to connect themselves is simply to carry out some plan that had been previously connected, etc. Now, my dear people, I, as a colored man, would ask of you to dispel all such ideas as they are not only false but

foolish and unwise. Think a moment and see if you cannot come to the conclusion that you yourselves are men, and that you have the same interest at stake as your white brother—I say white brother, because I believe that to be the proper phrase, inasmuch as I believe in the principle of the fatherhood of God and the brotherhood of all mankind no matter what the color of his skin may be. I am willing to accept the truthfulness of the statement that some white men don't want to admit the equality of all men, but I take this consideration of such men (that is in the shape of men) as these, and that is that they are of the most ignorant class; had they to go through a process of examination they would fall far below the average and this class you find in all parts of the country even right here in the state of Ohio. I will here just state one case concerning myself no long since at our last state convention. It was in this way: I had been nominated for vice president of the district. However, I declined, inasmuch as I thought that there were others who were more capable of serving the position. Well, at the time of the convention a number of delegates came instructed to vote for me, but I told them that I was not a candidate. A certain gentleman came to me and stated that he had been instructed to vote for me, but that he did not think a colored man should hold either of the three principal offices, viz., president, vice president or secretary. You may well judge my feelings at the time. But I did not judge all other white men by that one, because I know different. I knew that the rest of the white men in the state were not of the same mind as that one. Now what I am trying get at is this: Do not judge all men by the acts of one or two. My dear people, throw aside these foolish notions and come to the front like men and show to the world that, though you stand behind a dark skin beneath it beats the heart of a true man. I want to say further that the labor organizations have done more to eliminate the color line than all other organizations, the church even not excepted. Then let us all connect ourselves with the organization, I mean those who work in or around the mines, show a steady determination to be men and I will assure you that the whites will not only recognize you, but will take you by the hand and try to help you. Will you make an effort to better the conditions of yourselves and your fellowmen? If so now is the time to make the start; procrastination is said to be the thief of time, so start now, and show to the white people that you will not only join the organized ranks of labor, but that you are true men and the equals of any no matter who they may be. I know that in former days you used to sing "Give me Jesus, give my Jesus, you have all the world, just give me Jesus."

But the day has now come that we want a little money along with our Jesus, so we want to change that old song and ask for a little of the world as well. Don't you think so friends? I have been thinking so for some time."[79]

Perhaps to be recognized for following in footsteps of Jesus, two months later Davis wrote, "I think were I as good a Christian as I am an agitator, as some call me, I would surely get to heaven when I die."[80]

In May, Davis once again, this time unsuccessfully, "carried the gospel of union" to Nuttallburg, located in the New River region of West Virginia, a place "where whatever Mr. Nuttall says is law." Offering an insight into the hard physical strain of organizing labor, having at times to cross the mountains on foot, Davis wrote: "Oh boys! You ought to see me, now turned tramp at last, that is tramping railroad ties ... on shank's ponies and hoofed it all the way, a distance of about 10 miles for the top of the mountain and I haven't got over it quite yet."[81] After a poor showing, Davis lamented that more men chose to attend a nearby dance rather than a union meeting.[82]

In June, Davis again set off to organize the "virtual slaves" in the Pocahontas field in West Virginia. Foreshadowing the Mercer Hotel incident, in Peterstown, Davis was refused a bed in the main building and instead directed to "an old dilapidated building, out in the wood yard." However after Brother Page, a local white man, persuaded the proprietor, Davis was allowed to return to the main building, which resulted in "getting about the best bed in the house" and being "the first negro to eat at the table in that man's dining room." On a second occasion, in Lowell, Brothers Page and Moran intervened so Davis could have supper with them. If it had not been "for those two white brothers," Davis wrote, "I would have been behind bars" as he felt like, had he been by himself, he would have cursed and not known what the consequences might have been.[83] Having returned to Rendville and looking back on the experience, he again described the men in West Virginia as virtual slaves, working in a vein of coal merely three feet thick, lacking faith in organizing, and being cowards as a mine boss could walk into a meeting of 200 men, "rip out an oath and tell them to get away," and they would leave in a hurry. On one exceptional occasion however a "colored boy" refused to move, defying a rock throwing mine boss by telling him "he'd better not strike him," after which calmly walked away. At the same meeting, however, illustrative of the courage it must have taken Davis to organize, the mine boss "with stone in hand" threatened Davis by telling him: "Say, look here you --- --- black scamp, I want you to get off these premises right away, move along or I'll knock --- out of you in a minute." After moving off the premises to the nearby railroad, the boss followed Davis and told him, "--- --- your black soul, I want you to move either up or down the track, and that --- quick." Although Davis refused to do so none of the men dared follow him.[84]

Begun on June 30, and despite the fact that it made headlines across the country, Davis did not make any reference to the Homestead, Pennsylvania, strike. However, its failure must have emphasized to Davis and the leaders in the United Mine Workers the importance of having a strong labor organization. When the agreement between the Carnegie Steel Company and the Amalgamated Association of Iron and Steel Workers, under which wages were to be driven by the market price, expired, the company decided to go non-union. In order to break the strike, on July 5 the company tried to quietly bring 300 Pinkerton detectives up the Monongahela River. As the two barges carrying the Pinkertons approached Homestead early the next morning, a shot rang out that led to a battle that lasted until late afternoon and left nine steel workers and three Pinkertons dead. By the time the strike ended on November 20, the steel workers had lost and Carnegie Steel would remain non-union for the next 40 years.[85]

Meanwhile in the Sunday Creek Valley, Mine No. 3 had laid idle for nearly the entire month of July as Joseph P. Rend, one of Rend's sons, refused to pay the day scale. Serving in the capacity of checkweighman, and therefore not having "been in the mine in two years," Davis reported that Rend also refused to honor the docking system.[86] Trouble continued when confusion about the exact time drivers should arrive at the stable and return from the mine caused Rend to come down from Columbus to read the miners "the riot act." However, after a speech in which he gave "the cranks" a fit, a meeting with District 6 union officials settled the matter.[87]

That same month Davis also visited Mine No. 8 where the miners had gone home after refusing to work under a colored boss. When some of the colored miners argued that the union would never do them any good unless they organized their own, Davis became mad as "we are too far advanced a civilization to even entertain such foolish notions." Having "it got fixed up in my brain that a man is a man no matter the color of his skin," he once again argued strongly that is was "high time for the color line to be dropped" and that "we would accomplish a great deal more than we will by fighting among ourselves on account of race, creed, color or nationality."[88]

Trouble also continued at Mine No. 3 where unfair docking practices and disagreement about working hours for drivers led the miners to go on strike. When Rend came down from Columbus he "read them the riot act" after he first got off the train, but after a meeting the next day the matter was settled "in less than half an hour," after which the mine resumed operations."[89] In another revealing letter, reminding the miners of discriminatory practices, and having advocated for weighing coal before sending it over the screen. Davis saw no use in W.P. Rend's offer to give the colored men steadier work if they would agree to make up the majority in Mine No. 3. He remembered that when Mine No. 3 "was altogether colored [and] all the other mines were for the whites," the miners did not get paid for dead work and had to send the mined coal across a one-and-a-half-inch-screen. Demanding that the company adopt the same one-and-a-quarter-inch screen as in the other mines, Mr. Corcoran, the superintendent, said that if he did so he would put white men in the mine as well. This led to a "breaking of the ice" as ever since, "with the possible exception of Mine No. 19," white and colored miners were "now mixed up all through."[90]

Still, by August some colored miners now classed Davis "as a very dangerous man to be with," and a "traitor" while the "ring leaders" among them threatened to elect a new checkweighman on the tipple.[91] Reminding his colored brothers that capital was their common enemy, Davis argued that while capital organized "for the purpose of wringing from labor the greater share of the wealth that it creates," labor simply does so "for the purpose of demanding a fair day's pay for a day's work," and that "surely there is nothing wrong in that."[92]

Unlike in any of his letters, on August 29, Davis revealed some surprising personal information about himself. In response to an article in the previous *United Mine Workers Journal* issue, entitled "Beefsteak and Chicken the Rule Around Jellico," he wrote, "I just don't know how this caught my gaze, other than because of the fact that I am particularly fond of both of those diets, and chicken, oh, my!"[93] Having encouraged others in the same letter "to have the pluck and energy" to send letters to the *United Mine Workers Journal*, two weeks later fellow Rendvillian F.H. Jackson wrote a brief "word of advice" to Davis: "Go on, you are on the right road. Do your duty as you have in the past, though you may be called a traitor by some. I only wish we had all traitors like you are. Then we would all be men, not things as your accusers are. I am yours in the cause of labor."[94]

Also in September, when a fire, smaller than one that had occurred four years earlier, closed Mine No. 3, "wandering aimlessly," Davis "suddenly found himself in Congo. Not the Congo that we have so much read of in Stanley's works, but Congo, O.," an iron-clad model town about three miles west of Rendville, run by the Congo Coal Mining company, where miners could be evicted from their homes within five days of having been either laid off or having quit or gone on strike. Recommending to read it carefully and see for oneself what the miners would make of it, Davis decided to include a copy of the contract:

LICENSE TO EMPLOYES.

This is to certify that at my special request the Congo Coal Mining company has consented and does hereby consent that myself and family may, as tenant at will, occupy their tenement house No.—, at their coal works at Congo, Perry county, O.; upon and subject to the following terms and conditions and not otherwise:

First—To occupy peaceably and keep and return the said house at the expiration of said occupancy in the same good order and repair as when received, reasonable wear and tear excepted

Second—On any pay day to pay to said Congo Coal Mining company or allow to be deducted from my earnings as they prefer, the sum of—dollars, as a monthly rental for said house.

Third—Without any notice within five days after I have ceased to work for said Congo Coal Mining company by reason of any strike by any employees at said coal works, to deliver up to said Congo Coal Mining company peaceable possession of said house and at any time on five days notice to quit, to me, given by said Congo Coal Mining company or their agent, by service personally or left at said house, to deliver up peaceable possession of said property to said Congo Coal Mining company.

On my neglect or refusal to comply with any one of said terms or conditions, or to deliver possession of said house within five days after I quit work, as aforesaid, or within five days to quit, as aforesaid, I hereby agree that my family and myself may be treated as forcibly detaining possession of said house, and said Congo Coal Mining company, their servants or agents are hereby authorized to eject me or my family, and all personal property from said premises using such and so much force as they, the said Congo Coal Mining company, their servants or agents, or any of them, may deem proper, and I do hereby remiss and forever discharge and release the said Congo Coal Mining company, their servants and agents, from any and all liability to me or my family in any shape, manner or form, for forcibly ejecting me or any of us from said house and property.

Witness our hands and seals this—of ---, 1892.
Signed and sealed in presence of
_____

_____
Signed:
_____ [seal]
Congo Coal Mining Co., [seal]
Per _____ [95]

"Fenced in all-around, with two gates," Davis likened the town to the Ohio Penitentiary, where the colored miners were segregated underground from the white miners "over in Africa" and, when above ground, on "Nigger Hill" and where no peddlers were allowed and all transactions had to be conducted at the company store only.[96] Informed that Congo's superintendent asked "what in the h--- that fellow DAVIS meant by writing such letters about Congo," Davis thought that "seeing the bright side [of Congo] pictured so beautifully," it was necessary to "show the dark side of the picture" as well.[97] Facetiously suggesting that his letters might have "spoiled his chances of ever getting a job at Congo," Davis denied accusations that he was "a bighead" who was only in the union business for the money: "What I advocate is from a pure principle of unionism; nothing more, nothing less."[98] Wondering how someone could be a consistent Christian and not believe in unionism, and reminding his readers of his Knights of Labor roots that "an injury to one is the concern of all," Davis asked how it was possible that miners in "the home of the brave and the land of the free" refused to recognize the fact that it was rather the "land of the rich and the home of the slave."[99]

During the last two months of the year, Davis wondered whether Brothers Penna and Webb were having more success in organizing the miners in West Virginia than he did. He again affirmed his belief that one "can not be a consistent christian if he does not believe in unionism nowhere. I hear a man say he is a christian, but that he does not believe in unionism, I believe he lies."[100] Finally, as operators had increasingly begun to introduce cutting machines in the mines, he ended the year by attending a three-day convention in Columbus on the "Machine Entry Question" now that "pick mines" were "often compelled to be idle, except at such times as mines having machines are unable to supply the trade."[101]

The Depression of 1893

Arguing that weighing coal before screening "would be a grand achievement for the miners of Ohio" and stop the practice of "giving away several hundred pounds of good marketable coal on each and every mine car sent out," Davis started the new year continuing to debate the "anti-screen" bill that was being discussed in the Ohio legislature.[102] "For the life of me" he could not see how any miner might be opposed to a law that would forbid the weighing of coal before it passed over the screen and end "the robbery system." In favor of the anti-screen bill and noting that the miner had to work as just as hard for nut and pea coal as for lump coal," Davis argued that he should be paid accordingly. Once again he wrote:

> We must assert our manhood and no longer allow ourselves to be the slaves of the idlers, the drones sometimes called capitalists. No, boys, we should be men and not slaves, and should now with one mighty effort burst asunder the chains of wage slavery that now bind us.... Let us watch the actions of our representatives and those of them who are prejudiced enough against us as to vote against the bill, let us at the next election elect them to stay at home; relegate them to the rear and send men there to represent us that will work to the interest of the people.[103]

Two months earlier, having spoken out in favor of restricting immigration, in February, Davis once again lamented that while the importation of "Huns, Slavs and Italians" typically "classed with the whites," is still in its infancy," it would lead to increased competition for colored miners.[104] With work being "not very good" due to the scarcity of railroad cars but dedicated as ever to the cause, on March 3, the day Beatrice, his second daughter, was born, Davis did not fail to write his letter to the *United Mine Workers Journal*, this time to reject President Penna's proposal to reduce the journal's size and simultaneously increase its subscription price which was part the union membership. Instead Davis proposed it be printed in other languages as to keep its price as low as possible since some families already received multiple copies of the same as several members of the household would be members.[105]

Unfortunately, less than three weeks later Davis, having expressed his wish that "our children [be] better clothed, better fed, better educated, better housed and [have] better everything than we have now,"[106] reported that "the poor old Screen Bill [had] died of unconstitutionality." Expressing his disgust with the legislature and its politicians, Davis wrote:

> Strange is it not that any measure gotten up for the benefit of the workingman is always said to be unconstitutional, while, at the same time, a measure in the interest of some great corporation for the purpose of throttling and robbing the people can be passed almost without a dissenting vote. I have heard of morbid bodies, but such a one as the Ohio State Senate can not be found in existence, I don't think. Just think of it! This

same law has been passed in Illinois, Indiana, West Virginia and in remote Kansas, yet, when it comes that the Ohio miners demand it they are told it is unconstitutional, that it will work to the detriment of the consumer, increase the cost of production and a thousand other things. Now then what will we do about it? Will we quietly submit or will resent this most dastardly insult next fall? I say at all hazards we should show those gentlemen that we have some power left yet within us and that we intend to use it for the purpose of electing them to stay at home.[107]

Not until five years later did the legislature pass the Ohio Screen Bill which prohibited the mine operators from passing coal "over any screen or other device which shall take any part from the value thereof, before the same shall have been weighed and duly credited to the employee."[108]

Re-elected to the executive board of District 6 in April, Davis attended another Joint Meeting in Columbus on May 9, 1893, that led to an agreement with the mine operators to continue the previous year's wage scale.[109] While Davis was at the meeting, S. Glasgow, a white miner from Bellaire, Ohio, cautioned him in the *United Mine Workers Journal* to "not let the color idea run away with you" and "to let the white man get a chance to look at your race's condition." Glasgow wrote:

> We see no fault with the colored man, as long as he is true, because a man's skin is black, is no reason why his principles should be so. The colored man has the same right on this earth as any other, there is no law to prevent them. The church is their friend, I cannot see what brother D. wants. Is our union his enemy? Surely not. For a man who is true to the union, the union should be true to him. Brother D. don't let the color ideas run away with you. I don't see that you or any other of your race kicked at, so let us have a short rest on the color line and talk about something good for us all. I have the name of a chronic kicker, I accept it with fairness, and I may as well say it as I think it, I will kick until I am kicked out or shown that I am kicking wrongly.[110]

In his rebuttal letters Davis was puzzled why Glasgow did not seem to understand that the colored miner never yet had received a "fair shake" and that it was hard for him "to get above the pick and shovel no matter how competent he may be."[111] Davis emphatically denied that the church, in this "said-to-be Christian and civilized country," was a friend of the colored miner. Being a citizen of this country and arguing that "a man is a man no matter what the color of his skin may be," he praised the labor organizations for being "the only ones to recognize the Negro as an equal" and working to "wipe out all class and race distinctions to create "a government of the people, for the people and by the people."[112] Demanding equal representation, Davis argued that the unions needed the colored man and called for the election of colored miners to hold office, "not office in name, but office indeed," to include some financial pay. He then told Glasgow that he had "been called everything but a gentleman," and threatened with discharge, all for the sake of the union and without any pay.[113]

Unfortunately things would get worse for all miners. Early in 1893 the country plunged into a severe economic depression. On February 25, the Philadelphia and Reading Railroad went bankrupt, followed on May 4 with the failure of the National Cordage Company. Failing banks, shops and factories led to at least three million unemployed out of a total labor force of five million.[114] Fortunately, from January through August, except in June, Davis received approximately $10 to $30 each month "for work" from District 6 at the typical rate of $2.50 per day.[115] As work in the Sunday Creek Valley became "very poor," in part due to "most of the mines [being] overcrowded," Davis went on another week-long journey to Coshocton, Ohio, where, despite being twice told to get off the premises, he successfully organized a local. However, in nearby Conesville the miners wanted nothing to do with Davis because of his color.[116]

In August, as most of the mines in the Hocking Valley were overcrowded, the depression worsened and the men were unable "to get enough work to get bread," the operators began to issue 60-day notes rather than pay the miners in cash. Thinking that all business people would accept the notes, they "in voice of one accord" refused to do so. Despite his disgust with the notes, but as a member of the executive board that approved the notes, Davis later apologized for his "of the head and not of the heart" mistake to concede to the operators and called for a resumption of cash payment for work performed. However, part of the reason Davis believed why he was being attacked by his fellow miners was "because I am colored."[117]

As many of the miners were unable to pay their union dues as a result of being paid in notes rather than cash, by October the District 6 treasury had dwindled from more than $2,200 in April to $610. As the financial condition of District 6 continued to rapidly worsen, when auditing the union's books, Davis found them all to be in due order.[118] However, when Thomas McGough lamented that when he signed off he had wrongly trusted his fellow auditors, Davis in an uncharacteristically strong personal response, questioning the childish complaint, stated that he had never before heard "such a flimsy excuse" and that he had "a little girl [Edith] that is only two years old, and if she, today did not display more sense than [McGough] I don't know if I wouldn't whip the life out of her."[119]

As the year came to an end, work in the Sunday Creek Valley section of the Hocking Valley remained "somewhat slow" and left Davis wondering what the future would bring. Blaming the miners of Pennsylvania and West Virginia for enduring starvation wages and undermining the livelihood of the miners in Ohio rather than "taking concerted action to secure a uniform and living rate of wages," he once again called on all miners to stand together to "show the world that we are men worthy of the name."[120]

The Strike of 1894

On January 9, 1894, Davis attended a Special Session of District 6 in Druid's Hall, South Fourth Street, in Columbus, held "for the purpose of discussing the depressed condition of the coal trade," that rejected the operators' proposed scale.[121] By the middle of month work in the Sunday Creek Valley remained very poor. During the second week Mine No. 3 only worked one and one half days. Blaming the depression on the manipulation by "the money kings gambling in stocks and bonds," Davis reported hearing "the cry of hunger and starvation" from throughout the state. "How long," he despaired, "will we, the people allow it to continue?"[122] When the miners in New Straitsville, desperate for work, proposed to work at a 20-cent reduction regardless of the miners in the rest of the state, Davis once again reminded his readers that unless "united we stand, divided we [will] fall."[123] By the end of the month, while writing his letter to the editor and excusing himself for not being in church "where all good people ought to go," he started to suggest the possibility of a national strike: "Not only do I mean for the miners of Ohio to stop but Indiana, Illinois and Pennsylvania and as many of West Virginia stop as well … we will never know what we can accomplish until once we try it," he wrote, and "if down we must go let us go together."[124]

On March 25, 1894, a protest march of a hundred jobless men, led by businessman Jacob Coxey, left Massillon, Ohio, on its way to Washington, D.C., to demand the government create public work jobs. When the march arrived in the capital on April 30, Coxey's Army, as it became known, had increased to 6,000 men. After Coxey and others were arrested the next day for walking on the grass of the United States Capitol, the movement quickly dissipated. Interestingly, Davis did not comment on Coxey's Army. Neither did he write any letters to the editor until May. Chris Evans reported, however, that on Friday, April 5, 1894, at the Sixth Annual Convention of District 6, "Brother R.L. Davis was called on and thanked the miners of district 6 for the complimentary vote he had received and promised to continue his untiring efforts for and loyalty to the organization."[125] As during the year before, Davis was again paid monthly from January through June, except in March, and once more in November "for work" and attending convention and board meetings.[126]

The fifth annual convention of the United Mineworkers of America met in Columbus on April 10. As President McBride addressed the convention he reminisced that when they met the previous year they were "full of hope and expectancy as the future appeared bright" but that due to the financial panic of 1893 "the promised prosperity to our craft and country" had "gone glimmering" and it was uncertain what the future would hold. Due to what he called an "insane competition" mining rates had dropped to below a living standard. As the delegates debated the wisdom of organizing a national strike, McBride suggested that "oppression, low wages and hunger, aided and enforced by operators of mines have proved to be a more potent and efficient power in the work of organizing" than the work of union officials.[127] Committed to enforcing "the suspension of mining by peaceful and law abiding methods" and "promising to voluntarily assist in the work of protecting life and property whenever threatened, McBride called for a the strike to begin at noon on April 21 hoping to rapidly deplete the oversupplied national market."[128] He believed that it would increase the price of coal, ultimately leading to higher wages. When James Murray, a delegate from Illinois, asked all delegates in favor to stand up, "Every man arose. Cheer after cheer resounded through the vast hall, and it was some time before order could be restored."[129] According to the *New York Times*, on April 22 nearly 130,000 miners had laid down their picks that day knowing that the union's treasury would not allow it to pay any strike benefits. The union officers, as well as Samuel Gompers, were surprised by the vast number of men who went on strike and felt confident it would be of short duration. A telegram from Corning claimed that 8,000 miners in the Hocking Valley, where a 50 cent rate of mining had been established, had laid down their picks at 11:00 a.m., one hour ahead of the scheduled time. W.P. Rend who, according to the *New York Times*, employed 2,000 miners in Ohio let it be known from Chicago that if the miners and operators would meet in joint convention and arbitrate the strike would be over in two weeks. "I am personally in favor of that plan," Rend said, "and I know of other Presidents who agree with me. I have written to President McBride of the United Mine Workers of America, asking his co-operation."[130] While Rend believed McBride's estimate was exaggerated, a union bulletin on April 27 claimed more than 100,000 were out on strike. Three days later a second bulletin estimated the number at 160,000 and claimed that "it would not be long until there will not be coal enough left in the general market to boil a kettle, and a complete victory will be yours." As "a coal famine was staring the people in the face," the mine operators in West Virginia and Pennsylvania "came to the rescue and poured coal into the threatened markets" while "the strikers were living on a crust of bread and a glass of water, and their bare-footed children were crying with hunger." Aware that due to the depression most miners had had little to no earnings the union realized that the strike could only be of short lived.

Consequently, McBride called for a joint convention of operators and miners on May 15, to be held in Cleveland. Paying the miners a compliment on "the success met with the stoppage" in order "to secure living wages," referring to reports in the newspapers and reticent to use the word "strike" to describe the stoppage, McBride rather referred to the action as a suspension.[131] When the miners and operators met in joint convention the miners asked for 79 cent rate for the Pittsburgh district and a 70 cent rate for the Hocking Valley, the same scale as they had agreed upon since May 1, 1893. However, after the operators proposed 65 cent rate for the Pittsburgh district and a 56 cent rate for the Hocking Valley, the convention "ended in smoke."[132] Despite the resolution not to resort to violence, when soon after some strikers began threatening to burn bridges that were being used to transport the contraband coal, the Interstate Commerce Act, passed by Congress in 1887, prompted President Cleveland to call out the militia to protect the bridges. As this unfolded, in an official circular sent to the miners, McBride admitted that although no doubt violence had been committed it was not nearly as "outrageously lawless" as reported in the newspapers.[133] As the "wails of suffering from every part of the country [were] heart rending in the extreme," "unwilling to assume or bear the responsibility for acts over which he had no control," "being powerless to enforce discipline in our ranks," and as many of the larger operators threatened to open up the mines within the next week, "with the assistance of every lawful and unlawful Winchester," he realized that it would only be a matter of time before "the strike would fly to pieces," and that the time had come to reach a settlement. A joint convention held in Columbus on June 3, when approximately 180,000 of the nation's estimated 193,000 bituminous coal miners had joined the strike, reached an agreement to take effect on June 18 and last until May 1, 1895. It set the Pittsburgh scale at 69 cents and the Hocking Valley scale at 60 cents. Furthermore, the agreement granted the miners the right to elect their own checkweighman, stipulated that all wages be paid semi-monthly in cash at or above scale, and created an interstate board of arbitration and conciliation. While not having accomplished what he set out to do, McBride nonetheless argued to have accomplished more than could have been accomplished through local strikes.[134]

On May 21 as the strike was still unfolding, reporting on a labor organizing trip during the early part of May to the Flat Top Coalfield in Pocahontas County, West Virginia, Davis admitted having been in fear of his life. Although he had been in "some rough places" before, he thought "his time had come" as he had never been in a place before "where [his] life was so much endangered." Arguing that "those blood-suckers operators down there will not hesitate to stoop to anything low and dirty to carry their point," especially during a strike, Davis confessed to his readers that he was "not yet ready to become a martyr to the cause." Having been born in Virginia, he knew that when a threat was made against a black man that it was serious. Closely watched by "a number of spies through the region, both white and black," Davis vividly described the dangers he sometimes faced:

> Now to prove this I have been sitting or standing at different places when maybe two or three strange fellows would come along accompanied by one of the sucks of Pocahontas, when they would get to where I was I would hear one say, there he is, or there is the s-b-. Not only that, but I have heard myself spoken of in the same way of business men walking along the streets; besides I have heard threats made as to what they would do to me if I did not leave. Now, you might say, oh, he left because he was scared, but boys, let me say that I was then south of Mason's and Dixon's line, and there is little justice for the black man anywhere, and none down there, and for safety I thought it would be best for me to leave and even in doing this I had to be escorted to the station, the threat being so openly made about doing me up. Yes, and they were talking of doing Harris up, too, and his is a white man you know. Now, I was born in the State of Virginia, and I know that when they threaten a white man it is an absolute certainty about the negro and he better make himself scarce, that is, if he values his life."[135]

On May 28, five weeks since they "entered upon this, the greatest movement ever inaugurated by the American miners," Davis reported seeing "great train loads of coal passing through" Rendville, "coming from the scab mines in West Virginia, and going, we know not where." "The fight is on and it has been a noble one so far," he wrote, and "[we] must now be men enough to fight it out if it takes summer." Then he added, "When we have no longer resources of our own let us beg, and if we can't get it that way why then we will have to take it. Now I don't mean to steal, but go and get it while the fellow is looking. This I do not think we will have to do, I hope not at least."[136] On June 2, a "grand demonstration," led by the Rendville cornet band, marched from Rendville to Corning carrying banners and dummies representing the West Virginia miners, including "Rendville Solid for 70 cents Per Ton," "No Compromise," "No Scab Coal Hauled Here," and "Stand Out for Your Rights." Carrying dummies representing the West Virginia scabs and after listening to a series of speakers, including Davis himself, everyone went home "highly elated over the events of the evening" as this was "one of most demonstrative gatherings ever held in the valley." In praise of the strike, Davis concluded that "the men of the Sunday Creek valley are as solid as they were on the 21st day of April."[137]

Not writing much for more than a month, and not until July 16, as "the eyes of the entire country were turned on the great coal miners' strike" and "many others were having their say in regard to the late settlements," Davis repeated his demand for living wages and electing others to the legislature than "the fellow who has the most money and can set up the most beer and whiskey." Protesting that colored men, unlike "the Hungarian, Polander,

Italian, Chinaman and even the lazy, shiftless Indian" could not become members of the American Railway Union, then out on strike, Davis reminded his readers that the colored miners were "American citizens and should be treated as such." Finally, on behalf of the "Rendville Base Ball" club, he challenged any club in Perry, Hocking or Athens county "to cross bats" but that since they were church members they could not "play for a stake."[138]

With a union membership at a record low between 8,000 and 13,000 members,[139] the following week Davis apologized for having "said some things that were not very pleasant" after he had learned that "McBride and his associates" had settled the strike, contrary to the instructions the miners' delegates to the Cleveland convention to accept no settlement unless a 70 cent rate was agreed upon. The time had come, Davis said, "to heal the gaping wound and begin to get our forces ready for the next contest." Having learned a lesson, and as he had warned his readers almost three years ago, he cautioned his fellow colored miners to stop being blind partisans "voting tickets because your fathers before you voted that way" and "elect honest men" to the upcoming "convention of workingmen."[140]

Later in July, the Pullman Strike in Chicago drew national attention as the American Railway Union, led by Eugene V. Debs, on June 26, had called for a boycott of trains pulling the company's cars. First arrested, on July 17, 1894, Debs was sent to jail to serve a term of six months during which he became a socialist. By the time the conflict ended, 30 strikers were dead and by the time Debs got out of jail after having completed his sentence the union he had created no longer existed. Despite having won the strike, Pullman, worried that people might try to steal his body, requested that after his death his grave be lined in concrete.[141]

In October, Davis expressed his support for the law that was enacted at the annual convention that no person would be allowed to work in the mines unless he was card carrying member of the union. At the same time he opposed exchanging any union card unless the other union, including the railroaders, reciprocated the membership.[142] In a second letter he apologized for having erroneously assumed all along that Laurene Gardner of Linton, Indiana, was "an old boy." Instead he could only say that "he would to God that we had a thousand more such noble women friends" in the craft.[143]

In a final appeal to miners for the year, on November 19, Davis favored increasing the "entirely too cheap" cost of union membership in order to have more money on hand to support a strike as well as caution the operators to not try to "starve us into submission." "If we have a 10 cent organization we must expect 10 cent results," he wrote, "if we have a 25 cent or 50 cent organization we must expect results."[144] The following month, at its fourteenth convention held in Denver, Colorado, John McBride defeated Samuel Gompers with a vote of 1,041 against 1,023 to become president of the American Federation of Labor. Since he believed it to be inappropriate for the president and secretary to both represent the miners Chris Evans decided to resign his position as secretary of the Federation.[145]

CHAPTER 6

A Year of Transition

Continuing to write his letters during the weekend, Davis did not report any improvement in the "hard times" and "destitution" in Sunday Creek until July 1895 when he reported that "Mine No.3 of this place, after an idleness of five months durations ... again resumed operations."[1] He opened the new year reminding his readers that "most all reforms come from agitation, this is why I never minded being called an agitator." At the end of month, with work "practically at a standstill," Davis wrote: "Mine No. 3 has closed down and as a result has left many an honest man in straitened circumstances for when they were working they were not making a living, but merely eking out an existence; so, with no work, you all know how we are fixed, and just think of it in the midst of winter when every man's want is greatest, how we are going to pull through God alone can tell."[2]

As the economic depression continued to linger, the *United Mine Workers Journal* reported that half of the 10,000 miners in the valley were without work and that a committee of Hocking Valley miners had traveled to Columbus to appeal to Governor McKinley for assistance as "only starvation wages [were] being made by the miners" and "even [the] clay and brick factories [had] closed down."[3] In response to McKinley's appeal to the chambers of commerce in Cincinnati, Cleveland, Toledo and Columbus to offer support, the secretary of the Standard Oil Company, F. Rockefeller, notified the governor that his company had shipped "100 barrels of flour, 200 sacks of cornmeal, and 1,200 pounds of side meat" to the valley.[4] Desperate nonetheless, in April, Davis again wrote of desperation:

> We have no work, and have had none since January, and then we were not earning enough to keep body and soul together; and had it not been for charity no doubt many of us would have been starved by this time, or possibly have been compelled, through adverse circumstances, to have committed some depredation as a last resort to get something with which to support our wives and little ones. And charity is now at an end. We have no commissary now to go to for a morsel of bread; and what we

are going to eat, God alone knows for we have no work and nowhere to go to find work."⁵

In the midst of these desperate times, Lewis Coleman, an African American miner, submitted a letter to the *United Mine Workers Journal* that the time had come "for the election of a colored man upon the national executive board" of the United Mine Workers of America and "that that should be so at all times for it is representation that we as a race want and need most." Arguing that "it seems men forget the fact that the Hungarian, the Frenchman, the German, the Swede, the Polander and many others are recognized and treated as white men, but the poor colored man is snubbed and sneered wherever he goes," Coleman noted that "we have here, in our midst, a colored man that is well liked by white and black," and that "is none other than R.L. Davis of Rendville."⁶ In response Davis noted that, "'Friend Coleman' had taken it upon himself to give me a puff. I must say that I am proud to know that I have so many friends. I have certainly tried to do all that I could in the interest of labor and am willing to do more, and will if life lasts."⁷

Yet, three weeks after, Davis had to defend himself against "Friend Deloche" who in a letter to the *United Mine Workers Journal* had accused him of having traveled "thousands of miles and spent hundreds of dollars of the organization's money" but having contributed nothing but "(000000) or six times nothing." Recalling his travels in West Virginia, Davis reminded Deloche of the peril he was in during a return trip to the Pocahontas field in May of the previous year, after the local he had originally organized had failed to survive.

> I organized a local there again, even after an attempt had been made to kill me by a hireling of corporate greed. I yet have the mark and whenever you meet me just look at the left side of my face and you will see what I got at Pocahontas for doing nothing. How would you like a dose of the same medicine, my brother? I don't think you would stand fire. I did all I could while there but fate was against me.... The brother calls these trips excursions. I desire to say that whenever I went anywhere in the interest of the organization I went a matter of business, and not for pleasure, as the brother would have you believe.⁸

With Davis' name omitted, according to the Committee of Credentials, the Sixth National Annual Convention, which was held in Columbus, Ohio, on February 12, was attended by 122 delegates of whom 69 came from Ohio's District 6. John McBride, now ex-president of the union, delivered an opening speech in which he presented a detailed review of the strike of 1894. While admonishing the miners to curb violence as it would only weaken their cause by driving "every honest, conscientious man from official position in your ranks," he hoped that their deliberations would be marked by the "wisdom required to extricate your craftsmen from the necessity of depending upon charity to sustain life."[9]

Four days later, on February 16, "with President Penna in the chair," elections took place. Generally known as "Little Phil," Davis had suggested two years earlier that Penna should "fatten" some and that he could use "a little addition in some way to his size, that is, if some of those bosses get after him."[10] Having finished out McBride's term since December 15, Penna was now the duly-elected president, along with Cameron Miller of Ohio as vice-president, and Patrick McBryde of Pennsylvania as secretary-treasurer. One among 28 candidates for the remaining six seats on the Executive Board, Davis came in seventh with 173 votes after Fred Dilcher of Nelsonville who garnered 200 and one-half votes.[11] Less than two weeks later, labeled by the editor "a good a union man as ever," Davis wrote that, "although I was unsuccessful, I desire to say that I never asked anyone to vote for me or asked him anything in connection with his or their votes, I am proud to say that I was defeated by a very small majority, which to my mind proves very clearly that the question of color in our miners' organization will soon be a thing of the past." Trusting that the next time some good many of my race will be successful," Davis thanked his supporters.[12] In April, referring to the convention, Wm. O. Wareburton of Coaldale, West Virginia, wrote to the *United Mine Workers Journal* that "our colored brothers [were] all asking for R. L. Davis" so they would have "a chance to hear one of their race expound the doctrines of unionism."[13] Not to be discouraged, Davis further reminded his readers that "God only helps those who help themselves, and we cannot help ourselves only by united efforts; so again I say let us begin the work of organization."[14]

He also reported that the last District 6 board meeting had come to the conclusion that henceforth no district officer should hold office for more than two years. Arguing that it would make the union stronger locally, he also encouraged the miners to organize separate subdistricts for Hocking and Sunday Creek so they could establish their own rules and regulations in dealing with operators and the railroad company with which they had contracted. One such rule the Rendville miners had was that no one was to go into the mine before 7 a.m. and leave the mine later than 6 p.m., except on Saturdays when they had to be out no later than 1 p.m.[15]

Having written Secretary Coleman of Subdistrict No. 1 about the last day of February to decline being nominated for vice-president, Davis nonetheless received notice on Tuesday, March 5, that he had been elected on March 3, when ballots were due, and that he was invited to attend a convention in Shawnee that same day which he later learned had elected W.E. Farms as vice-president instead. Arguing the importance of following the constitution, he wrote, "Now I want to know how the change was brought about. If I wanted to contest the thing, I think I would have the whole thing declared illegal, and upon good grounds, for how are we to know but there was juggling in the whole election. I do not care for the office, but for God's sake let things be done right."[16] Arguing that although he did not think that Coleman was guilty of changing the vote, "setting aside the constitution to please a few at the displeasure of the many is a very lame idea." Settling the matter, Davis begged Coleman's pardon "for having marred his feelings," trusting that it would not happen again.[17]

Early March, when L.U. 296 threatened to withdraw from the United Mine Workers, disgruntled with its national leaders, Davis came to their defense. "United we stand, divided we fall," he wrote, adding,

> It cannot be denied that this organization is the best that the miners of this country ever had.... You say you are dissatisfied with the McBryde-Penna-Fahy & Company tyranny. Well, suppose you are, will a move as this do any good? You might as well say that if a man has trouble with a disordered stomach that the only means of effecting a cure would be to commit suicide. Now is not one as plausible as the other? For us to now withdraw from the United Mine Workers of America would be suicidal to ourselves, to our wives and children and our fellowman. Again, all of us know that the operators at all times take advantage of weakness."[18]

Subsequently, on March 15, President Penna made a visit to Rendville during which he held "the boys spellbound for an hour and a half." Next, Davis was listed as a candidate for vice-president of District 6 in the call for its annual convention which was to be held in Wirtheim's Hall in Columbus on Tuesday, April 2.[19] Although the Cash Book for District 6 lists $21 on April 8, 1894, as the only expenditure for Richard L. Davis during the entire year, in his annual report at the convention, indicative of Davis' active role, W.C. Pearce, Secretary-Treasurer of District 6, listed $97.65 for R.L. Davis as the district's seventh highest expenditure.[20]

On April 4, on the fourth ballot Henry Shires defeated Davis with 161 to 109 votes, thus ending Davis' presence on the executive board of District 6 after having served five terms. On the second day of the convention the delegates elected Michael Ratchford as their new president, "not what one would call a great talker" but "very persistent" and "great stickler." That same day the convention also passed a resolution in which the delegates tendered "a vote of thanks to Governor McKinley, the citizens of Ohio, all fraternities and organizations and individuals who responded so promptly to the cries for help from our fellow craftsmen."[21]

The same month, again reminding labor that "we must hang together or hang separately," Davis warned that the Pittsburgh operators were determined to wipe out the nine cent differential with Ohio coal and making a 60 cents scale. Since the Ohio operators were equally determined to keep the nine cents differential, this would mean that in order for the Ohio coal operators to remain competitive, the state's miners would have to accept 51 cents, damning the union. Furthermore, after warning against the menace posed by machine mines, he also, in somewhat surprising contrast to the inclusive nature of the Knights of Labor but consistent with contemporary views on gender roles, commented on an article he had read about women being employed in the rolling mills in Pittsburgh, exclaiming:

> Great Heavens! What are we coming to anyway? If this is true how long will it be until they are employed in the mines also? And this in free America! I have at all times hated the word anarchy, but if this is true then no doctrine that the anarchist can expound can be too strong, for it would be better that the government be overthrown than that the nation be degraded to a level lower than the lowest. Indeed it is enough to make a man's heart sink within him. Is it not time for men to come together and act? We have no room for the man who tries to sow seeds of dissention; the quicker he is out the way the better.[22]

In an effort to restore the joint scale of 1892, in May 1895, United Mine Workers President Penna called for an interstate joint conference of operators and miners to meet in Columbus. With an empty national treasury, having to borrow money for its officers to live on and pay operating expenses, and a membership of less than 7,000 in Ohio, the meeting failed to reach an agreement.[23] In June, District 6 President Ratchford and his Executive Board failed to organize an interstate strike

Michael D. Ratchford, fourth president, United Mine Workers of America, 1897–1898 (Evans, *History of the United Mine Workers of America, 1914–18*, 1920).

and approved an agreement that the price to be paid for pick mining of coal in the Hocking Valley would be 51 cents per ton in comparison to 60 cents in the Pittsburgh Field. In light of the ongoing economic depression, Davis came to the "no good" board's defense. Presenting a list of 13 poignant questions for the kickers, he believed himself to be lucky to no longer be one of the board's members and having to defend himself against "the evil slimy tongued scandal mongers" and "young buzzards [who] eagerly swallow the carrion injected into them by others." However, based on his experiences as a labor organizer these questions offer a broad frame of reference for his way of thinking.

1. Do you think Ohio now holds its same relative position in the coal markets as it did a few years ago?

2. If not, then please state why, in your opinion, conditions have changed?

3. Are you aware that there is a little state called West Virginia, which, if it continues as it has in the past few years will far outstrip Ohio as a coal producer?

4. Are you aware that because of the cheap production of this coal and with the present railroad facilities that coal can be placed on our markets as cheap, if not cheaper, than our own coal?

5. Do you think you can force high wages in Ohio as long as wages are low in West Virginia?

6. Do you think anything can be accomplished by withdrawing from the United Mine Workers organization and forming a hundred and one different forms of organization?

7. Do you believe that affiliating with the A.R.U. will be of any practical benefit to you as the miners?

8. Are you not aware that in case of a strike in Ohio that these same men would haul West Virginia coal right by your doors and would be unable to help themselves?

9. Are you aware that, according to the interstate commerce law, that this coal if loaded on railroad cars would be hauled if it took every available soldier in the United States to do it?

10. Are you not aware that a law under which a workingman may be convicted will be declared unconstitutional when a money corporation is tried under it?

11. Are you not aware that the money kings own the railroads, the land, the legislative halls and even our courts of justice?

12. Are you not aware that the railroad and coal corporations instead

of disuniting are steadily every day perfecting plans of forming one vast combination?

13. Do you not think you had better call a halt on some of our would-be leaders and instead of drawing away from our national organization draw our forces closer, and continue the work of organization more vigorously, co-operation of the miners of West Virginia, Pennsylvania and Illinois, so that we may be able to meet the common foe, instead of continuing the work of disintegration?[24]

Willing to "stake [his] head for a chopping block," in yet another articulate defense Davis compared the perceived lack of success of the union leaders with that of Christian missions:

> For years and years the people of all civilized countries, churches of all denominations, saints and sinners have been contributing their mite for foreign mission purposes, or in other words for the purpose of civilizing and Christianizing the heathens in foreign lands and after all these years of unceasing and persistent work, today, thousands, yes millions, of them are without the pale of civilization and yet bow down to wood and stone. Seeing that we have failed to accomplish the desired end in all this time would it not be well for us to close our churches, close our schools, wipe out everything pertaining to intellectual development, science, arts, and everything, stop the wheels of progress, turn about face and retrograde back to barbarism and heathen along with the others, when we will all be upon an equal basis? Probably some one will ask, do I believe that we should do this? Others will say I am crazy, but I am not; but would it not be as plausible to advocate withdrawing from the organization, say that it is no good simply because our officers have been unable to properly organize the miners of West Virginia, Illinois and parts of Pennsylvania? I think so. I think the one argument is as good as the other, for I can see nothing in the latter, only that since the officers have so far failed to get those people organized in the states named, then we will just for meanness, for lack of respect for our wives and children, for lack of love for comfort will disorganize themselves and get down and wallow the scabs.[25]

As Mine No. 3 after five months finally had resumed operations, on July 8, District 6 president Ratchford visited Corning and delivered "quite an able address" in which he advised the miners "to stick closer to their union, state and national, and to not allow themselves to be divided as they were."[26] Even though Mine No. 3 and a few other mines were at work again, the *Athens Messenger* reported that "suffering and destitution are again abroad in the Hocking valley" due to "a woeful lack of orders for coal." The paper further added that there were "entirely too many men engaged in digging coal than ever before in the history of the valley" and that "the mining industry … [was] being changed by the introduction of labor-saving machinery."[27]

That same month, Davis once again warned the men to stop quarreling amongst themselves and that the operators were simply "laughing up their sleeves at you and quietly planning how to fleece you." In response to a proposal by "Friend Wallace" to merge with the railway union in order to organize a successful national strike, Davis argued that he would never join a union that bars "the colored man."

> I will never allow myself to become connected in any way with an organization that says I cannot become a member, and just think of it too, I, an American citizen by birth, many of them are not yet dry from crossing the salt water pond, and yet they have the unlimited gall to say that an American citizen shall not take part in an American institution because of the color of his skin; it makes me mad whenever I think of it and I have no respect for the man or men who steps into a thing of the kind by holding out raise hope for them. Away with such rottenness.[28]

Asking the kickers whether they had forgotten that "in unity there is strength, and that a house divided against itself cannot stand," Davis had "nothing but good words to say" of the national officials, believing them to be honest men who were committed to advancing the union's cause, something that would be confirmed to him in the Mercer Hotel incident.[29]

The Mercer Hotel

On August 22, 1895, Davis organized two meetings in Congo and Corning when national president Phil Penna and District 6 president Michael Ratchford, accompanied by District 6 Secretary W.C. Pearce and Subdistrict No. 1 President W.H. Haskins paid a visit. The meeting at Congo was well attended and the men were well behaved, sitting quietly and listening. The meeting at Corning, however, was quite the opposite as "a few smart alecks started a disturbance" as soon as President Penna began his speech.[30]

After the meeting in Corning an incident occurred that resembled the experience nine years earlier at the Richmond Convention when Colonel Murphy, a Confederate war veteran, cancelled the contract after discovering that one of the delegates, Frank J. Ferrell, was African American.[31] The incident took place at the Mercer Hotel in Corning where Davis was invited to have dinner with Penna, Ratchford, Pearce and Haskins. Because some guests from West Virginia would be offended by his presence, Davis was asked to leave. Since Pearce had not yet arrived, recalling the incident, Davis asked the editor of the *United Mine Workers Journal* to convey to the three officials that they had "changed somewhat in their nature."

> I was invited to have dinner with them, and of course after having lived on beans and hominy all winter, the invitation was accepted; but, when poor old Dick got into the dining room just far enough to get a good view of the good things on the tables a hand was laid on me and a voice whispered in my ear that colored men could not eat there. So I had to get out, but when I came out Messr. Penna, Ratchford and Haskins followed,

Mercer Hotel, Corning (Little Cities of Black Diamonds).

refusing to partake of the delicacies laid for them. We proceeded to the Allen House and ate a better dinner than could have been served at the Mercer house. Now I understand that they have been cruel enough to say that all four of us were niggers. Now how is that?[32]

Comparing the struggles of the United Mine Workers of America to Paul's biblical ship successfully weathering the storm, Davis expressed his heartfelt respect for the union leaders' loyalty to his race.[33] While that same year the editor of the *New Lexington Tribune*, published 12 miles to the north in the Perry County seat, continued to refer to Rendville as "a pest place of industrial leprosy that has infested our valley [with] a horde of barbarian niggers,"[34] the editor of the *United Mine Workers Journal* reaffirmed the union's commitment to the belief that "there have only been two races on this earth since the world began—the working race and the exploiting one."[35]

Advised to take legal action, on November 27, Davis filed a claim for $500 in damages against the hotel owner, A.B. Mercer, in the Perry County Court of Common Pleas.[36] At the trial, held on Monday, February 28, 1896, Penna, Haskins, Pearce, Ratchford and Dennis H. Sullivan, who had served along with Davis on the District 6 Executive Board, were all summoned as witnesses.[37] However, since Mercer had already been fined as the first business under Ohio's then new anti-discrimination laws, county Judge Slough "dismissed [the case] at cost to the plaintiff without prejudice to a new action." Upon appeal, in a follow up trial, held on November 17, the court once again ruled in favor of the defendant and overruled Davis' motion for a new trial.[38]

Tough Times

As the Davis' court case continued to run its course, more trouble emerged. Six months earlier rumor had spread that Rend let it be known that of his two idle mines, No. 1 and No. 3, he was willing to re-open No. 3 if its miners would remove Davis as their checkweighman. Subsequently after Davis brought the matter to the attention of President Penna, in a meeting with Rend the latter denied any such demand. With the matter seemingly resolved, in June D.S. Williams, the superintendent, told some men that unless Davis was removed, Mine No. 3 would remain idle all summer. When Davis went to inquire Williams presented him with three requests from Rend:

> 1st. That the men would send clean coal.
> 2d. That they would get all their supplies from the company, which they would sell them as cheap as any one else.
> 3d. That I should be removed as checkweighman.

Not wanting to jeopardize the mine's reopening and work for some 200 men, Davis agreed to "get down" as long as an investigation was conducted into matter which Williams promised to do. Men who had supported him began backtracking. "Such a stampede you never saw," Davis observed. "So the old boy was defeated, the men most of all saying they wanted me, but they wanted the question settled first by the officers" in charge of the investigation. Davis speculated that perhaps it was his "writing to the JOURNAL" or his "persistence in organized labor" that had led Rend to take his position. Fortunately, according to Davis, Rend removed his objections when he came to realize that Davis was not "such a bad fellow after all" but instead found "that I try to be a fair, candid, liberty-loving citizen. How much better can a man be?"[39]

In the remaining months of the year, Davis worried about what would happen during the upcoming winter and focused his attention on the numerous price differentials with the Pittsburgh scale and below scale prices paid to miners in Ohio. Davis also came to the defense of D.H. Sullivan of Rendville, who had served on the Executive Board of District 6 with him in 1893.[40] Accusing his "Rendville friends who have played the Judas act," Davis warned that while he might have "some patience with a colored man, who, perhaps, may have been a slave and who had not had the chance of attaining an education" he would expose Sullivan's "white traitors ... so that everybody may know who you are, and what you are."[41] At Christmas time, as conditions for the American miner were getting ever worse and desperate miners in five separate mines in the valley were working six to 11 cents below the scale rates, facing winter and no work, Davis once again admonished all men to stand together:

> We have to get closer together and lay aside personal and petty jealousies, if we would wish to better and provide better homes and comforts for our wives and innocent babes. You may curse the operator all you please, but it won't do any good. It is all our own fault, for the operators or employers are only doing as we ourselves would do under the circumstances had we the same chances. We gave them the chance that they now have, and they are using it. Do you blame them? I believe in the adage "Heaven helps those who help themselves" and there is no way for us to help ourselves other than by getting together and staying together.[42]

CHAPTER 7

National Recognition

Hard times continued as another year began and the miners persisted in complaining that their wages were too low to make a living. The hardships they suffered led to a drop in the UMWA membership to around 10,000 as large numbers of miners "refuse[d] to pay the paltry sum of 10 cents to the national organization, simply because they do not like the officers." Facetiously Davis commented, "Yes sir, we miners of Ohio, at least some of us, are indeed glad that our wages are so small, because it gives us a chance to vent our spleen and d-n the officers for not doing that which is impossible for them to do.[1] In February, prospects remained "gloomy for the near future." In March, the mines were "practically doing nothing, one and one-half days per week [being] about all and turn slow at that." "Were anyone to ask how we manage to live," Davis wondered, "I am sure I could not tell."[2] In May, and continuing into June, Davis reported that Mine No. 3 had worked only one day the previous day and that Mine No. 8 had been completely shut down. Since the mines had been "practically laid idle all winter and spring, the miners and their families in Rendville and Corning were "in very poor shape."[3] Not until July did work in the mines improve somewhat.

Elected

Preceding the national convention, it was under these circumstances that the Seventh Annual Convention of District 6 met in Columbus, Ohio, on April 9. President Ratchford was highly pleased at the attendance which was better than "was expected under the depressed condition of the trade."[4] The dire financial straits in which the United Mine Workers of America found themselves appear to be reflected in the Cash Books of District 6 as well. While the Cash Book includes $81 for 1894 and $32 for 1895 in contributions by L.U. 398 and L.U. 1935 in Rendville, only one contribution of $15.10 by L.U. 398 was made in February 1896. No other contributions are recorded for the remainder of 1896, neither for 1897. Likewise there are only two Cash Book "Paid R.L. Davis for Work" entries in 1895: one for $36.65 on February 20 and one for $21 on April 8. Although the Cash Book includes entries for expenditures through April 6, 1896, none were paid to Davis. Finally, while the Cash Book does include salary expenditures in 1897 for the District 6 president, vice-president and secretary treasurer there are no other entries.[5]

When President Penna called the national convention to order at the Grand Central Hotel in Columbus on April 14, he described the preceding year as one of "disappointments, low wages, adverse conditions and an empty treasury," which were but the result of "open enemies and pseudo friends, masquerading in the garb of undying devotion to trade union principles, men with disappointed ambition, and those to whom slander is natural." Closing his speech, he recommended the miners to go into politics to "change this government from one of, by and for the gold syndicate and landlordism, into one of, by and for the people" or "all that remains to us will be lost."[6]

Richard L. Davis was one of 39 delegates from Ohio among an all-time low total of 81 delegates. As reported by the Committee of Credentials, while District 6's delegates still made up nearly half of all delegates, their presence had declined from 72 percent (102 among 142) in 1893, to 56 percent (72 among 128) in 1894, to 57 percent (69 among 122) in 1895, to 48 percent.[7] Secretary-Treasurer W.C. Pearce reported that while the organization had been nearly $500 in debt at the time of the previous year's convention, by now its balance has only slightly increased to over $1,150.[8]

Despite the lower turnout of Ohio delegates, when President Penna announced the vote for members of Executive Board, R.L. Davis had garnered 166 votes, more than any of the other 15 candidates.[9] Along with Vice-President Cameron Miller, Secretary-Treasurer Pearce, and Fred Dilcher from Nelsonville who had obtained the third largest number of votes, Richard L. Davis was now one four members from Ohio on the ten-member Executive Board. Promising "to do his utmost," Davis thanked the delegates for his election when the "financial situation of the organization at this time, however, [was] of such a nature that other members of the board as well as myself will have to remain at home." Expressing his hope that the next annual meeting would find the organization in "a better condition of affairs," Davis trusted that the miners across the country, in their struggle for "the emancipation of the wage slaves of the land" would be able to look out for their own interests, "for boys, you know what it takes to make the mare go."[10]

Remarkably, in the biographical sketches featuring the newly elected members, John Kane, editor of the *United Mine Workers Journal*, commended Davis' advocacy for his race while calling his intellectual abilities into question.

> R.L. Davis is a full-blooded colored man. He was born in the city of Roanoke, Va., December 24, 1863.[11] He began work at eight years of age in a tobacco factory; and worked at that trade until he was 17 years of age, going to school in the winter months. He began to work in the mines in the State of West Virginia along the New River and Kanawha, and remained in that district until 1882, when he removed to Renville, O., where he has since remained. He was elected a member of the executive board of District 6, United Mine Workers of America, April, 1890, and served continuously until 1895. His education seems to be very fair, at least he is a good reader, and writes a very good hand, and as our readers know, composes a very good letter. But it is impossible to find what there is in a man—unless you are a phrenologist, or a physiognomist[12]— unless he engages you in controversy, or in animated conversation, or lectures you. We have never had the pleasure of either with R.L. We cannot say whether his letters are in the nature of a combination of well remembered phrases, impressed on the memory at some remote time in the past, or whether they are the spontaneous utterances of an original mind. Were Brother Davis a conversationalist, we should long ere this have known which of these his letters manifested, but as he has never had occasion, or perhaps we have not, to engage him in this manner, it is difficult for us to tell. Nevertheless, his letters evince either originality or talent—talent of memory—and having cultivated it, he now enjoys the reward of his labor in being the representative of his race on the executive board of the United Mine Workers of America, for it would be too much to say that he has been signaled out from among the vast number of other men of all races represented in the United Mine Workers of America, for exceptional ability. The fact is that Dick (as he is familiarly known) was elected because he is a good representative of his race and because the miners believe that the colored men of the country should be recognized and given a representative on the board. At the same time it is only fair to say that he promises to give just as good service as any other man that might be elected, for albeit he is not exceptionally talented he possesses the average ability in the way of book learning and has other qualifications that hardly any other man in the organization owns. He will in a special way be able to appear before our colored miners and preach the gospel of trade unionism and at the same time will be able to prove to our white craftsmen how much progress might be made with very limited opportunities. We have heard him speak in conventions on several occasions, and he has generally given a good account of himself. We trust that by the time the next convention rolls around that Dick will have proven the wisdom of his selection. We will say this, that if it be a good principle to recognize races or nationalities on the board in preference to individuals, per se, the convention has done well to elect Dick, for he has certainly merited this recognition. In fact, he has merited it from either standpoint, for as man, and more especially as a union man, he has deserved well of the miners of the country. We wish him success and hope to congratulate both him and congratulate both him and the organization at the end of the year on the work he will have done in its behalf.[13]

The following week, in the April 30 edition, Davis offered a point by point rebuttal to the editor while deploring the desperate hardships the Rendville miners continued to suffer. "Work here is a thing of the past," he wrote, "I don't know what we are going to do. We can't earn a living, and if we steal it we will be prosecuted. So if some will kindly tell us what to do we will be very thankful."

In the last issue of your valuable paper, ye editor, in writing concerning the newly elected officers, in my opinion, did it well, and we must congratulate you for your very able effort. I must say, however, that ye editor seems to know more about me than I do myself; hence, you must be both a phrenologist and a physiognomist, i.e., if I know what those two big words mean. In regard to my being a conversationalist or not, I can only say that I have at all times avoided engaging myself in animated conversation only with those whom I have a thorough acquaintance, for I, believe that too much tongue is not conducive of any good. As a conversationalist, I will say that I have been engaged in controversy in newspapers and otherwise, and at all times tried to defend my position, but I have a dislike for these things and have several times promised to not do it again. You say that you can not tell whether our letters are in the nature of a combination of well remembered phrases, impressed on the memory at some remote time in the past or whether they are the spontaneous utterances of an original mind. I can assure you that be they ever so poor they are original, and I think ye editor knows it well. In reference to being the representative of my race, etc., I assure you and the miners of the country in general, that I am proud of this manifestation of kindness in recognizing my people, and not only am I proud, but my people also. I know that a great deal has not been said publicly, but I do know that our people are very sensitive, and upon many occasions I have heard them make vigorous kicks against taxation without representation. Now, then, they cannot kick this year, for although the representative himself may be a poor one, it is representation just the same, and I assure you that I shall try to so act that those who elected me shall not be made to feel ashamed.[14]

Blacklisted

Late May, addressing local discord among the miners in the Hocking Valley, Davis "anxiously" awaited a decision by the miners of Shawnee whether they would continue working under the "pernicious contract system."[15] Remembering "the day when Shawnee was considered the hotbed for unionism," Davis "despised" their decision early June to continue mining coal; "a very great mistake," he thought, even more so in light of the machine question.

> If Shawnee is allowed to continue (and I see no way of stopping her) then other pick mines must follow suit. Then you will have established a price for machine mining based on contract pick mining, which will mean a reduction to the poor under-paid loader of 8 or 10 cents per ton. The next move, then, will be another drop, for there is no use for men to be foolish enough to think that they can run the machines out for they cannot do it; they are here to stay. If anybody goes it will be us, and our places will be filled by the ignorant non–English speaking laborer. He, of course, can and will work for wages that the America miner would starve on. Oh, if the Shawnee people would reconsider and stop, how happy we would be, for they are only forcing themselves and others to a level but little better than serfs.
> Had it been colored men to start this contract system, no matter how destitute their families may have been, every mother's son of those now working under it would have marched with gun and club in hand to stop them even at the risk of some of them laying their lives upon the altar of human sacrifice. But, thank God, the negro did not start

it, nor is there one working at it. It may not be long until he too, will be at it, but he can conscientiously say he was forced to it by his white brother. Can you afford this to be said of you, ye men of Shawnee? I think not.

On a lighter note, Davis announced that Rendville's "new and elegant base ball park," likely financed by Rend, was about to be completed, that "our boys are ready to cross bats with any amateur team that might happen to come this way," and that they would be sure observe "the golden rule" to "treat others as they would desire others to treat them."[16]

By mid-summer the Rendville mine had been operating steadily, except for a few days, while men kept coming "from everywhere seeking work." However, due to a low scale rate of 45 cents per ton some men had to work 16 to 18 hours "at all hours of the night" to earn a living.[17] On July 30, District 6 president Ratchford held a poorly attended meeting in Corning during which he lamented the lack of support from the rank and file.[18] Reporting from "this God forsaken neck of the woods," Davis revealed another side of his personality by parodying the men of Mine No. 8 and Mine No. 3 for refusing to send a delegate to a special convention and opening themselves up to West Virginia conditions. Standing at the Rendville company store he overheard two men discussing the issue. "Say! Is you gwine down to de meetin'? If all de men was like me dey could call all de meetins dey wanted to but not a d-n delegate would dey send. Demn fellers down b'low is claimin' dat dey is starvin', and dat we done took dere work way from em an' how dey want to stop us, but we's gwine to work on dat's what we's gwine to do." Next, while drawing a comparison to the unorganized miners of West Virginia, Davis continued, "Bejabaers, Oive walked around here fur the last three years and the men at Shawnee and Hemlock was at work every day. We called conventions and had the officers to come, but the divil bit of good it done, and Oi for one mesilf am goin' to work, an' yez can all do to suit yez selves. Oi'm going to look afther my family if Oi have to dig for tin cints a ton."[19]

On September 6, Davis reported that when the miners in the Sunday Creek Valley had decided to go on strike on August 20 to demand the restoration of scale rates, kickers at Mine No. 3 in Rendville, among whom there were "men of [his] own race," had decided not to participate. When the drivers and day men decided, however, not to work below scale rates, these men went to the superintendent to tell him that Davis, and a certain Sam Martin, were the instigators behind the drivers and day men's actions and requested that Davis be discharged as checkweighman. Disgusted by their Booker T. Washington style anti-union treason,[20] and sorry to say these were men of his own race Davis questioned their morality.

Just how they could stoop so low I am unable to tell, and some of them, if not all call themselves Christians or children of the Most High God, but in reality they are the children of his satanic majesty for no others could commit such a dastardly deed as to try to starve a fellow-man's wife and family because he would not join them in the nefarious work. I can only say that it is the first time in the history of my life where men sought the removal of one of their number to keep him from blacklegging, and I am sure that it was quite unnecessary for them to have been so devilish particular.

Davis concluded the same letter by defending himself against criticism of his letter "containing [a] touch of negro and Irish dialect." He asserted that it was not an "attempt to throw or cast odium upon these two nationalities," that "nothing of the kind was ever intended," and that "No sane man could for a moment think that I would say or do anything that would reflect discredibility upon the negro (which race I am not ashamed to own that I belong to), and so far as the Irishman is concerned, some of my best friends are of that nationality, so why should I try to do anything to injure them? The fact is, everything was cut and dried, and when a man wants to find fault he can always find an opportunity."[21]

Three months later, in November, Davis wrote that he had not been "in very good spirits to write." Even though the mines in Rendville and Corning were "working steadily everyday" at a scale rate of 45 cents, he had "not worked any since August" due to his labor organizing. "I am not working today because of the slanderous tongues of some of these scoundrels. They can not speak of any dishonest act that I have done, but because things at first did not go to suit, they have been lying on me and even asked that I be discharged and today I can't work."[22]

Yet despite being blacklisted, ironically while serving on the National Executive Board, Davis chose to remain in Rendville awaiting, "the emancipation of industrial slavery."[23] Learning of the death of "the esteemed correspondent known as "Laurene Gardner," Davis wished "to God we had a few more such women, for surely it would make the world better." Desperate that he "had not as yet got work," whereas "others can get all the work they want," he declined to be nominated for the vice presidency of District 6 and announced that he would run for another term on the National Executive Board. At the same time, he painfully wondered why "I, who have never harmed anyone to my knowledge, must take chances with winter and its chilly blasts with the privilege of a job so as to earn a morsel of bread for my wife and little ones."[24] Encouraged, however, that some miners "were once more connecting themselves to the organization, he nonetheless compared his kickers to 'Old Judas[es],'" labeling them "some of the most despicable scoundrels as ever lived." In the spirit of the season, he nonetheless concluded the year with "Wishing to all a merry Xmas, I am as ever for labor rights."[25]

Re-Elected

In his first letter of the new year, which he wrote on January 25, Davis reported that Mine No. 3 had only worked one day the previous week and that prospects were "dark and gloomy." He also once again reminded his readers that "We are taught by the teachings of the Holy Writ that in unity there is strength," and that it is time for miners to organize as lawyers, doctors, preachers, teachers, and even employers of labor have done.[26] A month later he emphatically apologized for writing another letter:

> I know that these letters are not at all times enjoyed because they tell the old, old story, but nevertheless, I am compelled to follow the same strain.... Organized labor has been the means of bringing about every reform that has been made in the labor world. Every law that has been enacted in the interest of labor has been the result of organized labor but I think there is better way of answering this question at least in a more effective way, and that is to tell the first fellow who asks you the same question to go to West Virginia or Pennsylvania or even to some mining camps in Ohio where there is not organization.

"The man who is opposed to organization," he wrote, "is either grossly ignorant or too niggardly mean to do that which he himself believes to be right, he would rather stand idly by and enjoy whatever advantages that might be gained by others, this fellow is a coward and a knave."[27]

Interestingly Davis did not make any mention of his re-election to the National Executive Board. Due to the decision during the annual convention to move its date to January, the Eighth National Convention had met less than two weeks earlier from January 12 to 16, 1897, in Columbus, Ohio. With 72 delegates in attendance, nine less than the previous year, D(ick) L. Davis was among the 43 delegates from Ohio who made up 60 percent of all of those in attendance.[28] Opening the convention, President Penna expressed regret that even the separate joined agreements that had been reached in Pennsylvania and Ohio had failed because of "dishonor, avarice and greed on the one hand and indolence, ignorance and duplicity on the other." Dismissing the possibility of another joint convention with the operators, and not having been able during his term "to do more that routine work," he announced his retirement "made necessary by reason of domestic relations and duties."[29] Secretary Pearce, who "dwelt on the 1894 strike and its evil effect on the finances as well its membership, for some time past," reported a balance under $600, less than when the convention was held in April 1896.[30] Michael D. Ratchford, President of District 6, was elected as national president along with John Kane as vice-president and W.C. Pearce as secretary-treasurer. With 124 votes cast on his behalf, Davis garnered the second highest number of votes on the first and only ballot to become one of the five members from Ohio on the now nine-member National Executive Board.[31] Although still somewhat reserved, this time John Kane, still the editor of the *United Mine Workers Journal*, had kinder words for Davis.

> Dick, as he is generally called, is physically courageous, perhaps his physical boldness is stronger than that which sometimes requires less risk to the person, but more to the spirit. This little weakness, or rather less strength, speaking comparatively, is due to an overweening geniality, even with those who should be at times spoken to firmly. He is intelligent, and several years of practice in his local meetings as a debater, and an extensive practice even on more pretentious occasions, has made of him a very valuable talker under certain conditions."[32]

Congo Revisited

In March, as Mine No. 8 was idle due to water in the mine and Mine No. 3 only worked half a day every now and then Davis ventured over to Congo, "the only mine in this part that is doing anything." Apologetic that he had said "[his] fair share" of "many harsh words" against it when it first opened as a company-owned town, what he found changed his mind.

> The men are treated civilly and gentlemanly. I have heard of complaints from this source. Our organization is recognized and if there is a grievance the matter is adjusted by the mine committee and company's officials, that is, if it is not of too broad a nature, then the subdistrict officials are called to advice in the matter." I say these things in justice to the company because of what I have said in years gone by, and further because of the fact that my business called me there not long since and I could not have been treated better by company or miners.

Believing in "giving the devil his due," he did "not know of any company that gave to each head of the family a big fat turkey for their dinners on Thanksgiving." Referring to a list of holidays submitted by "Incog." in the *United Mine Workers Journal*, Davis added that the day he loved most was Emancipation Day, annually celebrated in Rendville on September 22. "By all means let us celebrate the day when the shackles were cut loose and four million black men were liberated from the galling yoke of chattel slavery."[33]

The Strike of 1897

During the next six months Davis did not submit any letters to the *United Mine Workers Journal*. By September, however, the United Mine Workers of America were engaged in a national strike that would mark a turning point in its history. According to Andrew Roy, the delegates had scarcely returned home from the national convention when the price of coal took another tumble in the market. When he was not satisfied with the response to a circular he sent out to the Executive Board and the district presidents, President Ratchford decided to call a meeting at the national headquarters in Columbus on June 26 and 27. The organization was in such a "wretched" condition it was unable to pay for any traveling expenses. After two days of deliberations the meeting decided to call a general strike in hopes of creating "a coal famine which would raise the price of coal and enable the operators to pay higher wages."[34] According to Chris Evans, when the operators decided to force the 45 cent rate for Ohio despite a higher 54 cent rate in the Pittsburgh district,[35] persisting in the union's demand for a 60 cent rate in Ohio, Ratchford ordered a strike to start on July 4, 1897, "believing it was the only way to prevent further reduction in mining rates, and stop the downward tendency of miners' wages, that was fast falling below anything near a living rate for the miners and those depending upon them for support." What made the situation particularly difficult was that the miners of Maryland, Kentucky, West Virginia, southern Illinois and DeArmitt's New York and Cleveland Gas and Coal Co. in Pennsylvania continued to go into the mines.[36] When the DeArmitt Company obtained an injunction prohibiting organizers on its grounds, some unknown party went so far as to "ship ... beer and whiskey into the camp by the barrel, which at Ratchford's order, was spilled in the ditches."[37] Described by Ratchford as "nothing less than the spontaneous uprising of an enslaved society, despite a United Mine Workers of America membership below ten thousand, more than one hundred thousand miners joined the walkout within the first four days of the strike."[38] According to a proud Chris Evans at the start of the strike the union estimated that out of 111,000 organized and unorganized miners only 10,678 belonged to the United Mine Workers of whom Ohio's 7,097, far outnumbering Pennsylvania's 1,075, the second largest membership.[39] As more miners continued to join the strike, their numbers further increased to about 150,000, or approximately three-fourths of all bituminous miners, "almost a million souls."[40]

In the Hocking Valley, between October 1896 and June 1897 the gross average earnings fell to $7.50 per man per month. After deducting the cost of mine supplies, this left many families destitute.[41] With the strike being nearly a hundred percent effective,[42] thousands of families were bordering on starvation. The newspapers published in the various coal fields mentioned cases of children of miners driving dogs away from refused bread, which had been thrown out, and eating it voraciously. Hundreds of families in various mining districts of the country were forced by necessity to appeal for charity because the monthly earnings were not sufficient to hold body and soul together. So serious had matters become that Governor Bushnell of Ohio, after directing the state board of arbitration to investigate the condition of the miners in the state, issued a call "To the people of the State of Ohio" for donations or money. Put in charge of distributing the donations, Robert M. Haseltine, Chief Inspector of the Mines, reported that children in the mining regions, "driven by the pangs of hunger are seen searching for food in the back yards of the more fortunate, and from slop barrels and from buckets of refuse, to fish scraps of bread and meat and cast-off remnants which they ravenously devour. Humanity revolts at such destitution and hunger."[43]

Whereas in 1886 West Virginia produced only half as much coal as Ohio, by 1893 it had increased to more than 66 percent. As the increase continued, in 1896 West Virginia became increasingly competitive with Pennsylvania and Ohio.[44] "Prior to the suspension, organization in West Virginia was an unknown quantity,"[45] Chris Evans wrote, and "when the work of organizing the miners of West Virginia first began, there was very little encouragement given to organizers that were sent there to carry on the work." It was not an easy task to convince the miners of West Virginia who were "receiving ten cents per ton advance on former prices" that it was to their own interest to strike, "more especially so where the same miners had not been able to get work prior to the suspension at hardly any price."[46]

To convince the West Virginia miners in the Kanawha and New River districts to join the strike Ratchford first sent District 6 vice-president Haskins, American Federation of Labor organizer Frank J. Weber, and Fred Dilcher, member of the National Executive Board, into the state followed by five additional organizers, one among whom was R.L. Davis. Eloquently describing the organizing efforts, Evans wrote,

> With the aid of President Mahon, of the Street Railway Employees, Joseph Vitchenstein, of the Pittsburg newspaper fraternity, President Robinson, of the Kanawha and New River districts, and the continued marches of Dilcher's and Weber's armies, crossing the mountains at all hours when least expected, keeping the enemy steadily on the run, and with the assistance of many local workers that are seldom found during such troublesome times, no wonder the miners of the Kanawha Valley have made the gallant fight recorded to their credit."[47]

Additional support came from the American Federation of Labor as Samuel Gompers himself spent several weeks in the Kanawha and New River districts, where he was joined by many others, including such notables as Grand Master James R. Sovereign of the Knights of Labor, Eugene Debs of the American Railway Union, and Mother Jones. Thankful for their support, Evans wrote that it would suffice "to say that the seed of unionism is sown in the Mountain State" and that "the United Mine Workers can be found now where they were never known before."[48]

Although Davis did not attend, on July 27, one day after the courts issued an injunction against Debs, Sovereign and Ratchford for their organizing activities, the latter called for a meeting of prominent labor leaders in Wheeling, West Virginia. Lamenting the deplorable condition of the miners "liv[ing] in hovels, unable to buy sufficient bread to ward off starvation; in many cases not sufficiently clothed to cover their nakedness; their children unfit to attend school because of lack of food and clothing, making them a danger to the stability of our republic,"[49] the labor leaders denounced the injunction and called for a meeting with Governor Atkinson to "demand the right of free speech and free public assemblage in the State of West Virginia." Meeting with Gompers, Sovereign and Ratchford, the governor stated that while he was "in entire sympathy with the miners," he could not interfere with the courts. In a subsequent letter on August 13, the governor restated his determination to defend every citizen's right of free speech, including his own, and that "so long as the working men of this state conduct their cause in a lawful and peaceful manner it will be my duty, as it will be my pleasure, to protect them; but should they, in an ill-advised hour, violate the law by interfering with rights or property of others" he would take action.[50]

On August 25, Weber wrote to Chris Evans from Montgomery: "R.L. Davis is here. I had him speak to the colored men."[51] According to J.E. George of Harvard University, "by the beginning of September the miners saw that the coal famine they had looked for had not come. Those mines in Southern Illinois and West Virginia which had failed to take part in the strike, and some of the mines of Iowa, Colorado, and other States, were shipping coal to Chicago and the East. The shipments were not large, but they were large enough to prevent a coal famine."[52] In view of these facts and the exhaustion of the funds of the miners' unions, a Special National Convention conference was called at which a compromise was reached. Attended by 152 delegates, Chris Evans, representing the American Federation of Labor, was one three organizers from the West Virginia fields who addressed the convention. Held at Wirtheim's Hall in Columbus, Ohio, September 8–11, 72 delegates came from Ohio, nearly half of those in attendance. On Saturday, September 11, the last day of the convention, the delegates approved a resolution "accept the proposition recommend by our national executive committee, viz.: 65 cents in Pittsburg district, all places in the above named states where a relative price can be obtained to resume work and contribute liberally to the miners who do not receive the advance, where the fight must be continued to a finish," which meant the scale rate of 56 cents for the Ohio miners. The delegates resolved that those who went back to work would be assessed ten percent of their earnings until those that remained out on strike would be paid the scale rate. After another speech, this time by General Master Workmen Sovereign, the convention passed a resolution condemning the previous day's what became known as the Lattimer massacre, the killing of a "number of innocent miners" in Hazleton, Pennsylvania, at the hands of sheriff Martin, "a deliberate murderer and wholly unfit to fill the position to which he was elected by the votes of honest workingmen."[53]

Although the strike continued in West Virginia, it was considered an important success for the miners as it resulted in an average 20 percent wage increase and included the promise of a joint conference to be held in January 1898 to negotiate a joint agreement.[54] On December 21, at a joint state convention of District 5 in Pittsburgh, attended by Chris Evans as well, W.P. Rend delivered a speech in which he paid "a grand tribute to the purpose of inter-state conventions."[55] On December 27, the miners and operators held a preliminary conference, once again at Chittenden Hall in Columbus to organize for "a conference or convention for reviving and establishing such inter-state agreements on rates and prices for the mining of coal, as properly and faithfully observed by the miners and operators respectively" and "promoting such amiable relations between the different states and between employers and employes [sic], at to advance the interest of both."[56] The next day, a call was issued to the operators and miners of Pennsylvania, West Virginia, Ohio, Indiana and Illinois for a joint conference to be held at the YMCA building in Chicago on January 17.[57]

The economic depression and strike of 1897 had a deep impact on Ohio's 22,131 miners and the 2,402 miners in the Sunday Creek Valley. Although coal production in the state fell by 3.6 percent compared to the previous year, it fell by 14.94 percent in Perry County to 1,449,178 tons, still leaving it the second largest producer after Jackson County. Compared to when the depression first began, total coal production in the state had dropped 16.05 percent from 14,828,097 tons in 1893 to 12,448.822 in 1897.[58]

West Virginia

Having returned to Rendville just two days before the Special National Convention meeting, Davis decided to break "his long silence" to report on the conditions in the West Virginia from where he had just returned "incessantly" trying to get its miners to join the national strike. Although he never had an injunction issued against him, he wrote they had faced "all kinds of dangers," that "were like taking one's life in his hands at times," when "we had men and Winchesters against us, which were in most cases just as effective."[59]

Lacking in any "spirit of independence whatever," Davis, writing from Columbus on September 13, suggesting that perhaps his name was left off the list of credentialed delegates and that he likely did attend, made three observations. First, he thought that even "the slave of 32 years ago exhibited as much or more freedom" than a thousand miners in the Flat Top field who could be scared into almost anything by "one man with the title of boss." Second, noting the pervasive sway the company store had over the miners, he observed:

> A man who deals largely has the preference of cars in the mine, while the fellow who does not deal so extensively can go to the mine day after day and practically get nothing to do; or in other words, he only gets to fill what coal the other fellow is unable to fill, and if this is not sufficient to induce him to deal in the store then he need not be at all surprised to get a red ticket in his envelope on pay day, a notice to come to the office and either agree to deal or get out.

Third, he condemned the laborer system, which three months later he encountered in Alabama as well. While they might pose as "great union men," those miners who hired their fellow brothers to work for them as laborers were "the worst scabs that lived." "Another thing they have to contend with is the good men from Ohio and Pennsylvania who go down there and take contracts or get a number of rooms in the mines and hire a number of poor, ignorant colored, and in many instances white, men to work for them at from 75 cents to $1 per day. These fellow are enable to make money out of the sweat of their fellow-men."[60]

Continuing to report on his organizing experiences in West Virginia, Davis reported that the while the operators in the Kanawha Valley, part of the Coal Exchange, admitted that the miners' demands for better wages were fair, they refused to meet with a committee of ten miners sent to Charleston on September 21 since doing so would amount to virtually recognizing the legitimacy of the union.[61] Having failed to return in the afternoon during a joint meeting on October 4, on October 10, at another joint convention held in Montgomery, when the miners learned of the "mean treatment" that President Ratchford and the committee of ten had received by the operators who sought nothing but "to whip the miners into submission," decided to continue the strike. In his letter, to illustrate some of the hostility the union encountered Davis included an editorial from the *Charleston Gazette* accusing the United Mine Workers of America of being part of a foreign conspiracy.

> The Kanawha miners who persist in the disastrous strike can no longer lay claim to the sympathy of the Community. The operators are willing to deal with them on a just and honorable basis. They went on a strike without a grievance of their own and merely out of sympathy with Ohio and Pennsylvania. The Ohio and Pennsylvania miners have returned to work. They have no sympathy evidently with the Kanawha miners. The

operators have conceded a wage scale that is perfectly satisfactory. There is no matter of importance in dispute between employer and employe [sic]. The men who engaged in the strike will be taken back in good standing. No persecution, no boycott, no bad blood. Mr. Ratchford demands that the operators shall place themselves in the power of the U.M.W. association. The operators in the light of the past, and in view of existing conditions, would not be justified in doing anything of the kind. The Pennsylvania and Ohio miners might quarrel with their bosses and the Kanawha miners who would have no quarrel with their bosses might feel compelled to walk out again. The U. M. W. association is controlled by Pennsylvania and Ohio, and the interests of West Virginia so long as the Kanawha men elect to serve a foreign controlled organization in opposition to the interests of the local community, they cannot expect either sympathy or support. They should go to work.[62]

To support the West Virginia miners on strike, the following week Davis implored the miners of Ohio and Pennsylvania to "come to [their] relief" or otherwise they would lose. "For heavens sake send what you can," he wrote, reminding them that this was not their fight alone but theirs too and therefore to "give them a morsel of bread to fill the mouths of their hungry wives and children."[63]

Alabama

Organizing miners in the South took courage, especially if one was "a dusky son of Ham."[64] Ten years earlier, on May 20, 1887, H.F. Hoover, a white organizer from South Carolina, had been shot dead in Warrenton, Georgia, while addressing an audience largely composed of African American workers.[65] And, although Davis' September 13 letter makes no mention of the Lattimer massacre, which occurred three days earlier near Hazleton, Pennsylvania, and had left 19 miners dead and 35 wounded, the massacre clearly showed once again that organizing labor, especially as an African American, was by all means a very dangerous endeavor.[66]

The end of November found Davis in Birmingham, Alabama where by his estimate about 70 percent of the 10,000 to 12,000 miners were African American.[67] He thought that in his lifetime he "had seen some colored people, but my, this is his home and they are almost innumerable." Encountering strong racial prejudice and intense Jim Crow segregation, with some exceptions, he believed that "the fellow from Ohio [should] be proud of his condition as compared to here."

> If I get on the railway train I must ride in a separate car, the same on the street car. If I want a drink I must go in to a separate bar, and I can only look at a hotel or restaurant. So the fellow from Ohio can be proud of his condition as compared here. Will say though that the old country man will treat you nice—he does not draw the line so

7. National Recognition

tight—and we hope to see the time when all will do away with such practices, and I think our organization will play a very important factor in wiping out this evil.[68]

Finding that the men at Pratt City, today a neighborhood section in Birmingham, were anxious to organize but without money and had never been able to "hold any kind of organization intact for any length of time," Davis reported that most all prices are based on Pratt, and no matter where we go we are asked what is Pratt going to do?" Having been treated "very nicely" by the miners, a number of whom "we were acquainted with in Ohio," Davis was happy to get "things stirred up," and hoped that "ere long we can report the negro of the South a part and parcel of the United Mine Workers of America—also whites as well, but of course our work is with the colored men in this field." Still he noted that "while there are intelligent people here as can be found anywhere, you can also find more illiterates than anywhere else." Furthermore, he cursed the labor system in which colored miners hired "colored men as laborers to work for them," thus making them "the servant of a servant," a practice which he vowed would be abolished "if we succeed in organizing them."[69] He also encountered miners who gloated "they had served time as convicts in the mines at Pratt and Coalburg." Although he "would [have] like[d] to give a description of these convict camps," Davis feared "it would take up too much of your space."[70] Fortunately, and although like Davis, he found "the system wrong for supplying coal to the market at prices that free labor is unable to compete with," Chris Evans offers a vivid description of a visit he made about the same time to a convict mine in Rockwood, Tennessee. Surrounded by "guards in large numbers and guns just as numerous," the mine employed about 525 convicts "about sixty of which were white men." Each convict had a daily task.

> In entries, two men mine eight cars of coal, said to weigh about thirteen hundred pounds. One man in entry has to load five cars. In rooms, two men's task is eleven cars and one man must fill six cars when he is alone. It is run-of-mine coal in every instance. Eight cents per car is paid for every car that is filled over the required task. When the mine is idle all convicts are in the mine as usual, and when the mine works again they must fill half task for each day lost unless there are several idle days together, then the extra task is made lighter. For any refusal to carry out rules the lash is applied. Some convicts are very little affected by lashes, while others take it as very severe punishment.

After leaving the mine, Evans was escorted to the prison where the convicts ate and slept.

> They are marched from their working places in the mines through an entry and to an opening near the jail on the mountain side. The remaining distance is securely covered until they enter the prison walls, made of boards and posts, 12 feet high. After entering they go direct to the bath room, undress, go through the process of shower baths, put clean suits on, and then march to the supper table, after which they retire to their beds

and remain there until next morning, when they breakfast, get their dinner bucket, enter the mine again at about half-past five o'clock in the morning to be released about five o'clock every night.[71]

While still in Pratt City, Davis wrote a letter to the *Southern Sentinel*, "a colored paper" purporting to support the miners, to criticize its editor for his devotion to "the interests of the coal and iron monopolies of the south" and "disintegration" of labor. The paper had advocated that the black Alabama miner "separate himself from the white laborer," and organize at the state level rather than join the United Mine Workers of America.

So that his readers could see what they had "to contend with down here" Davis included the editor's response to "a communication [elsewhere in the same issue], signed by one R.L. Davis in which he claims to be member of the executive board" and that the paper "did not care to dignify the writer by an argument in defense of its position," nor that it was "disposed to devote valuable time and space to a discussion of every passing breeze." Having learned that many of the colored men had "no confidence in their white brethren," Davis only wished that if he "could stay in the field long enough we would get our people in line."[72]

Knowing of no agent who could do more for "the upbuilding of labor's cause," in a final letter for the year, Davis decided to submit a single letter to the pro-union *Labor Advocate* in Birmingham. Again noting that the "white and colored miners" in Alabama, instead of burying their differences, acted more like slaves, he hoped that "the coal miners whose lot it seems is hardest will learn that a man is a man be he as white as the driven snow or as black as the vidian night." Published on Christmas Day, Davis felt compelled to cite one more instance he read about in the *Southern Sentinel* of an inconsistent "minister of the gospel" who during the week encouraged the men to go work in the already overcrowded mines. Using his Sunday pulpit to espouse the "cause of the lowly Saviour" only affirmed to Davis once again that "men will stoop to anything if the almighty dollar is there."[73]

Chapter 8

A Private in the Ranks

On January 1, 1898, "while everyone is out celebrating the ushering in of the New Year in their various ways," and "our people are celebrating the emancipation proclamation," Davis thought he would "while the time writing a few lines so that our acquaintances might know that we are still alive and talking organization down here in the Old Alabama, the so called Eldorado of the South." While it might be known as an Eldorado, Davis maintained once more that it is only for the "moneyed interest." "Everything is cheap here but a living," he wrote. "Life is cheap, but the necessities of life are out of sight, yet it seems that many of these people are perfectly contented." He reported having had "some very good meetings." Unlike the minister he had met the previous month, Davis this time spoke highly of the man. "The gentleman referred to is the Rev. W.M. Stores, and we can truthfully say that he is one of the most intelligent young colored men that we have in the South. We need a few more like him." Fully expecting to successfully organize a local at Pratt City on January 6, Davis noted that "our people are celebrating the emancipation proclamation ... but [that] we need another proclamation now of equal importance and that one is to emancipate wage slaves, both black and white."[1]

That same day, January 6, District 6 began its Ninth Annual Convention in Columbus without Davis' presence. As a result of the successful 1897 strike,[2] Secretary-Treasurer Thomas L. Lewis was able to report that the balance had improved from $4.13 on December 25, 1896, to $3,974.44 on December 31, 1897, and that its membership had increased to 14,000 from the 7,697 when the strike first began. In light of the improved conditions District 6 president W.E. Farms even suggested the use of "restriction" as a new method to improve scale rates by reducing the number of days worked each week, or the number of hours worked each day, or both."[3]

After adjourning on Saturday, January 8, the Ohio delegates, now including an absent but erroneously listed R.L. Davis among the Indiana delegates,[4] joined the Ninth Annual National Convention in Columbus on Tuesday, January 11. With less than 11,000 members when the strike began, but now with a threefold increase, Secretary-Treasurer W.C. Pearce, like T.L. Lewis, was able to report a tremendously improved balance from $582.93 on January 1, 1897, to $10,812.18 on January 1, 1898.[5]

Likewise the economy continued to improve. Whereas the tonnage of coal mined in Ohio had dropped by 3.6 percent during 1897, in 1898 it increased by 12.9 percent. Maintaining its rank, after Jackson County, as the second largest coal producing county in Ohio, the tonnage of coal mined in Perry County had dropped by 14.94 percent during 1897 but increased again by 23.5 percent in 1898. District Three Inspector R.H. Miller, who visited J.P. Rend's Mine No. 3 three times during the prior year, reported in 1898 that it had a shaft 35 feet deep, a double entry, two ventilating fans, and employed a total of 165 miners as well as 52 day hands.[6] The tonnage of coal mined in Ohio further increased by 15.1 percent in 1899 and by another 22.1 percent in 1900. Although production in Perry County decreased by 2.3 percent in 1899, dropping it to fourth place as the highest coal producing county in the state after Jackson, Hocking and Athens, in 1900 it once again increased by 44.0 percent, restoring it to second rank after Athens.[7]

By January 15, 1900, when the Eleventh Annual National Convention assembled in Indianapolis, the treasury balance had further improved from $22,890.31 on January 1, 1899, to $39,378.32.[8] Three months later, President John Mitchell reported a membership of 117,000. Two years later, due undoubtedly in part to the work of Richard L. Davis and other black organizers, the American Federation of Labor counted 40,000 African Americans among its members, half of whom belonged to the United Mine Workers of America, thus making up more than one-sixth of its total membership.[9]

In his address to the 206 delegates at the 1898 convention, President Ratchford reported "the greatest progress ever made during our organized existence." With 75 delegates Ohio's presence dropped to 36 percent compared to 60 the previous year.[10] Exuberant yet cautious that victory should inspire false hope, he declared:

> When you first elected me president over a year ago, we had a weak organization and a small group of delegates from Pennsylvania, Ohio, Indiana and Illinois. Today we have organizations from the anthracite coal regions on the east to the State of Wyoming on the west, and from the Klondike to Alabama. I promised you then that if you gave me support I would give you as aggressive an administration as you desired. Have I kept my promise?[11]

After unanimously re-electing Ratchford on Thursday, January 13, John

Mitchell of Illinois was elected vice-president. When the elections for the new National Executive Board were continued the next day after the delegates had attended a memorial mass at St. Patrick Church for John Kane who, having served as editor of the *United Mine Workers Journal* from 1891 to 1896 and as vice-president in 1897, had suddenly died on July 18 of the previous year. Kane was succeeded by Thomas W. Davis who served as editor until his resignation in July 1899, having been elected to become vice-president, and was followed in turn by W.C. Scott as editor. With "Chris Evans in the chair" serving as president of the convention, Richard L. Davis was one among 48 candidates. Being one of the 13 candidates to have received more than ten percent on the first vote, Davis reached the second round of ballots but failed to get re-elected.[12] His defeat marked a return to an all-white National Executive Board. Indicative of the ambivalence toward African Americans in leadership positions in the labor movement, as well as suggested by the subsequent inaction of the union leadership on his behalf in the coming years, an invisible Davis never received any mention by either Andrew Roy in his history or by Chris Evans who included him only as part of any list of names. Although Davis no longer served in a leadership capacity in the national union after the Indianapolis convention, the United Mine Workers of America entered a major period of growth and organization.

John Mitchell, fifth president, United Mine Workers of America, 1899–1907 (Roy, *History of the Coal Miners*, 1906).

Abandoning its dual structure, a mark that it had come of age, in addition to electing a new executive board, the convention also adopted a new constitution that struck out "any words that refer to anything other than the United Mine Workers of America."[13] Furthermore, it debated the creation of a defense fund and decided to publish the union journal "in such languages" as the editors "deem proper." And finally, after two ballots, the convention voted to move its headquarters to Indianapolis rather than remain in Columbus or move to Chicago, Cleveland, Toledo, or Evansville.[14]

Following the national strike of April 21, 1894, precipitated by the depression of 1893, the miners and operators had reached a final joint agreement that was meant to but did not take effect on June 18, 1894, and ended on May 1, 1895.[15] As part of the settlement of the strike of 1897, the miners and operators agreed to resume the joint conference system. Attended by 278 miners and 250 operators from Pennsylvania, Ohio, Indiana, Illinois, Indiana, Ohio and West Virginia, after ten days of deliberations, the interstate convention reached a joint agreement on January 26. The agreement, which went into effect on April 1, 1898, and lasted until April 1, 1899, adopted an equal price for mining screened coal to serve as a base scale, a screen that was uniform in size—"six feet wide and twelve feet long, built with flat bar iron not less than five-eighths of an inch surface with one and one-fourth inches between bars, free from obstructions," a nearly 18 percent raise of ten cents per ton for pick-mined screened coal, the adoption of the long-desired eight hour workday—to consist of six days per week, and, as 33 percent of all coal was being machine-mined, a continuation of the "same relative prices and conditions between machine and pick mining that have existed in the different states." Furthermore the operators agreed to "the eight-hour workday, with eight hours of pay, consisting of six days per week."[16]

"Now that district, national and interstate conventions are over," and having become "a private in the ranks," on January 29, Davis praised the joint agreement made at Chicago as "another evidence in favor of the method of settling disputes by conciliation" and once more condemned those who failed to join the organization as cowards and traitors. He strongly advocated the creation of a defense fund as a way to prepare for war in times of peace arguing that "the opposing forces will not be so ready to make war on us" knowing the miners had a war chest to support strikes.[17]

Alabama Revisited

On February 7, having returned from Alabama, Davis followed up on his promise to further inform his readers of the conditions. He found the answer to the question as to why the miners of the South failed to organize simple: "For the colored man there has been no inducement" and neither for the white miners who "to be honest would simply be giving away a simple thing." Not only did he encounter white miners who hired colored men to work for them so did some colored men which allowed them to make between $15 and $20 a week while "the servant[s] of a servant" earned a mere 75 cents to $1 per day.

Reluctant to be accused of "here he goes again trying to draw the color line," he nonetheless reported that "while white and colored miners worked in the same mines, and maybe in adjoining rooms, they will not ride even on a work-train with their dirty mining clothes on together, nor will they meet in a miners' meeting together in a hall with the whites going to one side of the hall, while the colored occupy the other side. You may even go to the post office at Pratt City, and the white man and the colored man can not get his mail from the same window. Oh, no, the line is drawn; the whites go to the right and the colored go to the left."

T.W. Davis, editor, *United Mine Workers Journal*, 1897–98 (Evans, *History of the United Mine Workers of America, 1914–18*, 1920).

Finally, he found that the convict system was hurtful to the white but more so to the colored miner.

> Now I do not wish to be understood that I approve of a man committing a wrong for I do not. I believe that all men should be amenable to the law, but in Alabama they will for the most trivial offense give you a term at Coalburg or Pratt mines, and especially if you happen to be a dusky son of Ham. One might think this would not cut much of a figure, but I am informed that at the Pratt mines alone convicts can produce 2000 tons of coal per day, and you can imagine the result in time of a strike in that section, and you must be a mighty good fellow or else they will send you over to help increase the capacity.[18]

War and Defense

Having recently addressed the need for the union to have a war chest, ironically, in his next letter Davis reported that although "almost all of our people are talking war" with "poor, old, dilapidated but impudent Spain," he was "of the opinion that it is a quick way to become a little angel" and would rather confine himself to "jotting a few lines to the miners' best." Reporting that the mines only weekly worked two days at the most and, in opposition to "a niggardly few" who opposed paying an extra 25 cents per month, Davis continued to advocate that now was the time to start a defense fund. At the same time, he also tried to keep up with the trial following the Lattimer massacre hoping that "every mother son of them, Martin and deputies, get the full extent of the law, and a duty evolves upon each and every miner, and this is to see that they are prosecuted by the laws of the land and not acquitted at the dictation of soulless corporations, for the time has come when men must be men or else we must sink to a level to which there is no hope of redemption." Begun on February 1 the trial would end in a "not guilty" verdict for Sheriff Martin and his deputies.[19]

On April 1, the day the eight-hour day went into effect, Davis, the Sage of Rendville, was invited to address the miners at Corning and Congo. Due to the roads being muddy and unable to afford the train fare, he stayed in Corning where "the boys [jollified] with music and speech making." Still dissatisfaction existed as due to passage of the Standard Time Act some operators did not open the mines until "7 o'clock standard time, which was a half hour later than during fast time, required the men to take an hour for dinner, and did not allow them to fire for the next day until 4 o'clock standard time," which made for a nearly ten-hour day.

Unfortunately, still blacklisted because of his membership on the National Executive Board and now having failed to be re-elected, Davis movingly finished his letter by deploring his personal hard times. "Well, I expect I had better stop for I can't get work here today because of my advocacy of right vs. wrong, and now for two years almost they have been giving me lessons how to live on wind. Well, I don't care for myself, but it is those innocent little children of mine that I care for, and yet they say this is free America. Hoping that this will end well for the miners of our country, if we have one. I am, as ever. R.L. Davis."[20]

On May 8, two weeks after the outbreak of the Spanish-American War, a conflict supported by the leadership of the United Mine Workers, because of its "salutary effect on the economy,"[21] Old Dog, an African American miner from Congo, wrote a compassionate letter calling upon the union to support Davis.

Congo, O., May 8—Editor Journal: Since I do not trouble you often I hope you will allow me a small space in the miners' friend for a few words.

Work in these parts is not so good as we would like to see it, especially at this time of the year. Very little is earned and the cost of everything is going up, so without a change I can't see how we poor miners are going to make it.

Mr. Editor, I notice our old true and tried friend, R.L. Davis, walking around. He can't get work in the mines and he says he can't get any work to do as an organizer. Why this should be I can not see. Dick, as he is familiarly called, has always been a staunch union man. He has done more to get the colored miners into the organization and hold them than any other man I know of in this part of Ohio. He has labored long and earnestly to build up the union, when men who now hold official positions had fallen by the wayside and would not dare utter a word in defense of the cause for fear of losing their jobs, but Dick always stuck to his post through thick and thin and because of his manhood along this line he is being fought with that most dastardly weapon, most commonly known as the black list. Knowing the man as I do I think he should be provided for in some way. I want to say right now that you do not often meet up with colored men like Dick, who have his grit in them, and it is only on account of his strong union principles that he is placed in the position that he is in today. Again, in this field there is not one colored man but who pays into the union and it is largely due to his persistent efforts that this has been brought about, every man in this section will bear me out in this, white and black. He has a family to keep and I think we owe him something. He nor his children can not live on wind, and further, if he is—mark that—but being a negro he does not get the recognition he should have. I want to say further that such treatment will not tend to advance the interest of our union, but will retard its progress and cause colored men to look with suspicion upon it. Now, as a colored man myself, I do not want any thing more than this: Give us an equal show. Dick deserves better usage. I would not write as I do, but I have talked with him and he feels sorely disappointed. He says he thought that the organization would afford him something to do, and I think so too. It will be as little as our officers could do to help him in this way, since we know that it is because of his love of unionism that has brought him and his family to almost want. For my part, I think if we would do right he could either go in the mines to work or we would see to it that he was started up in a small business or given field work. I want President Ratchford to show to all colored men that he values a man as a man irrespective of his color and he can best do this by giving Dick a helping hand.

I hope you will excuse my bad writing and language and also methods of speaking but I believe in calling a spade a spade. I am sure we are not being treated just as we should be. I will write again soon if this escapes the waste basket. I remain, the OLD DOG.[22]

The following week, in response to Old Dog's letter as well as another written by President Anderson of Indiana, Davis wrote of his desperation:

I wish to thank both gentlemen for their kind feelings towards me and my family. I have as yet never boasted of what I have done in the interest of organized labor, but will venture to say that I have done all I could and am proud that I am alive today, for I think I have had the unpleasant privilege of going into the most dangerous places in this country to organize, or in other words, to do the almost impossible. I have been threatened; I have been sand-bagged; I have been stoned; and last of all, deprived of the right to earn a livelihood for myself and my family. I do not care so much for myself, but it is my innocent children that I care for most, and heaven knows that it makes me almost crazy to think of it. I have spent time and money in the labor movement during the last sixteen years, and today I am worse off than ever, for now I have no money, nor no work. I will not beg, and I am not inclined to steal, nor will I unless compelled through dire necessity, which I hope the good God of the universe will spare me.

I again think of those who have spoken a kind word for me, and conclude this letter for I can not think of my present circumstances and write, for I fear I might say too much.[23]

Yet, despite being in dire straits and abandoned by the union, in June, as the mines had been "working fairly steadily" for three weeks, Davis as ardently as ever advocated the cause of unionism. Arguing in favor of "the best trades paper published" rather than subscribing to the "penny dailies," he encouraged the miners to subscribe to the *United Mine Workers Journal* as one more way to "patronize an enterprise of [their] own." Unfortunately, his canvassing efforts among the economic struggling miners throughout the Hocking Valley were rather unsuccessful.[24]

After a silence of four months, Davis would only write three more letters to the *United Mine Workers Journal*. Not until October 10, two weeks after "striking union coal miners and imported colored men engaged in a pitched battle in the main street of [Pana, Illinois] and several hundred shots were exchanged, the negroes using Winchesters, and the miners shotguns, rifles and revolvers, the result of which caused the death of several imported participants,"[25] Davis took notice of "the troubles now existing in the Sucker State," once again imploring the miners to organize.

> I am indeed sorry to see the State of affairs as exists there, and yet it teaches us that one lesson seemingly so hard to learn by a great many of us, viz., to organize. I do not mean to organize against the black man, as they are now doing, for that will do no good nor will there any good results accrue from it, and fight it as you may the result will be the same. I have watched it in the past and have never known it to fail. I would advise that we organize against corporate greed, organize against the fellow who, through trickery and corrupt legislation, seeks to live and grow fat from the sweat and blood of his fellow man. It is these human parasites that we should strive to exterminate, not by blood or bullets, but by the ballot, and try as you may it is the only way. You can't do it by trying to exterminate the negro or big black buck niggers, as they were referred to a few weeks ago through the columns of The Journal. I assure anyone that I have more respect for a scab than I have for the person who refers to the negro in such a way, and God knows that a scab I utterly despise. The negro North has no excuse, or very few excuses, for scabbing, but the negro South has lots of them, and while I give the North a great deal of credit, I fear that I make a mistake, for in many places even in the North, no matter how good a union man he may be, he can not get work only as a blackleg. And in the South he can work almost anywhere provided he is willing to be the other fellow's dog, and I don't mean the employer alone, but the white laborer as well. Now, the negro, like the mining machine, is here to stay and you may as well make up your minds to treat them right. I dare say that you seldom or never hear of negroes being brought into a locality to break a strike in which both white and black worked together, and even if

they were you always found the negro on the side of right. Hence, I say treat the negro right and he will treat you right. I earnestly hope to see the miners of Illinois win their battle, for I suppose they are like miners elsewhere. Their pittance is already too small.[26]

A few days later, on October 13, as Davis began another long silence, John Mitchell, who had become President on September 1 after Ratchford resigned to a accept position on United States Industrial Commission, faced his first major crisis when the Chicago Virden Coal Company tried to import "a trainload of colored laborers" at Virden, Illinois. Upon arrival at the station, hired guards presumably were the first to open fire from the train on the union miners. The ensuing gun battle left seven union miners dead and eight wounded as well as four to ten guards dead and a similar number wounded.[27]

On December 5, feeling that is was "time to come out of our shells," Davis eagerly anticipated the upcoming national and interstate conventions. Hoping the miners would get an advance, and that the union would vote to establish a defense fund, Davis lamented that although he was "still a miner" he could not "secure work as a miner." "Yet I love the old principles," he wrote, "that I have always advocated." "Even though a negro, I feel that which is good for the white man is good for me, provided however, it is administered in the right way. I want to see the negro have an equal show with the white man, and especially when he deserves it. I want this in every way in the local, in the district, and in the national, and that we have not had in the last year."[28]

Finally, more than seven months after Old Dog's plea that the union do something to support him, a few days before Christmas, Davis received $12.10 in compensation for railroad fare, hotel and time for three days, the only expense on his behalf recorded in 1898.[29]

Davis neither attended the Tenth Annual Convention of District 6, held January 5–7, 1899, in Columbus nor the Tenth Annual National Convention, held January 9–20, in Pittsburgh. With 79 miners from Ohio, former president Michael Ratchford, now serving on the United States Industrial Commission, complimented the 341 delegates for attending the largest national convention ever while Acting President John Mitchell thanked, and the delegates resolved to thank, Governor John R. Tanner of Illinois for refusing to send in the state troops during the Virden strike.[30] With a membership that had increased to 93,124 by the end of 1899,[31] Secretary-Treasurer W.C. Pearce reported a continuously improving balance from $10,812.18 on January 1, 1898, to $22,890.31 on January 1, 1899.[32] After officially electing John Mitchell as its new president, electing T.W. Davis as the new vice-president, and re-electing W.C. Pearce as secretary-treasurer, and the decision to add two members to the nine-member National Executive Board, W.C. Pearce and Fred Dilcher became its only members from Ohio.[33] The interstate joint conference, held January

17-24, decided to continue the previous year's agreed upon Chicago agreement until March 1, 1900.³⁴

On April 8, 1899, Davis wrote his last letter to report that he, joined among others by Fred Dilcher, had "had the pleasure of attending a demonstration in commemoration of the eight-hour day at Princeton, Indiana, on Saturday, April 1st," and that he had "never had a more enjoyable time" in his life. He noted that during the demonstration "not so much prejudice [was] shown as between white and colored as we generally find in mining camps." Wishing that it not be "consigned to the waste basket," in the last sentence of his letter he returned to one of his long held beliefs: "Hoping for the best interests of the miners everywhere and that those who are now without the fold of unionism may soon see the error of their way and enlist in the cause to help emancipate the wage slaves of this day and time."³⁵

Final Months

Although he continued to be blacklisted, as reported by the *New Lexington Tribune*, Davis was apparently able to find work as a public servant. At the time of his unexpected death, Davis was one among the 301 African Americans who lived in Rendville and made up 38 percent of its population of 790. They comprised 85 households of whom 33 owned their residencies. An additional 132 African Americans lived outside of town but within the precinct.³⁶

Delayed one week in reporting Davis' death, the *New Lexington Tribune* informed its readers that Rendville had been "robbed ... of one of its most prominent citizens, who was stolen away by that avaricious

W.C. Scott, editor, *United Mine Workers Journal*, 1899-1900 (Evans, *History of the United Mine Workers of America, 1914-18*, 1920).

robber, death" and that at the time of his death he "was holding the office of constable of our village; he also filled one term as city marshal the duties of which he fulfilled with great ability.... His death is regretted by everyone who knew him."[37] The funeral services, attended by visitors from as far away as Springfield, were held at the Baptist Church and conducted by the Rev. Williams. The internment at the Rendville Cemetery, where today a column marks his grave, took place on Thursday, January 18.[38]

Since contaminated water still posed a problem in Rendville typhoid fever may well have been the cause of Davis' death. One month after his death the *New Lexington Tribune* reported several cases of typhoid fever in Rendville

Rendville Cemetery, R.L. Davis (photograph by the author).

which doctors claimed were "due to germs contained in the water" of a condemned well.[39] However, according to the obituary notice, published in the *United Mine Workers Journal* on January 25, Davis died on January 16 as a result of "lung fever." The Records of Death in Perry County list the same cause, i.e., "pneumonia," and date of death at the age of "37 years, 1 month, 12 days."[40]

According to the *United Mine Workers Journal*, the delegates of the eleventh national convention received "the sad intelligence that former Board Member Richard L. Davis had suddenly died at his home in Rendville." On January 17, W.C. Pearce eulogized Davis:

> R.L. Davis was born in Roanoke, Va., Dec. 24, 1863. According to the usual custom of colored people of that age and clime he began work at eight in a tobacco factory working there and attending school during the winter months until he was 17 years old. At

the age of 17 he became disgusted with the very low wage rate and other unfavorable conditions of a Southern tobacco factory and, leaving there, he settled in the mining regions of West Virginia until 1882, when he moved to Rendville, Ohio, where he has since resided.

He was always a staunch union man and by reason of his activity in this direction and the evidences of his latent ability he was elected a member of the Executive Board of District 6 (Ohio) in 1890, and re-elected each year until 1895. At the National Convention of the U.M.W. of A., held in Columbus, Ohio, in April, 1896, he was elected a member of the National Executive Board, and re-elected again the year following.

"Dick," as he was always familiarly called, was an earnest, intelligent worker, and a representative man of his race. His able assistance and timely counsel will be missed by those with whom he associated and the United Mine Workers have lost a staunch supporter by his death.

We extend sympathy to his bereaved wife and orphaned children, and trust that they will receive the assistance and support merited by the husband, and father now deceased.

The following resolution was passed by the convention:

Indianapolis, Ind., Jan. 17, 1900.

"Whereas, We have learned with regret of the death of former Executive Board Member, R.L. Davis, of the United Mine Workers of America; and

"Whereas, In the death of Brother Davis our organization has lost a staunch advocate of the rights of those who toil, and his race a loyal friend and advocate; therefore, be it:

"Resolved, That the United Mine Workers of America, in convention assembled, barely expresses their deep sense of regret and extend to the bereaved family their heartfelt sympathy in this their hour of trial; be it further

"Resolved, That this resolution be spread upon the minutes of the convention and a copy forwarded to his relatives at Rendville, Ohio."

W.C. Cain, J.L. Clemo, W.T. Ryan, Committee[41]

Chapter 9

A Life of Devotion

Survivors

As life went on, six months after Davis' death on June 18, 1900, William Harris, enumerator for the U.S. Census, conducted the census of Rendville Village. He listed Mary Davis as being born in Ohio, black, head of the household, the widowed mother of two children, renting her house, and boarding a 65-year-old black male from Virginia by the name of Peter Bamer. According to John L. Jones, the Davis residence was probably just six doors down from his on Short Main Street. Due to her husband's untimely death Mary was left behind with two young daughters. Edith, who was now eight, and Beatrice, who was now seven. Both, like their mother, were listed as being able to read, speak and write English. In addition, both girls attended school seven months.[1]

A decade later, on September 10, 1910, Mary Davis of Rendville, a domestic and widow, age 43, born in Pomeroy, Ohio, to Tim Bailey and Nellie Coles, her married name being Davis, was married by J.W. Carroll, Minister of Gospel, to Joseph Watson of Rendville, a widowed miner, age 44, born in Waverly, Ohio, to John Thomas Watson and Ella Bundy. The marriage license, issued by Probate Judge James N. Hymes, lists both Joseph Watson and Mary Davis as "colored."[2] Someone, however, penciled "Do not publish" in the margin, which according to the Perry County clerk recorder was typical for a mixed marriage and might suggest that Joseph Watson perhaps was white.[3] If Mary Bailey was indeed five years old at the time of the 1870 U.S. Census she would have been born in 1865. However, if she was indeed 43 years old in 1910 she would have been born in either 1867 or 1866. Interestingly, presumably both were born in the county seat: Joseph Watson in Pike County and Mary Bailey in Meigs County.

Unfortunately, no birth record of Mary Bailey has been located in Meigs

County. According to his granddaughter,[4] Joseph Watson was a miner from Lawrence County, Ohio, who after the death of his wife in 1908 was left with three small children: Artie, Joseph and David. He subsequently married Mary Davis in 1910 and then moved the family to Columbus for about ten years before moving once again, this time to Cleveland in 1920. Both of Richard L. Davis' daughters, Edith and Beatrice, died without having any children. Mary, Edith and Beatrice are all buried in Cleveland, Ohio.

Legacy

On June 18, 1909, slightly over a year before Mary Davis remarried, the then editor of the *United Mine Workers Journal*, 56-year-old William Scaife, under the pseudonym "Old Timer," wrote a passionate tribute to Richard L. Davis.

> In this article I will change the color of the subject, or rather write something good about a colored man who was once a heroic fighter for the miners' organization in Ohio. His name is R. L. Davis and he resided at Rendville. Twenty years ago there was no more earnest worker in the Ohio miners' ranks than was Dick Davis. He died ten or twelve years ago and his loss was greatly felt in District 6.
>
> There have been a number of colored men who have been prominent in the miners' union from time to time. Warner was the first man of that race elected to the national board of the present organization. Others have had honors conferred on them, but none of them seemed to have the sticking qualities of R. L. Davis of Rendville, Ohio. Dick was in at the birth of the organization. He served as a member of the executive board of District 6 on several occasions. He was also vice-president of the same district and a member of the national board for more than one term, but my memory is so short I cannot tell with any degree of accuracy how many.[5] He talked organization as national organizer to the miners of Alabama, Kentucky, West Virginia and the Lord knows where he was not. We don't know of any man that had a more trying experience in West Virginia than did Dick, and to his credit it ought to be said he kept on with unflagging zeal and buffeted against trials and tribulations that would have daunted and discouraged the best of them.
>
> R. L. Davis, by his devotion to the miners' union, deserved better treatment than that accorded him in the last few years of his life. Perhaps he was regarded as a "has been." Nay; I have heard some of the mushroom growth of latter-day leaders be so unmanly and unremindful of the past as to designate him a "barnacle." Perhaps the same man, were he called upon to undergo the same hardship and experience as did Dick, would be like Jonah, when sent to Ninevah, "make tracks in another direction." This does not reflect on Dick, but it does show the uncharitable spirit of the man who was unmindful of the noble fight Dick made for union principles, when it took sand, pluck and grit to do it.
>
> Dick was a union man since when the memory of man runneth not to the contrary. The first time I met him was at the organization of the U. M. W. of A., nearly twenty years ago. He came in then as a delegate from No. 135 of the K. of L. How long he had been a member of that organization before 1890 I know not, but I do know he was an active, hard worker until his death, when the organization began to be a power and any

man could become a member of it without being in danger of the blacklist, although there might be a danger of his becoming regarded as a "barnacle" or a back number by some of the recent recruits to union principles. "Ah! me," I sometimes think the poet of nature was hitting the right head with a ten-pound hammer when he [Scottish poet Robert Burns] said, "Man's inhumanity to man makes countless thousands mourn." Had he been as well acquainted with the miners as many of our leaders have had reason to be, I have an idea he would have altered that and made it read "miners" in place of "man." Our ignorance has often led us to injure, abuse and crucify our best friends, and I must confess that there are lots of that kind at the present day, and many of our officials are today experiencing the effects of darts from the same shafts, as did all of their predecessors, 95 per cent of which I have no doubt are unmerited and entirely wrong.

W.M. Scaife, *Old Timer*, editor, *United Mine Workers Journal*, 1908–18 (Roy, *History of the Coal Miners*, 1906).

There are a few things that are of inestimable value to the miners, and if they could possess them I should feel more optimistic for the future than I am at present; and, I am very sorry to confess it, feel I could like to see them secure a better and wider grasp of the conditions that govern the craft. Had they this knowledge, then one-half of the carping criticism of the acts of the officials would be forever wiped out of their midst, and the lives of the officers freer from care and unpleasant moments.

For Dick Davis, let me say in conclusion that if he was black, he had a heart as white as any man and a devotion to union principles that was second to no man in the movement. His color he could not help, and I don't know that it matters a great deal anyhow. Quoting from the same poet: The rank is but the guinea's stamp, The man's the 'gowd' for a' that."

Let us not erect in the miners' organization a "color standard," but one of manhood, that every fallen "son of man," no matter his color, creed, religious or political belief, can flock for safety from the attack of incorporate greed, represented by combined capital. Let us all hang together, or we will perish singly in a pitiful struggle for a miserable existence. We need more colored men like Dick Davis, and we white men want to treat them right for the common good of us all.[6]

In part due to the loss of nearly all 19th century archives of the United Mine Workers of America[7] and the presumed burning of Rendville's municipal archives,[8] more than a century after his death, it is difficult to reconstruct the many nuances of Richard L. Davis' life. As he continues to speak to us through his letters, however, we can seek to gain what is undoubtedly an incomplete understanding of the complexities of the world in which he lived. While he did not reveal much about his personal life it was intertwined with his public life as a labor organizer and early voice for civil rights and social justice. He cared deeply about his children and everything he did for the cause of labor he did hoping that someday his children would have a better life.

Proud to be African American, he fought first and foremost to break the color line, deeply believing that whether a miner was white or black all were equal, as embodied first in the philosophy of the Knights of Labor and later in that of the United Mine Workers of America. Still, not unlike many of his contemporaries, he did not extend his advocacy for equal treatment to Chinese immigrants and had conflicting feelings about the fact that immigrants from eastern and southern Europe were often treated as white from the moment they arrived in the country whereas his fellow African Americans, although native born citizens, were treated unequally. In a similar contradictory manner he valued the role women might play in the labor movement, yet warned of anarchy if they were ever allowed to work in the mines.

Without doubt, Davis was a dedicated unionist and as such did not hesitate to reprimand his fellow black miners to stop "kicking" the union, time and time again reminding them that everyone, whether black and white, had to stand together. He was convinced that all miners, regardless of the color of their skin, were wage slaves in the land of the rich. Adverse to politics he spoke out against blind allegiance to either the Republican or Democratic party and urged miners to only vote for those who would support their cause.

A man of faith, although often an outspoken critic of organized religion, Davis regularly invoked God in the cause of labor which he did to such an extent that he believed he would enter heaven if he was as good a Christian as he was an agitator. Urging miners to organize and frequent reading rooms he valued education as an important avenue for advancing the labor movement. A man of courage he often willingly put his life in danger to spread the gospel of unionism. And, ever hopeful that the color line might someday soon become a thing of the past, he must have felt abandoned by the union after he no longer served on the National Executive Board.

George Swanson Starling

Although today there are no direct descendants of Richard L. Davis, he has left us an important legacy through his devotion to the labor movement and the struggle for racial equality. Quoting Adam Clayton Powell, Sr., in her sublime study *The Great Migration*, Isabel Wilkerson describes how a new generation of African Americans migrated in search a better life as Richard L. Davis had during his lifetime when he followed the railroad from Virginia into southeast Ohio crossing the Ohio River to the other side of Jordan. During the Great Depression, Adam Clayton Powell, Sr., as we have noted, a former resident of Rendville, reported that "there was hardly a member among [his] Abyssinian Church who could not count one of more relatives among the new arrivals" who were trying to escape the oppressive segregation of the South.[9]

Based on more than 1,200 interviews, Wilkerson's narrative of the Great Migration focuses on the lives of three African Americans who escaped from the South during the second wave of this exodus which lasted from the 1930s through the 1950s. The Great Migration began during World War I when the supply of immigrant workers dropped by more than 90 percent, creating employment opportunities in the North that set in motion a movement during which over the course of six decades some six million African Americans left the South in search of, as Richard Wright termed it, "the warmth of other suns."[10]

Following the failed promise of Reconstruction and the Supreme Court's "separate but equal" ruling in *Plessy v. Ferguson,* the life story of George Swanson Starling unfortunately offers many parallels to that of Richard L. Davis. Born on June 1, 1918, on a tobacco farm near Alachua, Florida, "Lil George," as he was called to distinguish him from his father "Big George," moved to St. Petersburg when his father grew tired of the treatment he suffered at the hands of Mr. Richard, the planter, who year after year claimed to have broken even and therefore did not have to pay the sharecropping family anything which eternally left it indebted. After his marriage broke up, Big George decided to move to Eustis where he found a job at the loading dock of a packing house and where Lil George joined him after having spent some time living with his maternal grandmother in Ocala. Valedictorian of the Class of 1936, Lil George was accepted at Florida Agricultural and Mechanical College (now FAMU) in Tallahassee. After two years, however, a remarried Big George wasn't willing to spend any more money to send his son back to college, arguing that he himself had done just fine with a fifth grade education and that Lil George could well make a living picking citrus in the orange groves. In love, but more than anything to spite his father, Lil George ran off with Inez Cunningham to a local judge and got married. Having to support his wife, Schoolboy, as the pickers started calling him, similar to Richard L. Davis, became an informal labor organizer. In 1943, with World War II well underway, leaving Inez behind, George decided to go to Detroit after the fruit season so he could earn extra income. Having tired of working in a cargo plane plant, yet having earned a decent wage, he decided to go back to picking fruit in Eustis. With a shortage of hands to pick the rationed highly prized fruit, George began to successfully organize the pickers encouraging them to refuse to pick the citrus unless they were paid a certain price. Starting the "unthinkable act" of negotiating with a white foreman,[11] word about his audacity began to spread through Lake County where a six-foot tall Willis Virgil McCall had been elected sheriff in 1944. A racist, wearing "a ten-gallon hat, size thirteen boots, and a Winchester rifle,"[12] McCall made it his business to intimidate the African American community and if necessary kill, as he did in 1951 in what came to be known as the Groveland case. In April 1945, after a yard man alarmed George that he had overheard the grove owners talking among themselves about getting rid of him and two other trouble making companions, he decided it was time to get out and take the next train, the Silver Meteor, out of Wildwood. An angry man because, not unlike Richard L. Davis' colored kickers, his own fearful people had betrayed him to the grove owners, George headed for New York, where he found a place to stay with an aunt in Harlem. Fortunately he immediately found a job as a luggage handler and coach attendant on the Seaboard Air Line, which ironically operated a railroad up and down the East Coast between New York and Florida.

According to Wilkerson, by the time George arrived in New York, Harlem was a "mature and well-established capital of black cultural life, having peaked with the Harlem Renaissance."[13] After bringing Inez to New York in June, George soon managed to save up enough of his earnings to buy a brownstone. Reminiscent of Richard L. Davis' venture into Alabama, work on the Silver Comet to Birmingham, the Silver Spur to Tampa and other Great Migration trains took him back into the very South he had sought to escape. Each time the train approached Washington, D.C. George had to assist those African Americans who were traveling south to move to the colored Jim Crow car. However, even in the New York of the 1950s he faced racism as bar tenders would shatter the drinking glass he had just finished to let him know African Americans were not welcome in their establishments, an experience similar to what Richard L. Davis experienced at the Mercer Hotel. Through it all Inez and George had two children, Gerard, born in 1947, and Sonya, born in 1954, joined temporarily in 1957 by Pat, the daughter of Inez' sister who had died back in Florida. By the 1960s, as the Civil Rights movement was changing the country, it fell to George to help enforce the new Civil Rights Act which granted African Americans the right to sit on the train wherever they pleased. As some of the Southern conductors and reluctant passenger refused to give up the old traditions, George would inconspicuously alert those who seemed open to refusing to move if asked. Perilous in doing so he would warn them not to implicate him in anyway as it might get him killed.

The strained marriage between George and Inez only worsened when thirteen-year-old Sonya became pregnant during a visit to Eustis and in 1968 gave birth to a son, Bryan, reminding George of how in the 10th grade he was named the father of a, to his relief, born dead baby. At this same time, George became involved with another woman who bore him a son named Kenny. Turning 52 in 1970, he realized that "the revolution had come too late for him." He began going back to church and started singing in the choir. Heartbroken by Gerard's addiction, Inez developed cancer and died in 1978. Following her death Gerard moved to Miami, continuing on a similar path, while Sonya moved Eustis, the very town George had fled. Sixty years old now, a having lived a life denied similarly to Richard L. Davis, George, despite many efforts to move up, had learned to accept life in a dead-end job.[14] In many ways his experience was not much different than what Ida Mae Brandon Gladney found in Chicago where many companies simply refused to hire colored workers because "their white workers just wouldn't stand for it." Just as during Davis' lifetime, African Americans often had to compete with descendants of immigrants "who were rewarded for their ability to leave their old world traits" and assimilate in a white world.[15] According to Wilkerson, "Jim Crow filtered through the economy, north and south, and pressed down on poor and working-class people of all races" as northern industrialists continued to hire colored workers as strikebreakers to keep wages down in ways similar to how coal operators hired black scabs in days of Richard L. Davis.[16]

In 1978, when he was 78 years old, Sonya's death in a car accident in Eustis brought him back to Florida. Although he had kept a small piece of property Big George had left him and he felt safe to return to visit Eustis, he decided he had become too much of a New Yorker to return to the old country. Losing friends to death and becoming frail, he ended up in a nursing home when a fall in 1978 left him in coma he never came out of. He died on September 3, 1998.

The Struggle Continues

While the Civil Rights movement of the 1960s has done much to advance the cause of equality, as attested to during the Great Recession of 2008, inequality continues to adversely impact the poor as argued by Tavis Smiley and Cornell West in their poverty manifesto *The Rich and the Rest of Us*. In August 2011, Smiley and Cornell conducted an 18-city bus tour to explore "the new face of American poverty and the extraordinary decades-long increase in wealth inequality in the American economic system."[17] Reminiscent of Richard L. Davis' struggle to cross the color line and for white and colored miners to stand together against wage slavery as well as his battle with poverty after being blacklisted, Smiley and Cornell argue that "income inequality is real" and that there continues to be "an institutionalized divide between the wealthy and the poor, so that what we now have are the rich and the rest of us."[18] Echoing Davis, they describe a society in which "poverty is the new slavery, and oligarchs are the new kings."[19] Their conclusion that a "growing divide between the rich and the poor" has "virtually eliminated" the middle class, and that "poverty is no longer confined by class or color," reminds us that more than a century later that Davis' vision for social justice is far from accomplished. Quoting Gandhi that "poverty is the worst form of violence," Smiley and West praise the homeless for squatting abandoned houses and their "courage to speak truth to power," a message that permeates Davis' letters.[20]

Similar to Smiley and West, in *Our Kids: The American Dream in Crisis*, Robert Putnam vividly describes the increasing class differences between rich and poor since the 1950s. While acknowledging that gender and race have remained powerful barriers for women and African Americans, he describes the 1950s as an era of full employment and strong unions during which few families experienced economic insecurity. Yet as in the days of Richard L. Davis, women had distinctly less educational and professional opportunities than men while African Americans in northern communities such as Port Clinton, Ohio, where Putnam grew up, lived in two worlds characterized by a "lack of socializing across racial lines."[21] Arguing that income inequality was "momentarily reduced by the immediate impact of the Great Recession," Putnam notes that since then there has been an "increasing affluence at the very top, coupled with stagnation or worse for the rest of society," which along with a "growing de facto segregation of Americans along class lines" has resulted in two Americas.[22]

The demise of the coal industry in southeast Ohio left the region, including Richard L. Davis' Rendville, with a severely depressed economy so much so that on May 7, 1964, President Lyndon B. Johnson chose the Ohio University campus in Athens to announce his War of Poverty. Ironically coal mining returned to region in 2004 when the Buckingham Coal Company opened up a box mine near Glouster, about ten miles south of Rendville. After extracting the remaining coal, in 2012 the company abandoned the mine, and in accordance with environmental protection laws, is currently in the process of reclaiming the land. That same year Buckingham opened up a second mine, five miles closer to Rendville. Purchased by Colorado-based Westmoreland Coal, the mine currently provides employment to nearly a hundred employees.[23] Located above the Marcellus and Utica shale, along with the return of coal mining, the region now is also experiencing the impact of fracking, a new extractive industry.

Richard L. Davis would likely be dismayed to learn that today many continue to question the role of labor unions and that the percentage of workers belonging to a union in the United States has dropped to slightly above ten percent.[24] Many of causes for which he so adamantly sought to organize his fellow miners continue to impact our world. When John L. Lewis became president of the United Mine Workers of America in 1920, the union represented about 300,000 coal miners. However as mechanization and competition from alternative fuels has increased, employment in the coal mines has dropped significantly. Today, the United Mine Workers of America has about 73,000 members.[25]

Chapter Notes

Introduction

1. Later editions of the *Journal* omit the apostrophe after *Workers*, a convention followed in the remainder of this book.

2. Annual Report of the Chief Inspector of Mines to the Governor of the State of Ohio, For the Year 1892 (Columbus, OH: The Westbote Co., State Printers, 1893).

3. U.S. Census Bureau, "American Factfinder: 2010 Census," accessed November 12, 2012. http://factfinder2.census.gov.

4. John A. Caruso, *The Appalachian Frontier: America's First Surge Westward* (Knoxville: University of Tennessee Press, 2003), 120–142.

5. "The Hocking Valley Railroad: First Through Freight Train from Nelsonville," *Daily Ohio Statesman*, August 19, 1869.

6. Ronald L. Lewis, *Black Coal Miners in America* (Lexington: University Press of Kentucky, 1987), 86.

7. "Free Trade in Imported Labor: The Colonial Barbarian Recognized," *Hocking Sentinel* (Logan, OH), September 16, 1886.

8. Lewis, *Black Coal Miners*, 86.

9. Untitled news article, *New Lexington Tribune* (New Lexington, OH), January 24, 1895.

10. Charles H. Nelson, "The Story of Rendville: An Interracial Quest for Community in the Post Civil War Era," *Buckeye Hill Country: A Journal of Regional History* 9 (1996): 32.

11. "Shot for Seduction: A Negro Suffers the Penalty of an Awful Crime, He Loses His Life at the Hands of a Brother for Leading a White Girl Astray," *Ohio State Journal*, June 3, 1894.

12. Nelson, "The Story of Rendville," 32.

13. Sara M. Evans, and Harry C. Boyte, *Free Spaces: The Sources of Democratic Change in America* (New York: Harper and Row, Perennial Library, 1986), 162–202.

14. Nelson, "The Story of Rendville," 32.

15. Herbert G. Gutman, "The Worker's Search for Power: Labor in the Gilded Age" in *The Gilded Age: A Reappraisal*, ed. H. Wayne Morgan (Syracuse: Syracuse University Press, 1963), 40–48.

16. Herbert G. Gutman, "The Negro and the United Mine Workers of America: The Career and Letters of Richard L. Davis and Something of Their Meaning," in *The Negro and the American Labor Movement*, ed. Julius Jacobson (Garden City, New York: Anchor Books, Doubleday & Company, Inc., 1986), 117, 125–126.

17. The holdings at Pennsylvania State University at University Park, the depository for the archives of the United Mine Workers of America, for the period 1890 and 1900 are scant and do not include any records pertaining to the National Executive Board. Jim Quigel, email communication, October 4, 2011, Barry Kernfeld, email communication, October 5, 2011; Unfortunately, Rendville's municipal records were destroyed during the 1990s when the village government did not operate due to lack of an elected village council. John Winnenberg, email communication, December 31, 2013.

18. George H. Meade, *Movements of*

Thought in the Nineteenth Century (Chicago: University of Chicago Press, 1936) in *Stanford Encyclopedia of Philosophy*, ed. Edward N. Zalta (Stanford, CA: The Metaphysics Research Lab, 2012), http://plato.stanford.edu/entries/mead/.

19. The Industrial Workers of the World, *Coal-Mine Workers and Their Industry: An Industrial Handbook* (Chicago: Industrial Workers of the World, 1922), http://www.workerseducation.org/crutch/pamphlets/coal/coal.html.

20. Old Timer, "Forty Years a Miner and Men I Have Known. Richard L. Davis of Ohio," *United Mine Workers Journal* 20, no. 28 (November 18, 1909): 6.

21. See also Chris Evans, *History of the United Mine Workers of America from the Year 1890 to 1900 with Illustrations of Officers during that Period*, vol. 2 (Indianapolis: United Mine Workers of America, 1918?, 1920), 24–25; Gutman, *The Negro and the United Mine Workers*, 81, in footnote reports not having been able to find anything further on Warner.

22. Gutman, "The Negro and the United Mine Workers," 49–127.

23. *Ibid.*, 58–59.

24. While the full name of the labor organization is the United Mine Workers of America, historically it has commonly been referred to as the United Mine Workers.

25. Gutman, "The Negro and the United Mine Workers," 59–60.

26. *Ibid.*, 79; "New Emancipation: The Wage Slaves Should Get Together for Protection," *United Mine Workers Journal* 1, no. 25 (October 1, 1891): 5; R.L. Davis, "Rendville. A General All-Round Talk on Miner's Duties. Let Us Cast Aside Prejudice and Work Together Like Men," *United Mine Workers Journal* 2, no. 29 (October 27, 1892): 4; R.L, Davis, "The Colored Race and Labor Organizations," *United Mine Workers Journal* 3, no. 7 (May 25, 2893): 5.

27. Gutman, "The Negro and the United Mine Workers," 85.

28. *Ibid.*, 114–115.

29. Philip S. Foner, *Organized Labor and the Black Worker, 1619–1981* (New York: International Publishers, 1982), 21.

30. As quoted in Foner, *Organized Labor,* 21.

31. *Ibid.*, 23, 26–27.

32. Robert E. Weir, *Knights Unhorsed: Internal Conflict in a Gilded Age Social Movement* (Detroit: Wayne State University Press, 2000), 12.

33. *Ibid.*, 28.

34. *Ibid.*, 70.

35. Foner, *Organized Labor*, 47; Robert E. Weir, *Knights Unhorsed: Internal Conflict in a Gilded Age Social Movement* (Detroit: Wayne State University Press, 2000), 10.

36. Foner, *Organized Labor*, 82.

37. *Ibid.*, 95–96.

38. Brier, "The Career of Richard L. Davis Reconsidered: Unpublished Correspondence from the National Labor Tribune," *Labor History* 2, no. 3 (1980): 423; Evans, *History of the United Mine Workers of America with Illustrations of early pioneers*, vol. 1 (Indianapolis: United Mine Workers of America, 1914, 1918), 111, 143–144.

39. McCormick, M.R, "A Comparative Study of Coal Mining Communities in Northern Illinois and Southeastern Ohio in the Late Nineteenth Century" (unpublished dissertation, The Ohio State University, 1978), 95, 114.

40. Herbert Hill, "Myth-Making as Labor History: Herbert Gutman and the United Mine Workers of America," *Politics, Culture, and Society* 2, no. 2 (Winter 1988): 133, 190, 195.

41. *Ibid.*, 147, see footnote.

42. *Ibid.*, 190.

43. *Ibid.*, 152–153.

44. *Ibid.*, 132.

45. *Ibid.*, 153–155.

46. *Ibid.*, 159–160.

47. *Ibid.*, 158.

48. *Ibid.*, 194.

49. Stephen Shulman, Nell Irvin Painter, David Roediger, Martin Glaberman, Francille Rusan Wilson, Stephen Brier, Irving Bernstein, and Albert Fried, "Labor, Race, and the Gutman Thesis: Responses to Herbert Hill," *International Journal of Politics, Culture and Society* 2, no. 3 (Spring 1989): 361–403.

50. Herbert Hill, "Rejoinder to the Sym-

posium on Myth-Making as Labor History: Herbert Gutman and the United Mine Workers of America," *Politics, Culture, and Society* 2, no. 4 (Summer 1989): 589, 594–595.

51. Ronald L. Lewis, "Coal Miners and the Social Equality Wedge in Alabama, 1880-1908," in *The United Mine Workers of America: A Model of Industrial Solidarity?*, ed. John H.M. Laslett (University Park: Pennsylvania University Press, 1996), 304–305. As recently as 1998, Nick Salvatore, in "Herbert Gutman's Narrative of the American Working Class: A Reevaluation,[qm] *International Journal of Politics, Culture and Society* 12, no. 1 (1998): 47, 57, 60, 72–73, criticized Gutman as a "sloppy thinker," given to "poor research." According to Salvatore, Gutman's unscholarly "interplay between test and footnote" sought "to privilege a political analysis that enthroned class conflict, oppositional consciousness, and popular activism as the central forces in American social life" so that he could create a "romantic conception of 'the community.'"

52. Stephen Brier, "R.L. Davis on Interracial Unionism: An 1886 Letter," *Labor: Studies in Working-Class History of the Americas* 5, no. 2 (2008): 7–12. doi: 10.1215/15476715-2007-074.

Chapter 1

1. Richard L. Davis never used his middle name. The only source to list his middle name was Ancestry.com.

2. Most sources indicate that Davis was born on December 24 in either 1863 or 1864; see for example, Gutman, "The Negro and the United Mine Workers," 52; K.A. Shapiro, "Davis, Richard L. (December 24, 1863–January 15, 1900 National Executive Board of Mine Workers of America)" in *Encyclopedia of U.S. Labor and Working Class History*, ed. Eric Arneson (New York: Routledge, 2007), 343. However, according to the Record of Deaths in Perry Country, Richard L. Davis was born in Virginia and died in Rendville on January 16, 1900, at the age of 37 years, 1 month, 12 days. According to his grave marker, Davis died on January 10, 1900, at the age of 37 years, 14 days. Yet another source, his obituary notice in the *United Mine Workers Journal*, states that Davis was born on December 24, 1863, which meant he would have been 36 at the time of his death.

3. "R.L. Davis. Member Executive Board," *United Mine Workers Journal* 6, no. 3 (April 23, 1896): 1.

4. Linda Steele, email message to the author, May 20, 2009.

5. "R.L. Davis," *United Mine Workers Journal* 10, no. 42 (Jan 25, 1900): 4; Gutman, "The Negro and the United Mine Workers," 53.

6. L.R. Harlan, "Booker T. Washington's West Virginia boyhood," *West Virginia History* 32, no. 1 (1971): 63–85; National Park Service, *African American Heritage at New River Gorge National River* (Boston), 22–25.

7. National Park Service, *African American Heritage*, 28–34, 187–208, 216–217.

8. Kenneth R. Bailey, "A Judicious Mixture: Negroes and Immigrants in the West Virginia Mines, 1880-1917," *West Virginia History* 34 (January 1973): 141–161; Charles W. Simmons, John R. Rankin, and U.G. Carter, "Negro Coal Miners in West Virginia, 1875-1925," *The Midwest Journal* 6 (Spring 1954): 60–69.

9. Stephen Brier, "Interracial Organizing in the West Virginia Coal Industry: The Participation of Black Mine Workers in the Knights of Labor and the United Mine Workers, 1880-1894," in *Essays in Southern Labor History: Selected Papers, Southern Labor Conference, 1976*, ed. Gary M. Fink and Merl E. Reed (Westport, CT: Greenwood Press, 1977), 20.

10. Joe W. Trotter, *Coal, Class, and Color: Blacks in Southern West Virginia, 1915-32* (Chicago: University of Chicago Press, 1990), 53; National Park Service, *African American Heritage*, 215–216, 248–49.

11. Gutman, "The Negro and the United Mine Workers," 53, 88. Unfortunately the Historical Society in Franklin County does not have any school lists in its collections for African-American students; Linda Steele, email message to the author, May 20, 2009.

12. "Endorsing the G.A., K. of L. Rendville, O., Oct. 24," *National Labor Tribune* 14, no. 40 (October 30, 1886): 3.

13. "Davis Of Rendville, Speaks on Action Of the Straitsville Men. Never Was Unity More Than The Present Time," *United Mine Workers Journal* 3, no. 42 (Jan. 25, 1894): 1; "R.L. Davis Condemns the System of Working Sixteen and Eighteen Hours a Day For One Day's Pay. Believes That Organization is the Only Hope for Workers in the Mines," *United Mine Workers Journal* 7, no. 17 (July 30, 1896): 8.

14. "A Noble Idea Presented by Davis of Rendville. Education and Its Blessings," *United Mine Workers Journal* 4, no. 36 (Dec. 13, 1894): 1.

15. O. Lester Smithers, Jr., "Homer Smithers," in: *Little Cities of Black Diamonds, Miners' Registry*, no date (Enon, OH).

16. Toledo Sunday Journal, "The Sunday Creek Valley. Great Railroad and Coal Co. Extension of the Central Ohio Railroad—Largest Coal Mines in Ohio-A Journal Reporter Visits Corning and Rendville and Notes their Improvements," *New Lexington Tribune*, July 1, 1882.

17. David H. Mould, *Dividing Lines: Canals, Railroads and Urban Rivalry in Ohio's Hocking Valley, 1825–1875* (Dayton: Wright State University Press), 29; Ivan Tribe, *Little Cities of Black Diamonds: Urban Development in the Hocking Coal Region, 1970–1900* (Athens, OH: Athens County Historical Society & Museum, 1988), 3.

18. Mould, *Dividing Lines*, 17–18.

19. Ibid., 32–33.

20. Ibid., 43.

21. Ibid., 48.

22. Clement Luther Martzolff, *History of Perry County* (New Lexington, Ohio: Ward and Weiland / Columbus, Ohio: Press of Fred J. Heer, 1902), 7–8.

23. Tribe, *Little Cities of Black Diamonds*, 18–22; Cheryl Blosser and John Winnenberg, *Agents of Change: The Pioneering Role of the Miners of the Little Cities of Black Diamonds in the Nation's Labor* Movement (Shawnee, Ohio: Little Cities of Black Diamonds Council, 2006), 6–7; "The Hocking Valley Railroad: First Through Freight Train from Nelsonville," *Daily Ohio Statesman*, August 19, 1869.

24. Herbert G. Gutman, "The Worker's Search for Power: Labor in the Gilded Age" in *The Gilded Age: A Reappraisal*, ed. H. Wayne Morgan (Syracuse: Syracuse University Press, 1963), 56–60.

25. Tribe, *Little Cities of Black Diamonds*, 40–48; Blosser and Winnenberg, *Agents of Change*, 7.

26. Tribe, *Little Cities of Black Diamonds*, 66–74; Blosser and Winnenberg, *Agents of Change*, 7.

27. Foner, *History of the Labor Movement, Vol. 2*, 439.

28. Andrew Roy, *A History of the Coal Miners of the United States: From the Development of the Mines to the Close of the Anthracite Strike of 1902, including A Brief Sketch of Early British Miners*, 3rd ed. (Columbus, OH: Trauger Printing Company, 1907), 66–67.

29. Roy, *A History of the Coal Miners*, 148–177; Anthony F.C. Wallace, *St. Clair: A Nineteenth Century Coal Town's Experience with a Disaster-Prone Industry* (New York: Knopf, 1987), 388–403.

30. Herbert G. Gutman, "Reconstruction in Ohio: Negroes in the Hocking Valley Coal Mines in 1873 and 1874," *Labor History* 3, no. 3 (1962): 243.

31. Ibid., 244.

32. Ibid., 247–250.

33. Ibid., 258; McCormick, "A Comparative Study of Coal Mining Communities," 31.

34. Gutman, "Reconstruction in Ohio," 260.

35. *Hocking Sentinel*, June 18, August 27, September 17, October 29, 1874.

36. Gutman, "Reconstruction in Ohio," 255, 262.

37. Philip S. Foner, *From Colonial Times to the Founding of the American Federation of Labor* of *History of the Labor Movement in the United States*, vol. 1 (New York, NY: International Publishers, 1947), 439–441.

38. Untitled news article, *National Labor Tribune* 1, no. 1 (June 27, 1874): 1.

39. McCormick, "A Comparative Study of Coal Mining Communities," 37; *Miners National Record* 1, no. 9 (July 1875): 160.

40. Eric Arnesen, "The Quicksand of Economic Insecurity: African Americans, Strikebreaking, and Labor Activism in the Industrial Era" in *The Black Worker: Race, Labor, and Civil Rights since Emancipation*, ed. Eric Arnesen (Urbana: University of Illinois Press, 2007), 54.

Chapter 2

1. *Chicago Tribune*, December 1, 1915; *Maysville Evening Bulletin* (Marysville, Kentucky), February 6, 1895.
2. Flora B. Doty, *Rend City: From Wilderness to Melting Pot Now a Memory: Memoirs of Hellen (Nellie) Russell Wood* (Fairfield, IL: Wayne County Press, 1994), 15; Donald L. Miller, *City of the Century: The Epic of Chicago and the Making of America* (New York, NY: Simon & Shuster, 1996), 240, 242–44.
3. Charles Ffrench, *Biographical History of the American Irish in Chicago* (Chicago and New York: American Biographical Publishing Company, 1897), 529; Arba Nelson Waterman, *Historical Review of Chicago and Cook County* (Chicago; New York: Lewis Publishing Co., 1908), 1056.
4. Ffrench, *American Irish in Chicago*, 524.
5. Christine Meisner Rosen, "Businessmen against Pollution in Late Nineteenth Century Chicago," *The Business History Review* 69, no. 3 (Autumn, 1995): 351–397.
6. Ffrench, *American Irish in Chicago*, 524; John W. Leonard, *Who's Who in America, 1899–1900* (Chicago: A.N. Marquis & Company, 1899), 597; John. W. Leonard, *The Book of Chicagoans* (Chicago: A.N. Marquis & Company, 1905), 482.
7. "Colonel W.P. Rend: Conversion of a Prominent Democrat in the Republican Faith," *New Lexington Tribune* (New Lexington, OH), September 16, 1880; Ffrench, *American Irish of Chicago*, 526; Arba N. Waterman, *Historical Review of Chicago and Cook County and Selected Biography* (Chicago: The Lewis Publishing Company, 1908), 1055.
8. Ffrench, *American Irish of Chicago*, 528; Leonard, *Who's Who*, 597; Miller, *City of the Century*, 242.
9. Ffrench, *American Irish of Chicago*, 528.
10. Mark Leff, *Rendville* (Athens, OH: WOUB Public Media, 2011), DVD, 14:50.
11. Waterman, *Historical Review*, 1051–1052.
12. Chris Evans, *History of the United Mine Workers of America from the Year 1860 to 1890 with Illustrations of Early Pioneers*, vol. 1 (Indianapolis: United Mine Workers of America, 1914, 1918), 444; Henry D. Lloyd, *A Strike of Millionaires Against Miners Or the Story of Spring Valley: An Open Letter to the Millionaires (1890)* (Chicago, IL: Belford-Clark Co., 1890), 206–207.
13. "A New Point of View—A Priest's Eloquent Plea for Just Treatment of the Laborer," *Hocking Sentinel* (Logan, Ohio), May 14, 1891.
14. Ffrench, *American Irish of Chicago*, 531–532.
15. "Would Hang Rend," *Hocking Sentinel* (Logan, OH), September 2, 1897.
16. "Came To Blows, Colonel W. P. Rend Figures in Sensational Encounter at Pittsburgh," *The Times Democrat* (Lima, OH), September 15, 1897; "Operator's Face Slapped, Quarrel in Pittsburg between Col. W.P. Rend and Capt. J.J. Steytler," *New York Times*, September 15, 1897.
17. Leff, *Rendville*, DVD, 13:22.
18. Doty, *Rend City*, 14.
19. "Big Coal Contract is Sold," *New York Times*, December 12, 1909.
20. Stu Fliege, *Tales and Trails of Illinois* (Urbana: University of Illinois Press, 2002), 160–163.
21. Bob Mayti, "Company Town," *Outdoor Illinois* 11 (May 1972): 12–13.
22. A.A. Graham, *History of Fairfield and Perry Counties, Ohio: Their Past and Present* (Chicago: W.H. Beers & Co., 1883), 222.; Matyi, "Company Town," 14–15.
23. Ffrench, *Irish Americans of Chicago*, 529.
24. "Still They Come," *Athens Messenger*, September 16, 1880; "Colonel W.P. Rend. Conversion of a Prominent Democrat in the Republican Faith," *New Lexington Tribune*, September 16, 1880.

25. W.P. Rend, "Dangers of Free Trade to the Industrial Workers of the Country" (speech, North Chicago Rolling Mills Company, 1880, published by Donnelly, Gassete & Lloyd, Chicago, 1880), 6–7.
26. W.P. Rend, "Dangers of Free Trade," 20.
27. Leff, *Rendville*, DVD, 24:15.
28. Doty, *Rend City*, 12.
29. Leonard, *Who's Who*, 85.
30. W.P. Rend's mother is buried in Lowell, Massachusetts. His father is buried in the Calvary Cemetery in Evanston, twelve north of downtown Chicago, the same cemetery where he was buried in a family crypt. Rend also had a brother, Ambrose J., who was born in 1863 in Lowell, Massachusetts, most likely a son by his father's second wife, Catherine Gannon Rend. Ambrose died in 1939 in Chicago. Like his brother, Ambrose J. Rend was a coal dealer who founded Rend & Co. Col. There are no Rends left in Chicago and no relative has been buried in the family crypt since 1970; Find a Grave. "William P. Rend." Accessed June 26, 2012. http://www.findagrave.com.
31. P.M. Cullinan, ed., *The Book of Perry County: An Historic, Industrial Portfolio* (New Lexington, OH: The New Lexington Herald, 1909), 2.
32. Nancy Aiken and Michel S. Perdreau, *Annotated Edition of the History of the Jones Family by John L. Jones and in Memoriam, J. McHenry Jones* (Berwyn Heights, MD: Heritage Books, 2001), 46.
33. Tribe, *Little Cities of Black Diamonds*, 75, 95, 97.
34. "Rendville," *New Lexington Tribune* (New Lexington, OH), April 1, 1880.
35. [Excerpted from Google Books: Joseph Patterson Smith, *The History of the Republican Party in Ohio*, vol. 2 (Lewis Publishing Company, 1898)]; Toledo Sunday Journal, "The Sunday Creek Valley. Great Railroad and Coal Co. Extension of the Central Ohio Railroad—Largest Coal Mines in Ohio—A Journal Reporter Visits Corning and Rendville and Notes their Improvements," *New Lexington Tribune*, January 5, 1882.
36. Charles Nelson, "The Story of Rendville: An Interracial Quest for Community in the Post Civil War Era," *Buckeye Hill Country* I (Spring, 1996), 26; "Rendville," *New Lexington Tribune* (New Lexington, OH), April 1, 1880; "Rendville," *New Lexington Tribune* (New Lexington, OH), April 15, 1880.
37. Tribe, *Little Cities of Black Diamonds*, 78.
38. "Rendville," *New Lexington Tribune* (New Lexington, OH), March 25, 1880; "Rendville," *New Lexington Tribune*, July 1, 1880; "Rendville," *New Lexington Tribune*, July 8, 1880.
39. Tribe, *Little Cities of Black Diamonds*, 75.
40. "Rendville," *New Lexington Tribune*, July 22, 1880.
41. "Rendville," *New Lexington Tribune*, August 26, 1880.
42. "Rendville," *New Lexington Tribune*, September 9, 1880; Aiken and Perdreau, *History of the Jones Family*, 63; John William Lozier, "The Hocking Valley Coal Miners' Strike, 1884–1885" (Master's thesis, The Ohio State University, 1963).
43. "Corning," *New Lexington Tribune*, September 23, 1880; Nelson, *The Story of Rendville*, 27.
44. "The Corning Trouble," *New Lexington Tribune*, September 30, 1880.
45. Nelson, *The Story of Rendville*, 27; "Corning," *New Lexington Tribune*, October 21, 1880.
46. "Corning," *New Lexington Tribune*, September 23, 1880.
47. "Converse and Foran, At Corning Tuesday Night—A Couple of Partisan Spouters," *New Lexington Tribune*, September 23, 1880.
48. "Corning," *New Lexington Tribune*, September 30, 1880; "Rendville," *New Lexington Tribune*, September 30, 1880.
49. "Rendville," *New Lexington Tribune*, October 7, 1880.
50. Nelson, *The Story of Rendville*, 27; "Rendville," *New Lexington Tribune*, October 21, 1880.
51. Tribe, 76–77.
52. "Found dead," *New Lexington Tribune*, November 18, 1880.
53. Untitled news article, *New Lexington Tribune*, March 17, 1881.

54. Untitled news article, *New Lexington Tribune*, August 25, 1881.
55. Tribe, *Little Cities of Black Diamonds*, 77.
56. Toledo Sunday Journal, "Sunday Creek Valley," *New Lexington Tribune*, January 5, 1882.
57. Untitled news article, *New Lexington Tribune*, April 6, 1882.
58. Toledo Sunday Journal, "Sunday Creek Valley," *New Lexington Tribune*, January 5, 1882.
59. Ibid.
60. Toledo Sunday Journal, "Sunday Creek Valley," *New Lexington Tribune*, May 18, 1882; *New Lexington Tribune*, June 1, 1882.
61. Untitled news article, *New Lexington Tribune*, September 11, 1883.
62. Untitled news article, *New Lexington Tribune*, August 10, 1882.
63. Untitled news article, *New Lexington Tribune*, August 24, 1882.
64. Untitled news article, *New Lexington Tribune*, February 7, 1884.
65. Untitled news article, *New Lexington Tribune*, May 8, 1884.
66. Untitled news article, *New Lexington Tribune*, December 27, 1888.
67. Untitled news article, *New Lexington Tribune*, February 9, 1893; Tribe, *Little Cities of Black Diamonds*, 6.
68. Aiken and Perdreau, *Annotated Edition of the History of the Jones Family*, 28–29; Untitled news article, *New Lexington Tribune*, October 5, 1882.
69. L.E. Erickson, "The Color Line in Ohio Public Schools, 1829-1890" (PhD diss., The Ohio State University, 1959), 419.
70. Ibid., 350.
71. Untitled news article, *The Perry Tribune*, September 17, 1883.
72. Untitled news article, *Daily Ohio State Journal*, September 12, 1887.
73. D.A. Gerber, *Black Ohio and the Color Line, 1860-1915* (Urbana: University of Illinois Press, 1976), 57; Erickson, "The Color Line in Ohio Public Schools, 1829-1890," 377–378.
74. Aiken and Perdreau, *Annotated Edition of the History of the Jones Family*, 26–27.
75. Untitled news article, *New Lexington Tribune* (New Lexington, OH), September 15, 1887.
76. Untitled news article, *Ohio State Journal*, September 12, 1887.
77. Nuptisp, *Cleveland Gazette*, June 28, 1884.

Chapter 3

1. "Letter from Rendville," *National Labor Tribune* 19, no. 18 (April 25, 1891): 5.
2. Evans, *History of the United Mine Workers of America*, vol. 2, 469.
3. Blosser and Winnenberg, *Agents of Change*, 171.
4. Evans, *History of the United Mine Workers of America*, vol.1, 87.
5. Ibid.
6. Blosser and Winnenberg, *Agents of Change*, 44–46.
7. Evans, *History of the United Mine Workers of America*, vol. 1, 117–119.
8. Blosser and Winnenberg, *Agents of Change*, 35–36.
9. Evans, *History of the United Mine Workers of America*, vol. 1, 189.
10. Blosser and Winnenberg, *Agents of Change*, 58.
11. Evans, *History of the United Mine Workers of America*, vol. 2, 8.
12. Fink, *Workingmen's Democracy*, 4.
13. Fink, *Workingmen's Democracy*, 23.
14. "Trevellick at Rendville," *National Labor Tribune*, June 21, 1883; Aiken and Perdreau, *Annotated Edition of the History of the Jones Family*, 64; Ivan Tribe, *Sprinkled with Coal Dust: Life and Work in the Hocking Coal Region, 1870-1900* (Athens, OH: The Athens County Historical Society, 1989), 58–59. Tribe, *Sprinkled with Coal Dust*, 58–59.
15. Aiken and Perdreau, *History of the Jones Family*, 64; Tribe, *Sprinkled with Coal Dust*, 58–59 [Table 15. The Knights of Labor in the Hocking Valley region].
16. Evans, *History of the United Mine Workers of America*, vol. 1, 97–107.
17. Ibid., 108–112.
18. Blosser and Winnenberg, *Agents of Change*, 20; McCormick, "A Comparative

Study of Coal Mining Communities," 14–16.

19. Lozier, "The Hocking Valley Coal Miners' Strike," 36.

20. *Proceedings of the Hocking Valley Investigation Committee of the General Assembly of the State of Ohio Authorized by H.J.R. No. 73*, Held at Columbus, Ohio, February 20, 1885 (Columbus, OH: The Westbote Co., State Printers, 1885). Testimony by Brashears, 178.

21. George Cotkin, "Strikebreakers, Evictions, and Violence: Industrial Conflict in the Hocking Valley, 1884–1885," *Ohio History* 87 (1978), 142.

22. Evans, *History of the United Mine Workers of America*, vol. 1, 121.

23. Blosser and Winnenberg, *Agents of Change*, 22–23.

24. *Proceedings of the Hocking Valley Investigation Committee*, 15.

25. Lozier, "The Hocking Valley Coal Miners' Strike," 103–104.

26. Andrew Roy, *A History of the Coal Miners of the United States, From the Development of the Mines to the Close of the Anthracite Strike of 1902* (Columbus, OH: J.L. Trauger Printing, 1907; Charleston, S.C.: Nabu Press, 2010), 217–218. Citations refer to the Nabu edition. Lozier, "The Hocking Valley Coal Miners' Strike," 57–60; McCormick, "A Comparative Study of Coal Mining Communities," 80.

27. *Proceedings of the Hocking Valley Investigation Committee*, 142.

28. John W. Lozier, "The Hocking Valley Coal Miners' Strike 1884–1885" (Master's thesis, The Ohio State University, 1963), 13–16; McCormick, "A Comparative Study of Coal Mining Communities," 57, 63.

29. Roy, *History of Coal Miners*, 218.

30. Cotkin, "Strikebreakers, Evictions, and Violence," 145; Lozier, "The Hocking Valley Coal Miners' Strike," 60–64; McCormick, "A Comparative Study of Coal Mining Communities," 31.

31. McCormick, "A Comparative Study of Coal Mining Communities," 18–20.

32. Lozier, "The Hocking Valley Coal Miners' Strike," 69; *Athens Messenger*, Dec. 11, 1884; Tenth Annual Report of the Inspector of Mines (1884), 39.

33. Roy, *A History of the Coal Miners*, 225.

34. Lozier, "The Hocking Valley Coal Miners' Strike," 68.

35. Cotkin, "Strikebreakers, Evictions, and Violence: Industrial conflict in the Hocking Valley, 1884–1885," *Ohio History*, vol. 87, 150.

36. Ibid., 143–144.

37. Ibid., 146.

38. Ibid., 147.

39. Ibid., 174; Lozier, "The Hocking Valley Coal Miners' Strike," 72–73, 77.

40. Blosser and Winnenberg, *Agents of Change*, 26; Lozier, "The Hocking Valley Coal Miners' Strike," 78–79.

41. Cotkin, "Strikebreakers, Evictions, and Violence," 148; "Riot and bloodshed," *Athens Messenger*, September 4, 1884.

42. "The Republican Party: It Follows Its Own Sweet Will—as Eloquent Tribute to Its Achievements," *Athens Messenger*, September 9, 1884.

43. Roy, *A History of the Coal Miners*, 234; Blosser and Winnenberg, *Agents of Change*, 28–29.

44. "Neighboring Counties," *Athens Messenger*, October 2, 1884.

45. "Your Paper," *Alarm* (Chicago, IL), October 4, 1884; "Modern Slavery: Our Starving Friends in the Hocking Valley," *Alarm*, October 4, 1884; "Timely Topics and Current Events," *Alarm*, October 18, 1884.

46. Lozier, "The Hocking Valley Coal Miners' Strike," 79.

47. *Proceedings of the Hocking Valley Investigation Committee*, March 19, 1885, 186.

48. Valda Lewis, *Devil's Oven: The Fire in the Heart of the Little Cities of Black Diamond* (Cleveland: Goodwin Video, 2008), DVD.

49. Lozier, "The Hocking Valley Coal Miners' Strike," 79–80.

50. "Neighboring Counties," *Athens Messenger*, December 4, 1884.

51. "The Hocking Valley Troubles: A Crisis Approaching—Relief Fund Mismanagement," *New York Times*, December 8, 1884.

52. Blosser and Winnenberg, *Agents of Change*, 27–28; Lozier, "The Hocking Valley Coal Miners' Strike," 80.

53. "The Valley of Death: Capitalistic Cannibals Devouring Their Propertyless Victims," *Alarm* (Chicago, IL), December 6, 1884; "Reports from the Hocking Valley," *Alarm*, December 27, 1884.
54. Roy, *A History of the Coal Miners*, 219.
55. "The Hocking Valley Miners: Failure of the Strikers and Their Pitiable Condition Now," *New York Times*, February 17, 1885.
56. Lozier, "The Hocking Valley Coal Miners' Strike," 86.
57. Evans, *History of the United Mine Workers of America*, vol. 1, 127.
58. Lozier, "The Hocking Valley Coal Miners' Strike," 87.
59. *Proceedings of the Hocking Valley Investigation Committee*, 5.
60. Ibid., 8–29.
61. Ibid., 29–51.
62. Ibid., 151–166.
63. Ibid., 167–178.
64. Ibid., 186–209, 237–243.
65. Ibid., 209–224.
66. Ibid., 243–251.
67. Ibid., 260–270.
68. Lozier, "The Hocking Valley Coal Miners' Strike," 83.
69. Evans, *History of the United Mine Workers of America*, vol. 1, 130.
70. Lozier, "The Hocking Valley Coal Miners' Strike," 88.
71. Evans, *History of the United Mine Workers of America*, vol. 1, 128–131.
72. Ibid., 131.
73. Blosser and Winnenberg, *Agents of Change*, 31; *Proceedings of the Hocking Valley Investigation Committee*, 29–51; Lozier, "The Hocking Valley Coal Miners' Strike," 89; Roy, *A History of the Coal Miners*, 234.
74. Evans, *History of the United Mine Workers of America*, vol. 1, 131–132.
75. Lozier, "The Hocking Valley Coal Miners' Strike," 90.
76. Ibid., 91.
77. Evans, *History of the United Mine Workers of America*, vol. 1, 136–137, 144–145; Lozier, "The Hocking Valley Coal Miners' Strike," 95–96.
78. Luce, "Chris Evans: Champion," 8.
79. *Proceedings of the Hocking Valley Investigation Committee*, 4.
80. Edward W. Bemis, *Mine Labor in the Hocking Valley*, paper read at Second Annual Meeting of the American Economic Association, Boston, May 23, 1887, 28–30; Blosser and Winnenberg, *Agents of Change*, 32–37; Evans, *History of the United Mine Workers of America*, vol. 1, 137–185; Lozier, "The Hocking Valley Coal Miners' Strike," 95–96.
81. Evans, *History of the United Mine Workers of America*, vol. 1, 184–185.
82. John H.M. Laslett, ed., *United Mine Workers of America: A Model of Industrial Solidarity?* (University Park: Pennsylvania State University Press, 1996), 39.
83. Edward W. Bemis, "Mine Labor in the Hocking Valley," *Publications of the American Economic Association* 3, no. 3 (July 1888), 27–28, 33–34.
84. Roy, *A History of the Coal Miners*, 224–225.
85. Ibid., 225–226.

Chapter 4

1. "The Sunday Creek Valley," *New Lexington Tribune* (New Lexington, OH), January 5, 1882.
2. *Fourteenth Annual Report of the State Inspector of Mines to the Governor of the State of Ohio for the Year, 1888* (Columbus, OH: The Westbote Co. State Printers, 1889); *Fifteenth Annual Report of the State Inspector of Mines to the Governor of the State of Ohio for the Year, 1889* (Columbus, OH: The Westbote Co. State Printers, 1890).
3. "From Rendville, Rendville, O., Sept. 21," *National Labor Tribune*, October 2, 1886; "Endorsing the G.A.K. of L., Rendville, O., Oct. 24," *National Labor Tribune*, October 30, 1886; "Knights of Labor in Rendville," *Cleveland Gazette*, November 13, 1886. Brier's (2008) article, which indicates that the letter in the *Cleveland Gazette* is Davis' earliest known letter, is incorrect. Brier, "R. L. Davis ... An 1886 Letter," 9.
4. While it is possible that Davis did write additional letters between 1886 and 1890; I have not been able to locate any.
5. "Endorsing the G.A. K. of L., Rend-

ville, O., Oct. 24," *National Labor Tribune* 14, no. 44 (October 30, 1886): 3.

6. Aiken and Perdreau, *Annotated Edition of the History of the Jones Family*, 64; Steven Brier, "R. L. Davis ... An 1886 Letter," 11.

7. Mahn Archives, United Mine Workers of America District 6, Cash Book, 1890–1894, MSS # 71, Box 23, Folder 14.

8. *Eleventh Annual Report of the State Inspector of Mines to the Governor of the State of Ohio for the Year, 1885* (Columbus, OH: The Westbote Co. State Printers, 1886).

9. Coroner's Office, *Papers relating to the Inquest Held upon the Body of Reese Jones, Shawnee, O., May 23, 1888*.

10. Bemis, *Mine Labor in the Hocking Valley*, 8–30; Blosser and Winnenberg, *Agents of Change*, 32–37; Evans, *History of the United Mine Workers of America*, vol. 1, 137–185; Lozier, "The Hocking Valley Coal Miners' Strike," 95–96.

11. Evans, *History of the United Mine Workers of America*, vol. 1, 189.

12. Leon Fink, *Workingmen's Democracy: The Knight of Labor and American Politics* (Urbana: University of Illinois Press, 1983), 47; Terence V. Powderly, *The Path I Trod: The Autobiography of Terence V. Powderly* (New York: Columbia University Press, 1940), 61; Weir, *Knights Unhorsed*, 237.

13. Powderly, *The Path I Trod*, 266.
14. *Ibid.*, 188–193.
15. *Ibid.*, 38–39.
16. *Ibid.*, 104.
17. Weir, *Knights Unhorsed*, 12.
18. Foner, *History of the Labor Movement*, vol. 1, 510; Foner, *History of the Labor Movement*, vol. 2, 61, 67.
19. Foner, *Organized Labor*, 56; *Cleveland Gazette*, October 23, 1886.
20. As quoted in Foner, *History of the Labor Movement*, vol. 2, 68; Fink, *Workingmen's Democracy*, 26 [writes this was June rather than October].
21. Foner, *History of the Labor Movement*, vol. 2, 86; Foner, *Organized Labor*, 53–56.
22. Foner, *History of the Labor Movement*, vol. 2, 73; Foner, *Organized Labor*, 55.
23. Foner, *Organized Labor*, 51; *Cleveland Gazette*, October 23, 1886.
24. Fink, *Workingmen's Democracy*, 26–30.
25. Foner, *Organized Labor*, 56; Weir, *Knights Unhorsed*, 308.
26. Foner, *Organized Labor*, 62–63.
27. Foner, *History of the Labor Movement*, vol. 2, 166–168.
28. Sara M. Evans, and Harry C. Boyte, *Free Spaces: The Sources of Democratic Change in America* (New York: Harper and Row, Perennial Library, 1986), 162–202.
29. *Cleveland Gazette*, April 5, 1884.
30. "Jefferson Medical College to J. Vilroy Simpson," *Cleveland Gazette*, January 17, 1885; "Judge Foraker," *Cleveland Gazette*, August 1, 1885; "The Republican Party," *Cleveland Gazette*, October 24, 1885; "Mayor Tuppins. Ohio's Only Colored Mayor Gives His Opinion," *Cleveland Gazette*, March 24, 1888, same article also April 7, 1888.
31. "Rendville Revelations," *The Free American*, March 19, 1886; Rendville," *Cleveland Gazette*, April 25, 1885; "Rendville Items," *Cleveland Gazette*, July 24, 1886; Tribe, *Little Cities of Black Diamonds*, 96.
32. "Death of Dr. Tuppins," "Obsequies of Dr. Tuppins," "An Obituary," *Cleveland Gazette*, January 19, 1889; Foner, *History of the Labor Movement*, vol. 2, 45–146; Aiken and Perdreau, *Annotated Edition of the History of the Jones Family*, 65.
33. "Dr. I.S. Tuppins, Mayor of Rendville, Ohio," *Cleveland Gazette*, October 15, 1885; August 7, 1886.
34. "Mayor Tuppins. Ohio's Only Colored Mayor Gives His Opinion, *Cleveland Gazette*, March 24, 1888.
35. Aiken and Perdreau, *Annotated Edition of the History of the Jones Family*, 65.
36. "The death of Dr. I.S. Tuppins," *Cleveland Gazette*, January 19, 1889.
37. Aiken and Perdreau, *Annotated Edition of the History of the Jones Family*, 64; "Obsequies of Dr. Tuppins," *Cleveland Gazette*, January 19, 1889.
38. A. Clayton Powell, Sr., *Against The Tide: An Autobiography* (New York: Richard R. Smith, 1938), 153.
39. *Ibid.*, 6–12.
40. *Ibid.*, 14.
41. *Ibid.*, 14–16.

42. *Ibid.*, 16-17.
43. *Ibid.*, 35.
44. *Ibid.*, 153.
45. Cheryl Blosser, "Women's Registry," *Little Cities Archives* (database). Accessed November 12, 2012. http://www.littlecities archive.org.

Chapter 5

1. R.L. Davis and Mary Bailey License. Marriage Record, Perry County, 1887, No. 393, 135.
2. *Index to Births*, Perry County, Ohio, 1871–1900. Mary Bailey might have had a light skin complexion. The Index to Birth erroneously listed Mary Bailey as white. The U.S. Census of 1880 lists her, Edith and Beatrice as black.
3. Evans, *History of the United Mine Workers of America*, vol. 1, 417–448; Blosser and Winnenberg, *Agents of Change*, 38–61.
4. Evans, *History of the United Mine Workers of America*, vol. 2, 4–19.
5. M.B. Fox, *United We Stand: The United Mine Workers of America, 1890-1990* (Washington, D.C.: International Union, United Mine Workers of America, 1990), 26.
6. Evans, *History of the United Mine Workers of America*, vol. 2, 4.
7. *Ibid.*, 25.
8. *Ibid.*, 248, 261; The convention of 1893 was labeled as the Fourth Annual Convention, hence skipping the third.
9. Evans, *History of the United Mine Workers of America*, vol. 2, 5.
10. "Amalgamation of Miners: Important Action of the Ohio Division of the N.P.U.," *Columbus Dispatch*, Tuesday, January 21, 1890.
11. "Miners and Mine Laborers. Large Convention held in the City," *Columbus Dispatch*, Wednesday, January 22, 1890.
12. "Amalgamation Favored by the Two Organizations of Miners," *Columbus Dispatch*, Thursday, January 23, 1890; Evans, *History of the United Mine Workers of America*, vol. 2, 12.
13. "The Joint Convention. The Work of Amalgamation Continued Rapidly," *Columbus Dispatch*, Friday, January 24, 1890; Evans, *History of the United Mine Workers of America*, vol. 2, 14; Roy, *A History of the Coal Miners*, 254.
14. "The United Mine Workers. Constitution Completed and Officers Elected," *Columbus Dispatch*, Saturday, January 25, 1890; "Miners Still at Work," *Columbus Dispatch*, Monday, January 27, 1890.
15. "The Miners Adjourn. To Meet Again in Columbus in February, 1891," *Columbus Dispatch*, Monday, January 27, 1890 [photograph in Evans, *History of the United Mine Workers of America*, vol. 2, 25].
16. Evans, *History of the United Mine Workers of America*, vol. 2, 18–23.
17. Foner, *Organized Labor*, 82.
18. Evans, *History of the United Mine Workers of America*, vol. 2, 70.
19. Blosser & Winnenberg, *Agents of Change*, 66; Evans, *History of the United Mine Workers of America*, vol. 2, 38 (1890), 59 (1891), 176 (1892), 295–96 (1893), omitted (1894), 387 (1895).
20. Evans, *History of the United Mine Workers of America*, vol. 2, 34–39.
21. United Mine Workers of America, District 6, Cash Book, 1890–1894, MSS #71, Box 23, Folder 13.
22. *National Labor Tribune* 18, no. 51 (December 13, 1890):5; *National Labor Tribune* 18, no. 52 (December 20, 1890): 5.
23. Roy, *A History of the Coal Miners*, 262, 277.
24. *United Mine Workers Journal* 2, no. 25 (September 29, 1892): 1.
25. MSS #71, Box 23, Folder 13, 62; "Work Dull at Rendville," *National Labor Tribune* 19, no. 6 (January 31, 1891): 5.
26. MSS #71, Box 23, Folder 13, 62; "A Tempest in a Teapot," *National Labor Tribune*, February 7, 1891.
27. "All Serene Again at Rendville," *National Labor Tribune* 19, no. 8 (February 14, 1891): 5.
28. Should Be Brought Into Share the Burdens," *United Mine Workers Journal* 1, no. 45 (February 18, 1892): 1.
29. "From Rendville," *National Labor Tribune* 19, no. 10 (February 28, 1891): 5.
30. Roy, *A History of the Coal Miners*, 279.

31. "Little or No Work," *National Labor Tribune* 19, no. 11 (March 7, 1891) 5; "Letter from Rendville," *National Labor Tribune* 19, no. 12 (March 14, 1891): 5; "Still Dull at Rendville," *National Labor Tribune* 19, no. 13 (March 21, 1891): 5; David Allan Corbin, *Life, Work and Rebellion in the Coal Fields: The Southern West Virginia Miners, 1880–1922* (Urbana: University of Illinois Press, 1981), 29–30.

32. "Still Dull at Rendville," *National Labor Tribune* 19, no. 13 (March 21, 1891): 5; Ronald L. Lewis, *Black Coal Miners in America: Race, Class, and Community Conflict 1780–1980* (Lexington: University Press of Kentucky, 1987), 138–139.

33. Lewis, *Black Coal Miners in America*, 138–139; "Davis Appreciates," *United Mine Workers Journal* 1 No. 42 (January 28, 1892): 5.

34. "Large Meeting—Good Results," *National Labor Tribune* 19, no. 14 (March 28, 1891): 5 ; "Letter from Rendville," *National Labor Tribune* 19, no. 15 (April 4, 1891): 5.

35. "Letter from Rendville," *National Labor Tribune* 19, no. 15 (April 4, 1891): 5.

36. "Letter from Rendville," *National Labor Tribune* 19, no. 18 (April 25, 181): 5.

37. MSS #71, Box 23, Folder 13, 151; "Letter from Rendville," *National Labor Tribune* 19, no. 21 (May 16, 1891): 5.

38. "From Rendville," *National Labor Tribune* 19, no. 23 (May 30, 1891): 5; "Work Very Dull," *United Mine Workers Journal* 1, no. 8 (June 4, 1891): 1.

39. "Work Very Dull," *United Mine Workers Journal*, June 4, 1891; "From Rendville," *National Labor Tribune*, June 6, 1891"; Letter from Rendville," *National Labor Tribune* 19, no. 25 (June 13, 1891): 5; "Dull in Sunday Creek," *National Labor Tribune* 19, no. 27 (June 27, 1891): 5.

40. "Letter from Rendville," *National Labor Tribune* 19, no. 25 (June 13, 1891): 5.

41. Evans, *History of the United Mine Workers of America*, vol. 2, 104; "A Big Convention," *United Mine Workers Journal* 1, no. 4 (Thursday, May 7, 1891): 4; Evans, *History of the United Mine Workers of America*, vol. 2, 128, 145.

42. "From Rendville," *National Labor Tribune* 19, no. 30 (July 18, 1891): 5.

43. "Now, Messr. Editors," *National Labor Tribune* 19, no. 31 (July 25, 1891): 5.

44. "New Emancipation," *United Mine Workers Journal* 1, no. 25 (October 1, 1891): 5.

45. "The Ohio Screen Bill," *United Mine Workers Journal* 2, no. 39 (January 5, 1893): 5.

46. "Gauzy Promises," *National Labor Tribune* 19, no. 33 (August 8, 1891): 5.

47. "From Rendville," *National Labor Tribune* 19, no. 35 (August 22, 1891): 5; "From Rendville," *National Labor Tribune* 19, no. 38 (September 12, 1891): 5; MSS #71, Box 23, Folder 13, 160–161.

48. "From Rendville," *National Labor Tribune* 19, no. 35 (August 22, 1891): 5; "From Rendville," *National Labor Tribune* 19, no. 36 (August 29, 1891): 5.

49. "From Rendville, *National Labor Tribune* 19, no. 36 (August 29, 1891): 5.

50. "From Rendville," *National Labor Tribune* 19, no. 38 (September 12, 1891): 5.

51. "New Emancipation," *United Mine Workers Journal* 1, no. 25 (October 1, 1891): 5.

52. "Marmet's Agents," *United Mine Workers Journal* 1, no. 26 (October 8, 1891): 1; "Rendville Mines," *National Labor Tribune* 19, no. 42 (October 10, 1891): 5.

53. "New Emancipation," *United Mine Workers Journal* 1, no. 25 (October 1, 1891): 5.

54. MSS # 71, Box 23, Folder 13, 164.

55. "Rendville Miners," *United Mine Workers Journal* 1, no. 24 (September 24, 1891): 1; "From Rendville," *National Labor Tribune* 19, no. 40 (September 26, 1891): 5.

56. "From Rendville," *National Labor Tribune* 19, no. 40 (September 26, 1891): 5.

57. "Good Suggestions," *United Mine Workers Journal* 1, no. 28 (October 22, 1891): 2; "What Is Organization!" *United Mine Workers Journal* 1, no. 28 (October 22, 1891): 8.

58. "What Is Organization!" *United Mine Workers Journal* 1, no. 28 (October 22, 1891): 8; "From Rendville," *National Labor Tribune* 19, no. 44 (October 24, 1891): 5.

59. "Good Suggestions," *United Mine Workers Journal* 1, no. 28 (October 22, 1891): 2.

60. MSS #71, Box 23, Folder 13, 169.
61. "Brother Davis' Letter," *United Mine Workers Journal* 1, no. 30 (November 5, 1891): 1; "Work Good in Ohio," *National Labor Tribune* 19, no. 46 (November 7, 1891): 5; "From Rendville," *National Labor Tribune* 19, no. 47 (November 14, 1891): 5.
62. "From Rendville, *National Labor Tribune* 19, no. 47 (November 14, 1891): 5.
63. "Brother Davis," *United Mine Workers Journal* 1, no. 34 (December 3, 1891): 5; "From Rendville," *United Mine Workers Journal* 1, no.36 (December 17, 1891): 3.
64. "Sudden Disappearance," *United Mine Workers Journal* 1, no. 32 (November 19, 1891): 2.
65. "A Frank Letter," *United Mine Workers Journal* 1, no. 37 (December 24, 1891): 5.
66. *United Mine Workers Journal* 1, no. 39 (January 7, 1892): 1.
67. "Davis Declines The Candidacy for Vice President of District 6," *United Mine Workers Journal* 1, no. 38 (December 31, 1891): 8; "Official Call for Annual Convention of District No. 6," *United Mine Workers Journal* 1, no. 40 (Thursday, January 14, 1892): 6.
68. "A Frank Letter," *United Mine Workers Journal* 1, no. 37 (December 24, 1891): 5.
69. MSS #71, Box 23, Folder 13, 196; "Ohio's Convention," *United Mine Workers Journal* 1, no. 42 (Thursday, January 28, 1892): 6; "The Facile Pen," *United Mine Workers Journal* 2, no. 35 (December 8, 1892): 5; Evans, *History of the United Mine Workers of America*, vol. 2, 159.
70. "Notes of Ohio Convention," *United Mine Workers Journal* 1, no. 42 (January 28, 1892): 4.
71. "Color Question," *United Mine Workers Journal* 2, no. 4 (May 5, 1892): 1.
72. "Davis Appreciates," *United Mine Workers Journal* 1, no. 42 (January 28, 1892): 5.
73. Brier, "The Career of R.L. Davis Reconsidered," 422.
74. United Mine Workers of America, District 6, Cash Book, 1890–1894, MSS #71, Box 23, Folder 14. Although the Cash Book presumably only covers 1890–1894, it includes Income 1892–1893 and Income 1894–1896.
75. "In Sunday Creek," *United Mine Workers Journal* 1, no. 46 (February 25, 1892): 1.
76. MSS #71, Box 23, Folder 13, 209; "Should Be Brought In to Share the Burdens," *United Mine Workers Journal* 1 no. 45 (February 18, 1892): 1; "Encouraging," *United Mine Workers Journal* 1, no. 47 (March 3, 1892): 1.
77. "Davis' Report," *United Mine Workers Journal* 1, no. 49 (March 17, 1892): 2; "Davis Laments," *United Mine Workers Journal* 1, no. 51 (March 31, 1892): 1; "Davis' Rambles," *United Mine Workers Journal* 1, no. 52 (April 7, 1892): 5.
78. "Davis Returns," *United Mine Workers Journal* 2, no. 1 (April 14, 1892): 5.
79. "Rendville, O.," *United Mine Workers Journal* 2, no. 2 (April 21, 1892): 8.
80. "R.L. Davis Discusses the Question of Race and Creed Prejudice," *United Mine Workers Journal* 2, no. 14 (July 21, 1892): 1.
81. "Missionary Work," *United Mine Workers Journal* 2, no.4 (May 12, 1892): 5.
82. "Rather Tough, R.L.," *United Mine Workers Journal* 2, no. 9 (June 9, 1892): 1.
83. "Missionary Work," *United Mine Workers Journal* 2, no. 4 (May 12, 1892): 5.
84. "Land of Bondage," *United Mine Workers Journal* 2, no. 12 (June 30,1892): 1.
85. David Brody. *Steelworkers in America: The Nonunion Era* (New York: Harper Torchbooks, 1969): 56–57; Foner, *History of the Labor Movement*, vol. 2, 206–218.
86. "Rendville," *United Mine Workers Journal* 2, no. 13 (July 7, 1892): 1; "R.L. Davis," *United Mine Workers Journal* 2, no. 14 (July 14, 1892): 1; "R.L. Davis Who wants a Satisfactory Answer to Certain Questions," *United Mine Workers Journal* 2, no. 15 (July 21, 1892): 1.
87. "What A Pity: No. 3 Lost Over Twenty Days," *United Mine Workers Journal* 2, no. 16 (July 28, 1892): 4.
88. MSS #71, Box 23, Folder 13, 216; "R.L. Davis Discusses the Question of Race and Creed Prejudice," *United Mine Workers Journal* 2, no. 14 (July 14, 1892): 1.
89. "What A Pity," *United Mine Workers Journal* 2, no. 16 (July 28, 1892): 4.
90. "Davis," *United Mine Workers Journal* 2, no. 17 (August 4, 1892): 5.

91. "Very Plain Talk," *United Mine Workers Journal* 2, no. 18 (August 11, 1892): 1.

92. "A Little Talk," *United Mine Workers Journal* 2, no. 20 (August 25, 1892): 3.

93. "Smacks His Lips," *United Mine Workers Journal* 2, no. 21 (September 1, 1892): 8. In 1892 Jellico, located on the border of Kentucky and Tennessee was the site of a strike in which the operators tried in convict laborers to replace the mostly white local miners. The local miners raided the railcars at least twice and freed the black convicts which created a major crisis that in 1896 led to the end of the convict lease system in Tennessee.

94. "A word of advice," *United Mine Workers Journal* 2, no. 23 (September 15, 1892): 1.

95. "A Contract," *United Mine Workers Journal* 2, no. 23 (September 15, 1892): 5.

96. "Congo," *United Mine Workers Journal* 2, no. 24 (September 22, 1892): 5; "Congo," *United Mine Workers Journal* 2, no. 28 (October 20, 1892): 1.

97. "May Want A Job," *United Mine Workers Journal* 2, no. 26 (October 6, 1892): 5.

98. *Ibid.*; "Davis Sends in the Last Chapter on Congo," *United Mine Workers Journal* 2, no. 28 (October 20, 1892): 1; "Sunday Creek Enjoys Smooth Times," *United Mine Workers Journal* 2, no. 33 (November 24, 1892): 4.

99. "Rendville," *United Mine Workers Journal* 2, no. 29 (October 27, 1892): 4.

100. "A Supplement," *United Mine Workers Journal* 2, no. 33 (November 10, 1892): 1; "Sunday Creek," *United Mine Workers Journal* 2, No. 33 (November 24, 1892): 4.

101. "Official Circular Calling for Action on Machine Matters," *United Mine Workers Journal* 1, no. 43 (Thursday, February 4, 1892): 8.

102. "Davis Answers," *United Mine Workers Journal* 2, no. 36 (December 15, 1892): 5.

103. "The Facile Pen," *United Mine Workers Journal* 2, no. 35 (December 8, 1892): 5; "The Ohio Screen Bill," *United Mine Workers Journal* 2, no. 36 (January 5, 1893): 5; "Davis Aroused," *United Mine Workers Journal* 2, no. 40 (January 19, 1893): 5.

104. "The Facile Pen," *United Mine Workers Journal* 2, no. 35 (December 8, 1892): 5; "Spare Moments," *United Mine Workers Journal* 2, no. 46 (February 23, 1892): 3; "R.L. Davis," *United Mine Workers Journal* 3, no. 8 (June 1, 1893): 1.

105. "Davis Dissents," *United Mine Workers Journal* 2, no. 48 (March 9, 1893): 5; "Davis Adds," *United Mine Workers Journal* 2, no. 49 (March 16, 1893): 5.

106. "The Ohio Screen Bill," *United Mine Workers Journal* 2, no. 39 (January 5, 1893): 5; "Davis Aroused," *United Mine Workers Journal* 2, no. 40 (January 12, 1893): 5.

107. "The Dead Bill," *United Mine Workers Journal* 2, no. 51 (March 31, 1893): 3.

108. Michael L. Benedict and John F. Winkler, *The History of Ohio Laws* (Athens: Ohio University Press, 2004), 890.

109. "R.L. Davis," *United Mine Workers Journal* 3, no. 3 (April 27, 1893): 1; Evans, *History of the United Labor Workers in America*, vol. 2, 280–289.

110. "Glasgow," *United Mine Workers Journal* 3, no. 5 (May 11, 1893): 1.

111. "Davis Replies," *United Mine Workers Journal* 3, no. 6 (May 18, 1893): 1; "R.L. Davis," *United Mine Workers Journal* 3, no. 8 (June 1, 1893): 1.

112. "The Colored Race and Labor Organizations," *United Mine Workers Journal* 3, no. 7 (May 25, 1893): 5.

113. "R.L. Davis," *United Mine Workers Journal* 3, no. 8 (June 1, 1893): 1.

114. Foner, *History of Labor*, vol. 2, 235–240.

115. United Mine Workers of America (UMWA), District 6, Cash Book, 1890–1894, MSS #71, Box 23, Folder 14.

116. "Cochocton News," *United Mine Workers Journal* 3, no. 12 (June 29, 1892): 1; "Rendville News," *United Mine Workers Journal* 3, no. 16 (July 27, 1893): 1, http://www.kent.edu/ehhs/ciie/cost/index.cfm.

117. "Rendville News," *United Mine Workers Journal* 3, no. 16 (July 27, 1893): 1; "A Mistake," *United Mine Workers Journal* 3, no. 19 (August 17, 1893): 1; "Wrong Impression," *United Mine Workers Journal* 3, no. 20 (August 24, 1893): 1; "Time!" *United*

Mine Workers Journal 3, no. 27 (October 12, 1893); "Davis," United Mine Workers Journal, 3, no. 22 (September 15, 1893): 1.

118. See UMWA, District 6, Cash Book, 1890–1894, MSS #71, Box 23, Folder 14.

119. "Davis Views," United Mine Workers Journal 3, no. 29 (October 26, 1893): 5; "Auditor Davis," United Mine Workers Journal 3, no. 32 (November 16, 1893): 1; "Auditor Davis," United Mine Workers Journal 3, no. 34 (November 30, 1893): 2.

120. "The Rendville Man," United Mine Workers Journal 3, no. 38 (December 28, 1893): 3.

121. Evans, History of the United Mine Workers of America, vol. 2, 302–312.

122. "Davis Mediates," United Mine Workers Journal 3, no. 41 (January 18, 1894): 1.

123. "Davis," United Mine Workers Journal 3, no. 42 (January 25, 1894): 5.

124. "Rendville News," United Mine Workers Journal 3, no. 43 (February 1, 1894): 5.

125. Evans, History of the United Mine Workers of America, vol. 2, 387.

126. UMWA, District 6, Cash Book, 1890–1894, MSS #71, Box 23, Folders 13–14.

127. Evans, History of the United Mine Workers of America, vol. 2, 319–326.

128. Ibid., 328–333.

129. Roy, A History of the Coal Miners, 303–304.

130. Roy, A History of the Coal Miners, 303; "130,000 Coal Miners Strike," New York Times, April 22, 1894.

131. Evans, History of the United Mine Workers, vol. 2, 336–338.

132. Evans, History of the United Mine Workers, vol. 2, 346–348; Roy, A History of the Coal Miners, 305–307.

133. Evans, History of the United Mine Workers, vol. 2, 336–338.

134. Evans, History of the United Mine Workers, vol. 2, 350–357; M.B. Fox, United we stand: The United Mine Workers of America, 1890–1990 (Washington, DC: International Union, United Mine Workers of America, 1990), 45; Roy, A History of the Coal Miners, 307–309.

135. "R.L. Davis," United Mine Workers Journal 4, no. 6 (May 17, 1894): 8; "R.L. Davis," United Mine Workers Journal 4, no. 7 (May 24, 1894): 1.

136. "Never Say Die," United Mine Workers Journal 4, no. 9 (June 7, 1894): 3.

137. "Grand Demonstration," United Mine Workers Journal 4, no. 9 (June 7, 1894): 4.

138. "R.L. Davis," United Mine Workers Journal 4, no. 15 (July 19, 1894): 8.

139. "R.L. Davis Sets Himself Right on the Question of Columbus Settlement—Three Things He Hates," United Mine Workers Journal 4, no. 16 (July 26, 1894); John H.M. Laslett, Labor and the Left: A Study of Socialist and Radical Influences in the American Labor Movement, 1881–1924 (New York, Basic Books Inc, 1970), 198.

140. "R.L. Davis," United Mine Workers Journal 4, no. 16 (July 26, 1894): 1; "The Right Step," United Mine Workers Journal 4, no. 18 (August 9, 1894): 1.

141. Foner, History of the Labor Movement, vol. 2, 261–278.

142. "A Difficulty," United Mine Workers Journal 4, no. 27 (October 11, 1894): 5.

143. "Dick Declaims," United Mine Workers Journal 4, no. 28 (October 18, 1894): 1.

144. "Davis," United Mine Workers Journal 4, no. 33 (November 22, 1894): 1.

145. Proceedings of the American Federation of Labor, 1894 (Bloomington, Illinois, Pantagraph Printing and Stationary Company, Reprinted 1906), 41–44.

Chapter 6

1. "Honest and Manly: Letter from Our Colored Correspondents R.L. Davis-Defeated for Office, but as Good Union Man as Ever," United Mine Workers Journal 5, no. 47 (February 28, 1895): 1; "A Few Tricks Have Been Played in the Sunday Creek Since the Miners Became Lax in Their Union," United Mine Workers Journal 5, no. 15 (July 18, 1895): 1.

2. "Davis Himself Takes Up the Cudgel to Deloche and Speaks about His Traveling," United Mine Workers Journal 4, no. 43 (January 31, 1895): 3.

3. United Mine Workers Journal 4, no. 40 (January 10, 1895): 4.

4. "Suffering among Ohio Miners, Gov. McKinley Calls Upon Chambers of Commerce for an Inquiry," *Washington Post*, February 17, 1895.

5. "Rendville, O., News. A Very Sad and Pitiable State of Affairs. A Reply to a Pittsburg Paper," *United Mine Workers Journal* 5, no.2 (April 18, 1895): 1.

6. *United Mine Workers Journal* 4, no. 39 (January 3, 1895): 8.

7. *United Mine Workers Journal* 4, no. 41 (January 17, 1895): 3.

8. "Davis Himself Takes Up the Cudgel to Deloche and Speaks About His Traveling," *United Mine Workers Journal* 4, no. 43 (January 31, 1895): 3.

9. Evans, *History of the United Mine Workers*, vol. 2, 359–364.

10. "Sunday Creek," *United Mine Workers Journal* 2, no. 33 (November 24, 1892): 4.

11. "For Executive Board," *United Mine Workers Journal* 4, no. 46 (February 21, 1895): 4.

12. "Honest and Manly," *United Mine Workers Journal* 4, no. 47 (February 28, 1895): 1.

13. "Cheering News From the Flat Top Region," *United Mine Workers Journal* 5, no. 2 (April 18, 1895): 6.

14. "Another Letter," *United Mine Workers Journal* 4, no. 48 (March 7, 1895): 1.

15. *Ibid.*; "Another Chapter," *United Mine Workers Journal* 4, no. 51 (March 28, 1895): 2.

16. "What R.L. Davis Thinks," *United Mine Workers Journal* 4, no. 49 (March 14, 1895): 1.

17. "Reconciled," *United Mine Workers Journal* 4, no. 51 (March 28, 1895): 1.

18. "What R.L. Thinks," *United Mine Workers Journal* 4, no. 49 (March 14, 1895): 1.

19. "Official Call for Annual Convention of District 6, With Nominations for Officers, Etc.," *United Mine Workers Journal* 4, no. 49 (March 14, 1895): 4.

20. "Expenditure," *United Mine Workers Journal* 4, no. 52 (April 4, 1895): 1; United Mine Workers of America, District 6, Cash Book, 1890–1894, MSS #71, Box 23, Folder 14.

21. *United Mine Workers Journal* 5, no. 1 (April 11, 1895): 2; Evans, *History of the United Mine Workers of America*, vol. 2, 384.

22. "R.L. Davis Takes Another Turn at Reviewing Things, Locally and in General, He is Horrified At the Employment of Women in A Pittsburg Mill-Feels Anarchistic," *United Mine Workers Journal* 5, no. 3 (April 25, 1895): 5.

23. Roy, *A History of Coal Miners*, 312–316.

24. "Circular Letter From the Executive Board of District 6, U.M.W. of A., to L.U.'s and L.A.'s," *United Mine Workers Journal* 5, no. 9 (June 6, 1895): 1; "Soft Sawder by R.L. Davis—He Handles the Genus 'Kicker' With Velvety Gloves and Fond Caresses. A Few Endearing Term Specially Manufactured for the Occasion," *United Mine Workers Journal* 5, no. 10 (June 13, 1895): 1.

25. "A Strong Plea," *United Mine Workers Journal* 5, no. 11 (June 20, 1895): 1.

26. "A Few Tricks Have Been Played In the Sunday Creek Since Miners Became Lax in Their Union," *United Mine Workers Journal* 5, no. 15 (July 18, 1895): 1.

27. "Alarming Conditions of the Miners in the Hocking and Sunday Valleys. Hunger and Want Staring Hundreds of Families in the Face. Governor McKinley and Legislature to be Called Upon for Aid," *Athens Messenger*, July 25, 1895.

28. "A Strong Protest From 'Dick' Davis Against the Move Made by Some Men in the Sunday Creek. He Never Will be a Party to an Organization Which Debars His Race," *United Mine Workers Journal* 5, no. 17 (August 1, 1895): 1.

29. "Another Exhortation by R.L. Davis in Behalf of Unity," *United Mine Workers Journal* 5, no. 19 (August 15, 1895): 1.

30. " A Report by Davis," *United Mine Workers Journal* 5, no. 21 (August 29, 1895): 5.

31. Eric Foner, *The New American History* (Philadelphia: Temple University Press, 1998), 71.

32. "A Report by Davis Of Penna and Ratchford's Meetings in the Sunday Creek. 'Poor Old Dick' Couldn't Eat at the Mercer House Because of His Color," *United Mine*

Workers Journal 5, no. 21 (August 29, 1895): 5; "Letter from D.H. Sullivan" *United Mine Workers Journal* 5, no. 49 (March 12, 1896): 8.

33. "Another Exhortation by R.L. Davis in Behalf of Unity. He deals With the Massillon Affairs and Exchanges a Few Words With Wallace," *United Mine Workers Journal* 5, no. 19 (August 15, 1895): 1.

34. *New Lexington Tribune* (New Lexington, OH), January 24, 1895; Blosser and Winnenberg, *Agents of Change*, 68; Ron L. Lewis, *Black Coal Miners in America*, 86.

35. Fox, *United We Stand*, 111.

36. Perry County Court Records, Box 163, No. 3192, Cost Book 12–87, 192, Perry County Court.

37. "Letter from D.H. Sullivan," *United Mine Workers Journal* 5, no. 49 (March 12, 1896): 8.

38. Blosser and Winnenberg, *Agents of Change*, 70–71; Perry County Court Records, Box 163, No. 3192, Cost Book 12–87 (February 10, 196): 15; (May 25, 1896) (November 17, 1896): 8, Perry County Court.

39. What Has he done? That is What R.L. Davis Wants to Know. The Company Objects to Him Being Checkweighman," *United Mine Workers Journal* 5, no. 26 (October 3, 1895): 5. "Fireside Musings of Our Old Friend 'Dick' Davis—Political Harangues and Operators' Perversity Reflected On," *United Mine Workers Journal* 5, no. 30 (October 31, 1895): 1.

40. Davis merely referred to accusations that were leveled against Sullivan without any further details. I was unable to locate any other sources to substantiate their nature.

41. "Grand Demonstration In the Sunday Creek Valley, Corning Visited Whose Hospitality Is Unbounded," *United Mine Workers Journal* 7, no. 9 (June 7, 1894): 4; "Davis's Ideas on Things Which Are Just Now Uppermost in the Minds of Miners. Dick Thinks He Sees a Black Cloud in the Horizon, Pittsburgward, and Incidentally Turns His Attention to a Few Local Judases, as He Terms Them," *United Mine Workers Journal* 5, no. 32 (November 14, 1895): 1; "R.L. Davis on Restrictions," *United Mine Workers Journal* 5, no. 35 (December 5, 1895): 1; "R.L. Davis Reviews the Shawnee Convention, and Speaks Commendably of the Men in the Lease Mines—Likes to Read the Restriction Articles," *United Mine Workers Journal* 5, no. 37 (December 19, 1895): 1.

42. "R.L. Davis Reviews The Shawnee Convention, and Speaks Commendably of the Men in the Lease Mines—Likes to Read The Restriction Articles," *United Mine Workers Journal* 5, no. 37 (December 19, 1895): 1; "What the Trouble Is. That's What R.L. Davis Claims to Point Out—Would Like to See Judge Little," *United Mine Workers Journal* 5, no. 38 (December 26, 1895).

Chapter 7

1. "Speaks his Mind Once More, Without Using Any Honeyed Word. If Men Who Think Themselves Much More Clever Than He Would Take His Advice. Things Would Get Righted a Good Deal Quicker Than Under Other Conditions," *United Mine Workers Journal* 5, no. 41 (January 16, 1896): 1; Blosser & Winnenberg, *Agents of Change*, 51; Roy, *A History of the Coal Miners*, 315.

2. "Report From Rendville. By the Ever Faithful R.L.—Work is Poor—Compliments to Our Other Correspondents—Good Words for Sec. McBryde, Ect.," *United Mine Workers Journal* 5, no. 46 (February 20, 1896): 5; "Couldn't Tell. If He Were Asked How the People Live at Rendville, Says R.L. Davis," *United Mine Workers Journal* 5, no. 49 (March 12, 1896): 1.

3. "Rendville, O.," *United Mine Workers Journal* 6, no. 8 (May 28, 1896): 5.

4. "Official Report. Of the Seventh Annual Convention of District 6, United Mine Workers of America. Containing the Annual Reports of President Ratchford and Secretary Pearce, In Which the Condition and History of the Organization is Graphically Portrayed," *United Mine Workers Journal* 6, no. 2 (April 16, 1896): 4.

5. Mahn Archives, United Mine Workers of America, District 6, Cash Book, MSS #71, Box 23, Folder 14.

6. Evans, *History of the United Mine Workers of America*, vol. 2, 410–412.

7. *Ibid.*, 247, 317, 357, 409.
8. *Ibid.*, 423.
9. "Official Report of the Seventh Annual Convention of the United Mine Workers of America—One of the Most Harmonious Conventions Ever Held in the City of Columbus," *United Mine Workers Journal* 6, no. 3 (April 23, 1896): 2.
10. "Thanks From Our Colored Member of the National Executive Board, R.L. Davis Who Promises to Do His Utmost," *United Mine Workers Journal* 6, no. 3 (April 23, 1896): 5.
11. Davis was most likely born December 24, 1862; see Chapter 2.
12. A phrenologist studies the size of the human brain; a physiognomist assesses a person's character or personality based on outer appearance, especially that of the face.
13. "R.L. Davis, Member Executive Board," *United Mine Workers Journal* 6, no. 3 (April 23, 1896): 1.
14. "Original. That's What Davis Says His Letters Are. He is a Representative of His Race and Proud of the Honor and Thankful," *United Mine Workers Journal* 6, no. 4 (April 30, 1896): 1.
15. "Rendville, O.," *United Mine Workers Journal* 6, no. 8 (May 28, 1896): 5.
16. "Sunday Creek Valley Pictured by R.L. Davis—Emotional And Scathing Observations on the Action of Shawnee Men—A Turn in Dick's Letter Which Shows the Ever Hopeful Spirit of Miners. Amid Threatening Forebodings the Rendville Boys are Still Prepared To Meet Rivals at the Bat," *United Mine Workers Journal* 6, no. 6 (June 4, 1896): 1.
17. "R.L. Davis Condemns the System of Working Sixteen and Eighteen Hours a Day For One Day's Pay. Believes That Organization is the Only Hope for Workers in the Mines," *United Mine Workers Journal* 7, no. 17 (July 30, 1896): 8.
18. "R.L. Davis Writes an Interesting Letter Giving the News of the Upper End Of Sunday Creek Valley," *United Mine Workers Journal* 7, no. 18 (August 6, 1896): 4.
19. "R.L. Davis Complains of the Indifference and Carelessness Manifested in Some Parts of the Sunday Creek Valley," *United Mine Workers Journal* 7, no. 19 (August 13, 1896): 1.
20. Lewis, *Black Coal Miners in America*, 100.
21. "Betrayed Is Brother R.L. Davis, in the Home Of His Friends—Dick's Unionism Is too Aggressive For Some People of Rendville Who Ask for His Discharge," *United Mine Workers Journal* 7, no. 23 (September 10): 1.
22. "Davis's Ire is Up Because of the Treatment Meted Out To him by Those Who Should Be Brothers," *United Mine Workers Journal* 7, no. 35 (December 3, 1896): 4.
23. "R.L. Davis Again to the Fore with a Few Interesting Suggestions—Time We Thought About Unity," *United Mine Workers Journal* 7, no. 32 (November 15, 1896): 1; "Working Steadily At Rendville, Ohio, But Earnings Are Very Small—R.L. Davis Declines Nomination for The District Vice Presidency," *United Mine Workers Journal* 7, no. 37 (December 17, 1896): 17.
24. "Working Steadily At Rendville, Ohio, But Earnings Are Very Small—R.L. Davis Declines Nomination for The District Vice Presidency," *United Mine Workers Journal* 7, no. 17 (December 17, 1896): 1.
25. "Notes from Rendville By R.L. Davis, Who Describes Rather Hotly the Attitude of Some Back-Sliders," *United Mine Workers Journal* 7, no. 38 (December 24, 1896): 1.
26. "Davis," *United Mine Workers Journal* 7, no. 42 (January 28, 1897): 1.
27. "Glad," *United Mine Workers Journal* 7, no. 44 (February 11, 1897): 1.
28. Evans, *History of the United Mine Workers of America*, vol. 2, 453.
29. *Ibid.*, 441–442.
30. *Ibid.*, 436–441, 444.
31. *Ibid.*, 453; "Official Report of the Eighth Annual Convention of the United Mine Workers of America," *United Mine Workers Journal* 7, no. 41 (January 21, 1897): 2, 5.
32. "R.L. Davis," *United Mine Workers Journal* 7, no. 41 (January 21, 1897): 1.
33. "R.L. Davis Of Rendville Breaks the Silence of The Last Couple of Weeks On his Part By Once More Advising His Fellow

Miners to Do Their Duty By the Organization," *United Mine Workers Journal* 7, no. 48 (March 11, 1897): 1.

34. Selig Perlman and Philip Taft, *History of Labor in the United States, 1896–1932, Vol.4 , Labor Movements* (New York: Macmillan, 1935), 21; J.E. George, "The Coal Miners' Strike of 1897," *Quarterly Journal of Economics* 12, no. 2 (January 1898): 199–200. Retrieved from http://www.jstor.org/stable/1882118; Roy, *A History of the Coal Miners*, 326–327.

35. Evans, *History of the United Mine Workers of America*, vol. 2, 512.

36. Roy, *A History of the Coal Miners*, 327.

37. Ibid., 328.

38. Laslett, *Labor and the Left*, 198; Perlman and Taft, *History of Labor in the United States*, 22.

39. Evans, *History of the United Mine Workers*, vol. 2, 512–13.

40. "The Story of the Wheeling Conference," *American Federationist*, August 1897, 119; Fox, *United We Stand*, 51.

41. George, *The Coal Miners' Strike of 1897*, 188–189.

42. Fox, *United We Stand*, 51.

43. "Condition of Labor Strikes," *Twenty-Third Annual Report of the Chief Inspector of Mines to the Governor of the State of Ohio, For the Year 1897* (Norwalk, OH: The Laning Printing Company, 1898), 55–59; George, "The Coal Miners' Strike of 1897," 206; Roy, *A History of the Coal Miners*, 324–325.

44. George, "The Coal Miners' Strike of 1897," 193.

45. Chris Evans, "The Miners' Strike," *American Federationist*, December 1897, 241.

46. Evans, *History of the United Mine Workers of America*, vol. 2, 492–493.

47. Corbin, *Life, Work, and Rebellion in the Coal Fields*, 44; Evans, *History of the United Mine Workers of America*, vol. 2, 494.

48. Evans, *History of the United Mine Workers of America*, vol. 2, 495.

49. "The Story of the Wheeling Conference," *American Federationist*, August 1897, 121.

50. Evans, *History of the United Mine Workers*, vol.2, 464–466; Laslett, *Labor and the Left*, 203; Perlman and Taft, *History of Labor in the United States*, 24; "Conference with Governor Atkinson," *American Federationist*, August 1897, 122.

51. Evans, *History of the United Mine Workers*, vol. 2, 469.

52. George, *The Coal Miners' Strike of 1897*, 296–297.

53. Evans, *History of the United Mine Workers*, vol. 2, 469–478.

54. Ibid., 474; Fox, *United We Stand*, 52; Perlman and Taft, *History of Labor in the United States*, 25.

55. Evans, *History of the United Mine Workers*, vol. 2, 506.

56. Ibid., 497–498.

57. Ibid., 498.

58. *Twenty-Third Annual Report of the Chief Inspector of Mines to the Governor of the State of Ohio, For the Year 1897* (Norwalk, OH: The Laning Printing Company, 1898).

59. "R.L. Davis," *United Mine Workers Journal* 7, no.22 (September 9, 1897): 1.

60. "R.L. Davis" *United Mine Workers Journal* 7, no. 23 (September 16, 1897): 5; "R.L. Davis," *United Mine Workers Journal* 7, no, 36 (December 16, 1897): 1.

61. "R.L. Davis," *United Mine Workers Journal* 7, no. 25 (September 30, 1897): 1.

62. "R.L. Davis," *United Mine Workers Journal* 7, no. 28 (October 21, 1897): 1.

63. "R.L. Davis," *United Mine Workers Journal* 7, no. 29 (October 28, 1897): 4.

64. "R.L. Davis," *United Mine Workers Journal* 7, no. 44 (February 10, 1898): 1.

65. Foner, *Organized Labor*, 58–59.

66. Foner, *History of the Labor Movement*, vol. 2, 409, Evans, *History of the United Mine Workers of America*, vol. 2, 610.

67. "R.L. Davis," *United Mine Workers Journal* 7, no. 44 (February 10, 1898): 1.

68. "R.L. Davis Reports the News From Alabama—Since Being in the State He Has Visited Blocton, Pratt, Bessemer And Other Small Places, and Finds the Needs of Organization. He Contemplates the Organization of Several New Local in the Near Future," *United Mine Workers Journal* 7, no. 33 (November 25, 1897): 4.

69. "R.L. Davis," *United Mine Workers Journal* 7, no. 36 (December 16, 1897): 1.

70. "R.L. Davis Reports Conditions in Alabama, and Says that it takes time. But He hopes to establish the Organization there. Many obstacles to overcome, the Principal ones being illiteracy and race prejudice," *United Mine Workers Journal* 7, no. 36 (December 16, 1897): 1.

71. Chris Evans, "Tennessee Convict Mine Visit, October, 1898," *United Mine Workers, Journal* 9, no. 27 (October 13, 1898): 1; Evans, *History of the United Mine Workers of America*, vol. 2, 612–614.

72. "R.L. Davis Reports Some of the Obstacles Met With White Planting the Banner of Organization in the Sunny Southland. Believes that the Editor of an Afro-American Paper is in the Employ of the Coal Companies As an Obstructionist—The Organization Likely to Prove the Winner in the End," *United Mine Workers Journal* 7, no. 37 (December 23, 1897): 1.

73. "R.L. Davis Administers a Scathing Rebuke to the Colored Ministers and Southern Sentinel," *Labor Advocate* 52 (December 25, 1897): Col. D.; Evans, *History of the United Mine Workers of America*, vol. 2, 588.

Chapter 8

1. "R.L. Davis, Board Member, Reports From the Alabama Fields, and Says That the New Eldorado Is A One-Sided Affair, and That Money Rules There as it Does in Most All Other Places," *United Mine Workers Journal* 7, no. 39 (January 6, 1898): 1.

2. Selig Perlman, *A History of Trade Unionism in the United States* (New York, NY: The MacMillan Company, Google Books, 2006), 95; Evans, *History of the United Mine Workers of America*, vol. 2, 512–513, 515–517.

3. Evans, *History of the United Mine Workers of America*, vol. 2, 509–519.

4. *Ibid.*, 530.

5. *Ibid.*, 528–529; Roy, *A History of the Coal Miners*, 349.

6. *Twenty-Third Annual Report of the Chief Inspector of Mines to the Governor of the State of Ohio, For the Year 1897* (Norwalk, Ohio: The Laning Printing Company, 1898); *Twenty-Fourth Annual Report of the Chief Inspector of Mines to the Governor of the State of Ohio, For the Year 1898* (Columbus, Ohio: The Westbote Co., State Printers, 1899).

7. *Twenty-Fifth Annual Report of the Chief Inspector of Mines to the Governor of the State of Ohio, For the Year 1899* (Columbus, Ohio: Fred J. Heer, State Printer, 1900); *Twenty-Sixth Annual Report of the Chief Inspector of Mines to the Governor of the State of Ohio, For the Year 1900* (Columbus, Ohio: Fred J. Heer, State Printer, 1902).

8. Roy, *A History of the Coal Miners*, 349–350.

9. Foner, *History of the Labor Movement*, vol. 2, 345; Foner, *Organized Labor*, 84.

10. Evans, *History of the United Mine Workers of America*, vol. 2, 519.

11. Fox, *United We Stand*, 53; Evans, *History of the United Mine Workers of America*, vol. 2, 522–528, 531.

12. "Official Call," *United Mine Workers Journal* 7, no. 37 (December 23, 1897): 1, 5; "Friday Session," *United Mine Workers Journal* 7, no. 41 (January 20, 1898): 4; Evans, *History of the United Mine Workers of America*, vol. 2, 533.

13. Evans, *History of the United Mine Workers of America*, vol. 2, 538–544.

14. Evans, *History of the United Mine Workers of America*, vol. 2, 544.

15. Roy, *A History of the Coal Miners*, 303–310.

16. Evans, *History of the United Mine Workers of America*, vol. 2, 546–552; Roy, *A History of the Coal Miners*, 333–337; *Twenty-Third Annual Report of the Chief Inspector of Mines to the Governor of the State of Ohio, For the Year 1897* (Norwalk, Ohio: The Laning Printing Company, 1898).

17. "R.L. Davis Of Rendville, Writes Interestingly of the Conventions, and Urges the Necessity of A Complete Unity of the Mining Forces and Calls Upon All To Support the Establishment of a Defense Fund," *United Mine Workers Journal* 7, no. 43 (February 3, 1898): 5.

18. "R.L. Davis, Writes Interestingly of

Conditions in Alabama and Depicts a Regrettable State of Affairs. Laboring People Cannot Afford to Draw the Color Line—It Means Industrial Degradation and Slavery to All" *United Mine Workers Journal* 7, no. 44 (February 10, 1898): 1.

19. "R.L. Davis Briefly Reviews Conditions in Connection With Organization And The Defense Fund," *United Mine Workers* Journal 7, no 47 (March 3, 1898): 1; Evans, *History of the United Mine Workers of America*, vol. 2, 610–612.

20. "The Sage of Rendville Writes Interestingly of Conditions in the Sunday Creek Valley of Ohio," *United Mine Workers Journal* 9, no. 1 (April 14, 1898): 1.

21. Foner, *History of the Labor Movement*, vol. 2, 411–417.

22. "Old Dog Reports Work at Congo Poor and Price of Living Advancing. Also Speaks a Kind Word For a Friend and Offers Some Suggestions For His Benefit," *United Mine Workers Journal* 9, no. 5 (May 12, 1898): 8.

23. "R.L. Davis Of Rendville, O., Thanks Those Who Have Expressed Sympathy for Him," *United Mine Workers Journal* 9, no. 6 (May 19, 1898): 8.

24. "R.L. Davis Of Rendville Breaks the Silence of a Few Weeks and Recounts His Experience While Canvasing for the Journal," *United Mine Workers Journal* 9, no. 11 (June 23, 1898): 3.

25. Evans, *History of the United Mine Workers of America*, vol. 2, 605.

26. R.L. Davis of Rendville Make a Plea for Proper Treatment for the Negro and Says That Like The Mining Machine He is Here to Stay," *United Mine Workers Journal* 9, no. 27 (October 13, 1898): 2.

27. Evans, *History of the United Mine Workers of America*, vol. 2, 608, 640; Roy, *A History of the Coal Miners*, 339.

28. "R.L. Davis Thinks that as Time for Holding the Annual Convention at Hand He and Other Should Come Out of Their Shells; Is Unable To Suggest a Plan of Betterment But Favors a Defense Fund. And Would Like to See An Advance In Mining Rates, *United Mine Workers Journal* 9, no. 35 (December 8, 1898): 3.

29. Mahn Archives, United Mine Workers of America, District 6, Cash Book, MSS #71, Box 23, Folder 16.

30. Evans, *History of the United Mine Workers of America*, vol. 2, 633–642, 653.

31. Roy, *A History of the Coal Miners*, 349.

32. Evans, *History of the United Mine Workers of America*, vol. 2, 642–643; Roy, *A History of the Coal Miners*, 241.

33. Evans, *History of the United Mine Workers of America*, vol. 2, 652.

34. *Ibid.*, 663–671.

35. "R.L. Davis Of Rendville, Ohio, Report His Visit at Princeton, Ind., Was Royally Received and Retains Pleasant Recollections of Friends There—Princeton Well Organized," *United Mine Workers Journal* 10, no.1 (April 13, 1899): 6.

36. Tribe, *Little Cities of Black Diamonds*, 96.

37. "Rendville, Obituary," *New Lexington Tribune*, February 1, 1900; Tribe, *Little Cities of Black Diamonds*, 96.

38. "Rendville, Deferred Letter, Obituary," *New Lexington Tribune*, February 1, 1900.

39. Tribe, *Sprinkled with dust: Life and work in the Hocking coal region*, 15.

40. "R.L. Davis," *United Mine Workers Journal* 10, no. 42 (January 25, 1900): 4; Record of Death, Perry County, 83–84, row 68.

41. "R.L. Davis," *United Mine Workers Journal* 10, no. 42 (January 25, 1900): 4. Due to the loss of records it is unknown whether any monetary compensation was ever extended to his family.

Chapter 9

1. Aiken and Perdreau, *Annotated Edition of the History of the Jones Family*, 65; Twelfth Census of the United States. Schedule 1—Population—Rendville Village, Monroe, Tw.

2. Marriage Record, Probate Court, Perry County, Ohio, 1910, 248.

3. Barbara Fox, personal communication, May 15, 2009.

4. Rachel Fair, email communication, July 14, 2000.

5. Davis never served as vice-president of District 6.

6. Old Timer, "Forty Years A Miner And Men I Have Known. R.L. Davis of Ohio," *United Mine Workers Journal* 20, no. 28 (June 18, 1909): 6.

7. Email communication, Barry Kernfeld, Historical Collections and Labor Archives Special Collections Library, Paterno Library, The Pennsylvania State University, University Park. October 5, 2011.

8. Frans Doppen, discussion with John Winnenberg, Sunday Creek Associates, August 18, 2011.

9. Isabel Wilkerson, *The Warmth of Other Suns: The Epic Story of America's Great Migration* (New York, NY: Random House, 2010), 249; Powell, 70.

10. Isabel Wilkerson, *The Warmth of Other Suns*, 249, 161.

11. *Ibid.*, 137.

12. *Ibid.*, 152.

13. *Ibid.*, 251.

14. *Ibid.*, 420.

15. *Ibid.*, 417.

16. *Ibid.*, 316–317.

17. Tavis Smiley and Cornell West, *The Rich and the Rest of Us: A Poverty Manifesto* (Carlsbad, CA: Smiley Books, 2012), 4–5.

18. *Ibid.*, 9.

19. *Ibid.*, 153.

20. *Ibid.*, 79, 98.

21. Robert Putnam, *Our Kids: The American Dream in Crisis* (New York, NY: Simon & Schuster, 2015), 1–18.

22. *Ibid.*, 35–37.

23. Buckingham Mine #6, Available: http://mines.findthedata.com/l/48278/Buckingham-Mine-6 [Retrieved February 20, 2016].

24. U.S. Department of Labor, Bureau of Labor Statistics, *Economic News Release*, January 23, 2013. Available: http://www.bls.gov/news.release/union2.nr0.htm [Retrieved February 20, 2016].

25. *Union Facts: United Mine Workers.* Available: https://www.unionfacts.com/union/United_Mine_Workers [Retrieved February 20, 2016].

Bibliography

Primary Sources

Books

Aiken, Nancy, and Michel S. Perdreau. *Annotated Edition of the History of the Jones Family by John L. Jones and in Memoriam, J. McHenry Jones*. Berwyn Heights, MD: Heritage Books, 2001.

Cullinan, P.M., ed., *The Book of Perry County: An Historic, Industrial Portfolio*. New Lexington, OH: The New Lexington Herald, 1909.

Evans, Chris. *History of the United Mine Workers of America from the Year 1860 to 1890 with Illustrations of Early Pioneers*, Vol. 1. Indianapolis: United Mine Workers of America, 1914, 1918.

Evans, Chris. *History of the United Mine Workers of America from the Year 1890 to 1900 with Illustrations of Officers during that Period*, Vol. 2. Indianapolis: United Mine Workers of America, 1918, 1920.

Ffrench, Charles. *Biographical History of the American Irish in Chicago*. Chicago: American Biographical Publishing Company, 1897.

Graham, A.A. *History of Fairfield and Perry Counties, Ohio: Their Past and Present*. Chicago: W.H. Beers & Co., 1883.

The Industrial Workers of the World, *Coal-Mine Workers and Their Industry: An Industrial Handbook*. Chicago: Industrial Workers of the World, 1922. http://www.workerseducation.org/crutch/pamphlets/coal/coal.html.

Leonard, John W. *The Book of Chicagoans*. Chicago: A.N. Marquis & Company, 1905.

Leonard, John W. *Who's Who in America, 1899-1900*. Chicago: A.N. Marquis & Company, 1899.

Lloyd, Henry D. *A Strike of Millionaires Against Miners or the Story of Spring Valley: An Open Letter to the Millionaires (1890)*. Chicago: Belford-Clark Co., 1890.

Martzolff, Clement Luther. *History of Perry County*. New Lexington, OH: Ward and Weiland / Columbus, OH: Press of Fred J. Heer, 1902.

Proceedings of the American Federation of Labor, 1894. Bloomington, Illinois, Pantagraph Printing and Stationary Company, Reprinted 1906.

Roy, Andrew. *A History of the Coal Miners of the United States: From the Development of the Mines to the Close of the Anthracite Strike of 1902, including A Brief Sketch of Early British Miners*, 3rd ed. Columbus, OH: Trauger Printing Company, 1906.

Smith, Joseph Patterson. *The History of the Republican Party in Ohio*, vol. 2. Lewis Publishing Company, 1898.

Waterman, Arba Nelson. *Historical Review of Chicago and Cook County*. Chicago: Lewis Publishing Co., 1908.

Articles

Bemis, Edward W. *Mine Labor in the Hocking Valley*. Paper read at Second Annual Meeting of the American Economic Association, Boston, Massachusetts. May 23, 1887.

Bibliography

George, J.E. "The Coal Miners' Strike of 1897." *Quarterly Journal of Economics* 12, no. 2 (January 1898): 188–200. Retrieved from http://www.jstor.org/stable/1882118.

Rend, W.P. "Dangers of Free Trade to the Industrial Workers of the Country." Speech, North Chicago Rolling Mills Company, 1880, published by Donnelly, Gassete & Lloyd, Chicago, 1880.

Archives

Little Cities Archives, Shawnee, OH. Blosser, Cheryl. "Women's Registry."

Little Cities Archives, Shawnee, OH. Smithers, O. Lester, Jr. "Homer Smithers," in: *Little Cities of Black Diamonds, Miners' Registry*, no date. (Enon, OH).

Mahn Center for Archives and Special Collections, Athens, OH. United Mine Workers of America. District 6, Cash Book, 1890–1900, MSS # 71, Box 23, Folder 13–16.

Perry County Archives, New Lexington, OH. Marriage Records, Probate Court, 1887, 1910; Index to Births, Perry County, Ohio, 1871–1900; Records of Death, 1900; Perry County Court Records, 1896.

R.L. Davis Letters

Cleveland Gazette, 1886.
Labor Advocate, 1897.
National Labor Tribune. 1886–1891.
United Mine Workers Journal, 1891–1899.

Journals

Alarm, 1884.
American Federationist, 1889.
Athens Messenger. 1880, 1884, 1895.
Chicago Tribune, 1915.
Cleveland Gazette, 1883–1900.
Columbus Dispatch, 1890.
Daily Ohio State Journal, 1887.
Daily Ohio Statesman, 1869.
Hocking Sentinel, 1871–1900.
Maysville Evening Bulletin, 1895.
Miners National Record, 1875.
National Labor Tribune, 1876–1900.
New Lexington Tribune, 1873–1900.
New York Times, 1884, 1885, 1894, 1897, 1909.
Ohio State Journal, 1887, 1894.
Perry Tribune, 1883.

The Times Democrat, 1897.
United Mine Workers Journal, 1891–1900, 1909.
Washington Post, 1895.

Reports

Annual Report of the Chief Inspector of Mines to the Governor of the State of Ohio, For the Years, 1874–1900.

Proceedings of the American Federation of Labor, 1894. Bloomington, Illinois, Pantagraph Printing and Stationary Company, Reprinted 1906.

Proceedings of the Hocking Valley Investigation Committee of the General Assembly of the State of Ohio Authorized by H.J.R. No. 73, Held at Columbus, Ohio, February 20, 1885. Columbus: The Westbote Co., State Printers, 1885. Testimony by Brashears.

Databases

Find a Grave. "William P. Rend." Accessed June 26, 2012. http://www.findagrave.com.

U.S. Census Bureau. "American Factfinder: 2010 Census." Accessed February 6, 2016: http://factfinder2.census.gov

U.S. Department of Labor, Bureau of Labor Statistics, *Economic News Release*, Accessed February 6, 2016: http://www.bls.gov/news.release/union2.nr0.htm

Secondary Sources

Books

Benedict, Michael L., and John F. Winkler. *The History of Ohio Laws*. Athens: Ohio University Press, 2004.

Blosser, Cheryl, and John Winnenberg. *Agents of Change: The Pioneering Role of the Miners of the Little Cities of Black Diamonds in the Nation's Labor Movement*. Shawnee, OH: Little Cities of Black Diamonds Council, 2006.

Brody, David. *Steelworkers in America: The Nonunion Era*. New York: Harper Torchbooks, 1969.

Caruso, John A. *The Appalachian Frontier: America's First Surge Westward*. Knoxville: University of Tennessee Press, 2003.

Corbin, David Allan. *Life, Work and Rebellion in the Coal Fields: The Southern West Virginia Miners, 1880–1922*. Urbana: University of Illinois Press, 1981.

Cotkin, George. "Strikebreakers, Evictions, and Violence: Industrial Conflict in the Hocking Valley, 1884–1885." *Ohio History* 87 (1978), 142.

Doty, Flora B. *Rend City: From Wilderness to Melting Pot Now a Memory: Memoirs of Hellen (Nellie) Russell Wood*. Fairfield, IL: Wayne County Press, 1994.

Erickson, L.E. "The Color Line in Ohio Public Schools, 1829–1890." PhD dissertation, The Ohio State University, 1959.

Evans, Sara M., and Harry C. Boyte. *Free Spaces: The Sources of Democratic Change in America*. New York: Harper and Row, Perennial Library, 1986.

Fink, Leon. *Workingmen's Democracy: The Knight of Labor and American Politics*. Urbana: University of Illinois Press, 1983.

Fliege, Stu. *Tales and Trails of Illinois*. Chicago: University of Illinois Press, 2002.

Foner, Eric. *The New American History*. Philadelphia: Temple University Press, 1998.

Foner, Philip S. *From Colonial Times to the Founding of the American Federation of Labor* of *History of the Labor Movement in the United States*, vol. 1. New York: International Publishers, 1947.

Foner, Philip S. *From the Founding of the American Federation of Labor to the Emergence of American Imperialism* of *History of the Labor Movement in the United States*, vol. 2. New York: International Publishers, 1955.

Foner, Philip S. *Organized Labor and the Black Worker, 1619–1981*. New York: International Publishers, 1982.

Fox, M.B. *United We Stand: The United Mine Workers of America, 1890–1990*. Washington, D.C.: International Union, United Mine Workers of America, 1990.

Gerber, D.A. *Black Ohio and the Color Line, 1860–1915*. Urbana, IL: University of Illinois Press, 1976.

Laslett, John H.M. *Labor and the Left: A Study of Socialist and Radical Influences in the American Labor Movement, 1881–1924*. New York, Basic Books Inc., 1970.

Laslett, John H.M., ed. *United Mine Workers of America: A Model of Industrial Solidarity?* University Park: Pennsylvania State University Press, 1996.

Lewis, Ronald L. *Black Coal Miners in America*. Lexington: University Press of Kentucky, 1987.

Lozier, John William. "The Hocking Valley Coal Miners' Strike, 1884–1885." Master's thesis, The Ohio State University, 1963.

McCormick, M.R. "A Comparative Study of Coal Mining Communities in Northern Illinois and Southeastern Ohio in the Late Nineteenth Century." Unpublished dissertation, The Ohio State University, 1978.

Miller, Donald L. *City of the Century: The Epic of Chicago and the Making of America*. New York: Simon & Shuster, 1996.

Mould, David H. *Dividing Lines: Canals, Railroads and Urban Rivalry in Ohio's Hocking Valley, 1825–1875*. Dayton: Wright State University Press, 1994.

National Park Service. *African American Heritage at New River Gorge National River*. Boston: U.S. Department of the Interior, 2010.

Perlman, Selig, and Philip Taft. *History of Labor in the United States, 1896–1932, Vol. 4, Labor Movements*. New York: Macmillan, 1935.

Powderly, Terence V. *The Path I Trod: The Autobiography of Terence V. Powderly*. New York: Columbia University Press, 1940.

Powell, A. Clayton, Sr. *Against The Tide: An Autobiography*. New York: Richard R. Smith, 1938.

Putnam, Robert. *Our Kids: The American Dream in Crisis* New York: Simon & Schuster, 2015.

Simmons, Charles W., John R. Rankin, and U.G. Carter. "Negro Coal Miners in West Virginia, 1875–1925." *The Midwest Journal* 6 (Spring 1954): 60–69.

Smiley, Tavis, and Cornel West. *The Rich and the Rest of Us: A Poverty Manifesto*. Carlsbad, CA: Smiley Books, 2012.

Tribe, Ivan. *Little Cities of Black Diamonds: Urban Development in the Hocking Coal Region, 1970–1900*. Athens, OH: Athens County Historical Society & Museum, 1988.

Tribe, Ivan. *Sprinkled with Coal Dust: Life and Work in the Hocking Coal Region, 1870–1900*. Athens, OH: The Athens County Historical Society, 1989.

Trotter, Joe W. *Coal, Class, and Color: Blacks in Southern West Virginia, 1915–32*. Chicago: University of Chicago Press, 1990.

Wallace, Anthony F.C. *St. Clair: A Nineteenth Century Coal Town's Experience with a Disaster-Prone Industry*. New York: Knopf, 1987.

Weir, Robert E. *Knights Unhorsed: Internal Conflict in a Gilded Age Social Movement*. Detroit: Wayne State University Press, 2000.

Wilkerson, Isabel. *The Warmth of Other Suns: The Epic Story of America's Great Migration*. New York: Random House, 2010.

Book Chapters

Arnesen, Eric. "The Quicksand of Economic Insecurity: African Americans, Strikebreaking, and Labor Activism in the Industrial Era," in *The Black Worker: Race, Labor, and Civil Rights since Emancipation*, ed. Eric Arnesen. Urbana and Chicago: University of Illinois Press, 2007.

Brier, Stephen. "Interracial Organizing in the West Virginia Coal Industry: The Participation of Black Mine Workers in the Knights of Labor and the United Mine Workers, 1880–1894," in *Essays in Southern Labor History: Selected Papers, Southern Labor Conference, 1976*, ed. Gary M. Fink and Merl E. Reed. Westport, CT: Greenwood Press, 1977.

Gutman, Herbert G. "The Negro and the United Mine Workers of America: The Career and Letters of Richard L. Davis and Something of Their Meaning," in *The Negro and the American Labor Movement*, ed. Julius Jacobson. Garden City, NY: Anchor Books, Doubleday & Company, Inc., 1986.

Gutman, Herbert G. "The Worker's Search for Power: Labor in the Gilded Age," in *The Gilded Age: A Reappraisal*, ed. H. Wayne Morgan. Syracuse: Syracuse University Press, 1963.

Lewis, Ronald L. "Coal Miners and the Social Equality Wedge in Alabama, 1880–1908," in *The United Mine Workers of America: A Model of Industrial Solidarity?*, ed. John H.M. Laslett. University Park: Pennsylvania University Press, 1996.

Meade, George H. *Movements of Thought in the Nineteenth Century*. Chicago: University of Chicago Press, 1936, in *Stanford Encyclopedia of Philosophy*, ed. Edward N. Zalta. Stanford, CA: The Metaphysics Research Lab, 2012. Accessed February 6, 2016: http://plato.stanford.edu/entries/mead/.

Articles

Bailey, Kenneth R. "A Judicious Mixture: Negroes and Immigrants in the West Virginia Mines, 1880–1917." *West Virginia History* 34 (January 1973): 141–161.

Brier, Stephen. "The Career of Richard L. Davis Reconsidered: Unpublished Correspondence from the National Labor Tribune." *Labor History* 2, no. 3 (1980): 423.

Brier, Stephen. "R.L. Davis on Interracial Unionism: An 1886 Letter." *Labor: Studies in Working-Class History of the Americas* 5, no. 2 (2008): 7–12. doi: 10.1215/15476715-2007-074.

Gutman, Herbert G. "Reconstruction in Ohio: Negroes in the Hocking Valley Coal Mines in 1873 and 1874." *Labor History* 3, no. 3 (1962): 243.

Harlan, L.R. "Booker T. Washington's West Virginia's Boyhood." *West Virginia History* 32, no. 1 (1971): 63–85.

Hill, Herbert. "Myth-Making as Labor History: Herbert Gutman and the United Mine Workers of America." *Politics, Culture, and Society* 2, no. 2 (Winter 1988): 132–195.

Hill, Herbert. "Rejoinder to the Symposium on Myth-Making as Labor History: Herbert Gutman and the United Mine Workers of America." *Politics, Culture, and Society* 2, no. 4 (Summer 1989): 589–595.

Mayti, Bob. "Company Town." *Outdoor Illinois* 11 (May 1972): 12–13.

Nelson, Charles H. "The Story of Rendville: An Interracial Quest for Community in the Post Civil War Era." *Buckeye Hill Country: A Journal of Regional History* 9 (1996): 32.

Rosen, Christine Meisner. "Businessmen against Pollution in Late Nineteenth Century Chicago." *The Business History Review* 69, no. 3 (Autumn 1995): 351–397.

Shulman, Stephen, Nell Irvin Painter, David Roediger, Martin Glaberman, Francille Rusan Wilson, Stephen Brier, Irving Bernstein, and Albert Fried. "Labor, Race, and the Gutman Thesis: Responses to Herbert Hill." *International Journal of Politics, Culture and Society* 2, no. 3 (Spring 1989): 361–403.

Audiovisual

Leff, Mark. *Rendville*. Athens, OH: WOUB Public Media, 2011. DVD.

Lewis, Valda. *Devil's Oven: The Fire in the Heart of the Little Cities of Black Diamond*. Cleveland: Goodwin Video, 2008. DVD.

Index

Numbers in **_bold italics_** refer to pages with photographs.

Abernathy, Ralph 3
Adelphon Kruptos 12, 61
Agents of Change 5
Alabama 128–130, 134–135
Alarm 47–48
Amalgamated Association of Iron and Steel Workers 91
Amalgamated Association of Miners of the United States 13, 41–43
American Federation of Labor 38, 41, 73, 103, 124–125, 132
American Miners Association 19, 38
American Railway Union 102, 124
Ames, Miner T. 20
Andrew, Thomas 58
Appalachia 8, 15
Arnett, Benjamin W.: Arnett Law 37
Athens 1, 2, 8, 18, 19, 26
Athens Messenger 8, 47–48, 110

Bailey, Mary 37, 70, 143
Bailey, Tim 143
Bailey, William H. 60
Bamer, Peter 143
Bargar, G.H. 49
Barry, Elizabeth C. 23
Battle of Point Pleasant 8
Becker, Joseph 47
Bemis, Edward W. 56
Big Lick Township 15–16
Biographical History of the American Irish in Chicago 22
blacklegging 84
blacklisted 118–120, 136
Blosser, Cheryl 2–6; *Agents of Change* 5
Blythe Coal Company 25
Board of Canal Commissioners 18
The Book of Perry County 27
Brancroft, Thomas B. 59
Brier, Stephen 13–14
Bristol tunnel 49
Broadis, Sadie D. 36–37

Buchtel, John 47, 51, 53
Buckingham Coal Company 150–151
Bundy, Ella 143
Burke, Stevenson 48, 51
Burton, J.P. 44

Carnegie Steel Company 91
Carpenter, Samuel 18
Carroll, J.W. 143
Charleston Gazette 127
Chesapeake & Ohio Railroad 16
Chicago Tribune 22
Chicago Union League Club 22
Chicago Virden Coal Company 139
Chief Cornstalk 8
Chief Logan 8
Chillicothe 8
Cincinnati Inquirer 81
Civil War 8, 11, 15–16, 19, 21, 23, 25
Clark, Septima 3
Cleveland (city) 18, 20
Cleveland Central Labor Union 24
Cleveland Gazette 14, 37, 58, 63–65, 70
Clifford, Peter 34, 36
coal fields 16–18, 39–45, 75, 83, 123
coal operators 43–47, 53, 71, 102, 108, 126–128
Coleman, Lewis 105–107
Coles, Nellie 143
color line 8, 11, 13, 63, 85, 87–94
Columbus and Hocking Valley Railroad 18–19, 38, 45
Columbus and Sunday Creek Valley Railroad 28
Columbus Dispatch 74–75
Congo 5, 93–94, 111, 122, 136
Congo Coal Mining Company 93–94
Corning 2, 5, 11, 19, 30–33, 36, 82, 99, 101, 110–111, 115, 119–120, 136
Corning, Erastius 27–28
"Corning War" 31
Cotkin, George 46

181

Index

Crafts, Walter 53, 55
Craney, Dick 36

Davis, Beatrice 143–144
Davis, Edith 143–144
Davis, John M. 40
Davis, Lee 15
Davis, Maria 15
Davis, Mary 143–144
Davis, Richard L. *17, 71, 72, 141*
Davis, Thomas W. 133, *140*
Debs, Eugene V. 102, 124–125
Depression of 1873 16, 27
Depression of 1892 95–97
Depression of 1893 134
"Devil's Oven" 48
Dilcher, Fred 106, 116, 124, 139–140
District 6 78–87, 92–98, 105–124, 131; Cash Books 78, 88, 107, 115–116
Drakes 5
Dunmore's War 8

economic depression 19–20, 43, 97, 104, 109, 150
Eller, Ron 6
Elliot, George F. 49
Emancipation Day 6, *35*, 122
Evans, Chris 3, 38, *39*, 40, 41–46, 51–55, 71–73, 98, 103, 123–129, 133; *History of the United Mine Workers of America from 1890 to 1900* 3

Farms, W.E. 106, 131
Ferrell, Frank J. 62, 111
First International 12
First Joint Conference of Operators and Miners 60
Foner, Philip 11; *Organized Labor and the Black Worker, 1619–1981* 11
Foraker, Joseph B. 47
Foran, M. A. 31
Foreman, Worthy 75
Fort Charlotte 8
Fort Gower 8
Foster, Charles 28, 30
Fraternal Order of Red Men 2
"Friend Deloche" 105
"Friend Wallace" 111

Gaines, Maj. Kemp 15
Gainesborough 15, 16
Gardner, Laurene 102, 120
Garfield, James 25
George, J.E. 125
Gilded Age 9
Glasgow, S. 96
Gompers, Samuel 41–42, 73–74, 99, 103, 124
Gowen, Franklin B. 19
The Great Hocking Valley Strike 38–58
The Great Migration 147
Great Railroad Strike 40
Great Recession of 2008 149–150
Gutman, Herbert 9–17; Gutman Debate 10;
The Negro and the United Mine Workers of America 11
Guy, Ella 64

Hare, William 46
Harlem Renaisssance 148
Harper's Weekly Illustrated Magazine 47
Harris, William 143
Haseltine, Robert M. 7, 124
Haskins, W.H. 111, 124
Hayes, Max 24–25
Henry, Patrick 17
Hickey, Richard 34–35
Highlander Research and Education Center 3
Hill, Herbert 13–14
History of the United Mine Workers of America from 1890 to 1900 3
Hoadly, George 46–47, 59
Hock, Christopher 31
Hocking Canal 18
Hocking District 44–45
Hocking Field 54
Hocking River 8
Hocking Sentinel 21, 24
Hocking Valley 3–8, 18–25, 38–48, 54–59, 83–84, 97–100, 104, 110, 118, 138
Hocking Valley & Toledo Railroad 44, 48, 51
Hocking Valley Coal Field 18, 39
Hocking Valley Investigation Committee 49–53, 55; *Proceedings* 50
Hocking Valley Miners' Union 20
Hoover, H.F. 128
Horton, Miles 3
Hymes, James N. 143

Illustrated Newspaper 47
immigration 16, 38, 95, 146, 149
Industrial Workers of the World 10
International Working People's Association 47

Jackson, F.H. 93
Jacksonville Agreement 4
James, John 20
Jay Cooke and Company 19
Jim Crow 9, 128, 148
Johnson, Alexander 55
Johnson, Lyndon B. 150; War on Poverty 150
Jones, John L. 27, 36, 68, 143
Jones, Reese 60

Kanawha Valley 16–19, 126–127
Kane, John 79, *81*, 117, 133
Das Kapital 12
Kellogg Foundation 5
Kennedy, John F. 4
King, Martin Luther, Jr. 3
Kintz, J. E. 37
Knight, James 18
Knights of Labor (*also* Noble and Holy Order of the Knights of Labor) 10–21, 38–45, 59–

63, 73, 76, 85, 88, 108, 124, 146; *Adelphon Kruptos* 12, 61
Kohler, Jacob A. 49–50

Labor Advocate 14, 130
labor movement 4, 8, 10, 21, 37, 43
Lafferty, Arch 9
Lattimer massacre 126, 128
Lawson, Thomas 55
Lee, Fitzhugh 63
Lemert, Colonel Wilson C. 28–33
Leslie, Frank 47; *Illustrated Newspaper* 47
Lewis, Andrew 8
Lewis, John L. 3–4, 49, 151
Lewis, Ronald L. 8, 14
Lewis, Thomas 131–132
Lewis, William T. 71
Lick Run Mine 20
Little Cities of Black Diamonds 1–8, 18–19, **28**; *The Story of Our Community* 5
Little Cities of Black Diamonds: Urban Development in the Hocking Coal Region 8
Longstreth, Thaddeus 20–21

Martin, John D. 19, 40
Martin, Sam 119
Marx, Karl 11; *Das Kapital* 12
McBride, John 41–48, 51, 55, 71–74, **75**, 98–106
McBryde, Patrick 106
McCall, Willis Virgil 148
McCarthy, J.J. 46
McClung, W.F. 21
McCormick, Michael 13
McCormick Building 26, **27**
McGough, Thomas 97
McKinley, William, Jr. 7, 26, 104
Meade, George Herbert 10
Mercer, A.B. 112
Mercer Hotel 11–13, 62, 91, 111, **112**, 113
Miller, Cameron 89, 106, 116
Miller, R.H. 132
Miners' and Laborers' Benevolent Association 39
Miners' National Association 19–20, 40
Miners' National Record 21
Mitchell, John **133**, 139
Monday Creek 8, 18, 19; Restoration Project 4
Morgan County 8
Moxahala tunnel 28
Mulharren, Charles 29
Murray, Owen 34, 111
Myers, Isaac 12

National Cordage Company 97
National District Assembly 135 74
National Federation of Miners and Mine Laborers 13, 41, 58, 60, 71
National Guard 47
National Labor Tribune 7, 13–14, 17, 21, 37, 40, 43, 55–59, 70, 79–80, 86
National Labor Union 11–12

National Progressive Union 41, 71–78
The Negro and the United Mine Workers of America 11
Nelson, Charles 9
Nelsonville (formerly York Township) 8, 18–20, 30, 48
New Lexington Herald 27; *The Book of Perry County* 27
New Lexington Tribune 9, 29–37, 112, 140
New River 16–18
New Straitsville 3–9, 19–20, 40–43, 48, 54–55
New York Times 48, 99
Nugent, John 76, 81, 84, 89

Odd Fellows 29, 59
Ohio and Hocking Coal and Iron Company 53
Ohio Canal 18
Ohio Central Coal Company 18, 31–34
Ohio Central Railroad Company 28, 43, 58
Ohio Coal Exchange 45, 48, 53
Ohio Humanities Council 4–5
Ohio Miners' Convention 88
Ohio River 8, 18
Old Dog 136–137, 139
Old Lick 16; *see also* Roanoke
Old Timer 10–11, 144, **145**
Organized Labor and the Black Worker, 1619–1981 11
Our Journey Continues: The History of New Straitsville, Ohio 4–5
Our Kids: The American Dream in Crisis 150

Parks, Rosa 3
Payne, Glenroy 9
Pearce, W.C. 107, 111, 116, 121, 132, 139, 141
Penna, Phil H. **83**, 94–95, 106–116, 121
Perry County 1–8, 112, 132, 143; *The Story of Our Community* 5
Perry County Republican Convention 65
Philadelphia and Reading Railroad 97
Pinkerton guards 45–48, 77, 91
Plessy v. Ferguson 147
Porter, Lorle 4
Powderly, Terence V. 12–13, 42, 60, **61**, 63, 71–74
Powell, Adam Clayton, Sr. 37, 66, **67**, 68–69, 147
Pratt City 128–131, 135
Proceedings of the Hocking Valley Investigation Committee 50
Pullman Strike 102
Putnam, Robert 150; *Our Kids: The American Dream in Crisis* 150

Rae, John B. **74**, 75–84
railroad 8, 18–20, 28, 45, 102
Ratchford, Michael 25, 107, **108**, 110–115, 119–127, 132, 139
Rend, Col. William P. 18–22, **23**, 24–30, 34, 45–46, 50, 55–56, 63–64, 71, 79–82, 92, 99, 113, 119, 132; *Biographical History of the*

American Irish in Chicago 22; W.P. Rend & Company 22–23, 26, **27**, 28, 31, 63
Rendville **28**, **29**; Academy 36; Arts Works 6; Baptist Church **32**, **33**, 67; Emancipation Day 6, **35**, 122; Historic Preservation Society 6, 86; Town Hall **36**
Residential Incorporated 3
The Rich and the Rest of Us 150
Roanoke (also Old Lick and Big Lick Township) 15–16
Robinson's Cave 3, 40
Rockefeller, F. 104
Rodgers, Ned 29
Roy, Andrew 44, **45**, 49, 57, 75, 122, 133
Ruffner, Gen. Lewis 16

Sandusky, Newark, Somerset & Straitsville Railroad 19
Scaife, William (*also* Old Timer) 10–11, 144, **145**
Scott, W.C. 133, **135**
Seeger, Pete 3
segregation 8–9, 13, 17, 128, 147, 150
Shawnee 2, 5, 8, 19, 30, 40, 43, 47–48, 54, 106, 118
Shawnee: Reflections Upon the First 125 Years 5
Sheffield, Ric 4
Shires, Henry 107
Siney, John 19–20
slavery 8, 11–13, 23, 51, 84, 114, 122; *see also* wage slavery
Smiley, Tavis 149, 150; *The Rich and the Rest of Us* 150
Smith, Capt. Thomas J. 28–29
Southern Sentinel 130
Sovereign, James R. 13, 63, 124–125
Spanish-American War 136
Special National Convention 126
Sprinkled with Coal Dust 8
Stalter, D.J. 50
Standard Time Act 136
Starling, George Swanson 146–149
Stephens, Uriah S. 12
Steytler, J. J. 25
The Story of Our Community 5
Straitsville Great Vein 18, 44
strike 3, 19–24, 38–49, 54–55, 60–62, 76, 85, 99–102, 123–125, 131, 134; breakers 8, 11, 17, 20–21, 44–48; *see also* blacklegging
Strike of 1894 98–105, 121, 134
Strike of 1897 122–126, 131, 134
Sullivan, Dennis H. 112–113
Sunday Creek Coal Company 22, 31, 82–83
Sunday Creek Valley 4–8, 18, 28–34, 88–106,

119; Associates 4–5, 8; *Our Journey Continues: The History of New Straitsville, Ohio* 4–5; *Shawnee: Reflections Upon the First 125 Years* 5
Sylvis, William H. 12
The Syndicate 43–44, 48, 55

Tanner, John R. 139
Tecumseh Theater 2
Tennessee Railroad 16
Tribe, Ivan 3, 8; *Little Cities of Black Diamonds: Urban Development in the Hocking Coal Region, 1870–1900* 8; *Sprinkled with Coal Dust* 8
Tuppins, Isaiah S. 37, 63–64, **65**, 66, 69

union 10–16, 19–21, 26, 43, 55, 77, 94, 102, 110–111, 136–137, 151
United Mine Workers of America (UMWA) 1–4, 10–14, 25, 40–42, 56–58, 70–83, 91, 98–99, 105–107, 112–115, 123–129, 132–134, 142, 145, 151; Constitution 76–78; First National Convention **72**; National Executive Board of UMWA 1, 13–14, 70, **71**, **76**, 106, 116, 120, 123, 133, 136, 142, 145
UMWA Journal 7, 10, 13–14, **17**, 79–80, 84, 87, 93, 95, 104–106, 111–112, 121–122, 133, 138, 141, 144
United States Industrial Commission 139
Upson Mine 48

Virginia Railroad 16

wage slavery 79–87, 116, 131
Walker, Edwin 23
War on Poverty 150
Warren, R.F. 73
Washington, Booker T. 16, 119
Watchorn, Robert 75, 78
Watson, John Thomas 143
Watson, Joseph 143–144
Weaver, Daniel 19
Weber, Frank J. 38
Weitzel, G.C. 30
West, Cornell 150; *The Rich and the Rest of Us* 150
West Virginia 126–128
Wilkerson, Isabel 147–148; *The Great Migration* 147
Williams, D.S. 113
Williams, T.H. 58
Williston, John 30
Winnenberg, John 2–6; *Agents of Change* 5
Wolcott, Simon P. 49
Wright, Richard 147